W9-AVR-216

DEADLY COMPANY

Norman Daniels was not aggressive enough for The Company's liking. Daniels came up with one excuse after another why he couldn't kill Carole Garton. He asked The Company for more time. In response, The Company e-mailed Daniels a series of threatening messages. One message said, *If you don't do what you're told, you or your son could end up either hurt or dead.*

That was the final incentive as far as Norman Daniels was concerned. He already half believed he was a dead man no matter what he did. But the safety of his son concerned him greatly. It was this threat that finally forced his decision.

Norman Daniels agreed to act then. He was afraid of killing Carole Garton. She was someone he liked and also feared, because The Company had told him what a crack shot she was during her Irish Republican Army days. But as much as he feared her, he feared The Company even more. He screwed up his courage and decided May 16, 1998, would be the day he would kill her—come hell or high water.

Other Pinnacle Books by Robert Scott:

SAVAGE
ROPE BURNS
LIKE FATHER, LIKE SON
DANGEROUS ATTRACTION
MARRIED TO MURDER

KILL
OR
BE
KILLED

ROBERT SCOTT

PINNACLE BOOKS
Kensington Publishing Corp.
http://www.kensingtonbooks.com

Some names have been changed to protect the privacy of individuals connected to this story.

PINNACLE BOOKS are published by

Kensington Publishing Corp.
850 Third Avenue
New York, NY 10022

Copyright © 2004 by Robert Scott

All rights reserved. No part of this book may be reproduced in any form or by any means without the prior written consent of the Publisher, excepting brief quotes used in reviews.

If you purchased this book without a cover you should be aware that this book is stolen property. It was reported as "unsold and destroyed" to the Publisher and neither the Author nor the Publisher has received any payment for this "stripped book."

All Kensington Titles, Imprints, and Distributed Lines are available at special quantity discounts for bulk purchases for sales promotions, premiums, fund-raising, and educational or institutional use. Special book excerpts or customized printings can also be created to fit specific needs. For details, write or phone the office of the Kensington special sales manager: Kensington Publishing Corp., 850 Third Avenue, New York, NY 10022, attn: Special Sales Department, Phone: 1-800-221-2647.

Pinnacle and the P logo Reg. U.S. Pat. & TM Off.

First Printing: September 2004
10 9 8 7 6 5 4 3 2

Printed in the United States of America

Acknowledgments

Many people helped in the preparation of this book. I would particularly like to thank Vicki Holman, Virginia Griffiths, Collin Colebank, Shannon Colebank and Marty Federici. I'd also like to thank Laron Johnson, Detective Steve Grashoff and Deputy District Attorney Greg Gaul. Finally, thanks go out to my terrific literary agent Damaris Rowland and wonderful editor at Pinnacle Books, Michaela Hamilton.

Chapter 1

The Package

Cottonwood, California, April 28, 1998—Midnight

Darkness covered the hills over the sleeping northern California town of two thousand souls as the clock struck midnight. Winding Cottonwood Creek ran silently through the dense trees as a pair of headlights swept along Gas Point Road and swung into a driveway near a mobile home. It was mainly a rural area with long distances between houses, and the locale was deserted at this hour. The driver dimmed the lights of his SUV, cut the engine and stepped into a yard. He carried a large, orange-colored, 11" x 14" manila envelope in his hand as he walked toward the mobile home on the wooded property. Underneath his jacket, protected from the cool air and preying eyes, his right arm displayed an Irish Republican Army (IRA) tattoo. The tattoo portrayed an American flag and an Irish flag, with ONE BUT NOT THE SAME written beneath the banners.

The tattooed man who stepped out of the shadows and into a pool of light in front of the mobile home was twenty-seven-year-old Todd Jesse Garton.

Slowly another man stepped into the circle of light and faced him. Even though the man's face was boyish-looking for a twenty-eight-year-old, his jaw was now set with grim determination, reflecting the seriousness of the moment. The boyish-looking man was Norman Daniels III and occupant of the mobile home.

The two men were not strangers. In fact, they had been on an assassination mission together. It had taken them across state lines up into Oregon with a vehicle filled with weapons, a huge cache of ammunition, disguises and silencers. As Garton handed the package to Daniels, Norman looked down at the lettering on its cover. Two strips of clear plastic tape revealed letters spelled out in block form. The letters read, NEWBIE RECRUIT, PATRIOT RECRUITER. Daniels knew that he was the "newbie recruit" and that Garton was "Patriot." It was a code name given to him by a shadowy organization of hired killers. The organization seemed to be filled with ex-CIA operatives, former military Black Ops specialists and just plain soldiers of fortune. Daniels had gathered all this information by listening to Garton's stories about his dangerous exploits on behalf of the organization.

Daniels turned the package over and noticed a wax seal that appeared to bear the head of a ram. But his eyes deceived him. In fact, it was an impression from Garton's Navy SEAL pin. The wax displayed the headpiece of a diving bubble, the insignia of the SEALs. It was an emblem steeped in stealth, covert operations and quick death.

Just as Daniels began to place his thumb under the wax seal, Garton spoke up and said, "Hold on. Wait a second! I warn you, before you open that, if you open it, you are going to have to do what it tells you in that package. Or you will end up dead."

Daniels responded, "Well, I already opened the seal, so it looks like I'm going to have to go through with this."

Garton grunted and said, "Okay."

As Daniels looked at the contents of the package, he immediately noticed a small pager. It had instructions and an 800 number to call on how to make the pager operational. There were also instructions made of labeling tape, the same kind of labeling tape used on the front of the package. These instructions advised Daniels that he must give his recruiter the pager number. In other words, Todd Garton.

Also in the package were several news articles related to the turmoil in Northern Ireland. They spoke of the Irish Republican Army and Sinn Fein, their political affiliate. One of the articles dealt with an IRA leader who had died recently and showed a picture of people mourning at his funeral. Another photo was of a crowded Belfast street in Northern Ireland. One of the articles discussed an anonymous female who dealt with IRA "political prisoners." Another was about an unknown female who planted a bomb at a British bookstore. Daniels vaguely wondered if the women in the articles might be Todd's wife, Carole Garton. Todd had told him previously that Carole had been an IRA operative in Ireland when she was a teenager. He'd indicated that she'd helped plant bombs and even gun down British soldiers. He said she was a crack marksman.

The most potent material in the package were three photographs. The first photograph portrayed Carole Garton, a woman that Norman Daniels knew well, wearing a completely black outfit and dark sunglasses. She was looking back over her shoulder at the photographer. It was hard to read the expression on her face.

The second photo was of Carole Garton at a waterfall near a bridge and rocky cliff area along a stream. There were dense woods in the photo. Strangely enough, the scene looked like an area east of Cottonwood, where Norman Daniels and Todd Garton had gone rappelling in years past. As a matter of fact, the photo itself looked familiar. Daniels was sure he'd seen it in Garton's home. Maybe in a photo album. He asked Garton about this, but Garton replied, "I've never seen this photograph before."

The third photograph was the most potent of all. It portrayed Carole Garton, Todd Garton and an anonymous male on a stage. There was sound equipment in the background and a large audio speaker. Todd was sitting on the stage up against a wall. The unknown male was standing with his arms crossed. Carole was front and center. She wore a hat and sunglasses and held one arm aloft with her head tilted to the side. She seemed to be posing for the camera. The most unusual thing about the photo was that both Todd and the unknown male's heads were x-ed out with a marking pen, but Carole's head had a large circle drawn around it in yellowish green ink. Daniels knew from previous instructions that his target to kill was whoever had his or her head circled in a photograph. He was not to do it with a rifle from ambush. He was to kill his target up close and personal with a pistol.

On the back of this photograph, in clear tape with black lettering, was information and instructions. The information gave Carole Garton's birth date, social security number and the license plate number of her Jeep Wrangler. The instructions read, *Carole Garton—TO*. TO meant target of opportunity.

The instructions also stated, *WO—12:01 on the 28th of April until May of the 20th*. WO meant window of opportunity—in other words, the amount of time Daniels had to carry out his mission.

The very last thing on the instructions was the admonition, *If you don't complete this mission, you will be terminated*. Daniels understood this to mean that he would be killed.

Even though Daniels had been on the assassination mission to Oregon, this one startled him. He knew and admired Carole Garton. He turned directly toward Todd and said, "No way!"

Todd took the photo of Carole from Daniels, looked at his wife's face and sighed heavily.

"I can't do this!" Daniels exclaimed. "I'll get caught. You've got to call someone and change this."

Todd reluctantly took Daniels's cell phone and began to dial some numbers. Then suddenly he pressed the power button and hung up. He ran his hand over his head as Daniels kept repeating, "I can't do this. I'm going to get caught. I'm a dead man."

"You've got to do it," Garton finally replied. "There's no way out."

Then Garton sat down heavily on a chair near the

porch of the mobile home, saying that they both ought to get drunk. He looked as forlorn as Daniels felt.

Finally after staring at his wife's circled face in the photo once again, Todd sighed and said, "Well, at least it isn't me."

Norman Daniels first met Todd Garton at Shasta College on the north side of Redding, California, in the spring of 1993. With its buildings tucked in a beautiful, rolling wooded area, the campus looked more like a park than a college. To the northeast, fourteen-thousand-foot snowcapped Mount Shasta rose majestically over the countryside. Surrounded by myths and legends, ethereal Mount Shasta at times seemed to float above the terrain as if it were not really connected to the earth. There were stories of underground passages beneath the mountain and lost kingdoms. New Age devotees flocked there seeking enlightenment. More sportsmanlike devotees flocked there for good hunting and fishing. The area lived up to its chamber of commerce title, "the Shasta Cascade Wonderland."

Norm Daniels bumped into Garton in the college's Mac lab, a room filled with Macintosh computers for students to do homework and assignments. Garton happened to be doing homework on a Mac when Daniels noticed him wearing a military shirt. Since Daniels had been an army paratrooper, he asked if Garton had been in the military as well. Garton said that he was still in the military. They struck up a conversation and Todd said that he was a lieutenant in the marines and had injured both of his legs in a mission. He was currently in the process of being rehabilitated and not on active duty at the present time. During this period of convalescence he was taking classes at Shasta College to further his education. As a matter of fact, that was the reason why he was in the Mac lab. He was doing an assignment for his geography class.

Daniels sat down beside Garton and they continued to talk about the military and the world in general. As they talked, Daniels noticed that Garton was having trouble with his computer program and it was obvious that he was a novice in this regard. The same could not be said of Norman Daniels.

In 1993 Daniels was a computer science major with experience in programming in Basic and C++ 3.1. He knew DOS, Disk Management Plus Systems operation for Linux machines and had Internet experience. He was also a computer program designer.

As Daniels watched Garton fumble around with his program on world geography, he offered to help. Soon they were both looking at maps of the world. Todd Garton pointed at Central America and said, "I've been there." The conversation that followed led Norman Daniels into a world he had never dreamed of. It was filled with romance, danger and excitement.

Garton explained that he was a field grade officer; in other words, he had not gone to officers' school but had enlisted as a private and risen in the ranks to lieutenant because of his abilities in the field. He pointed at Guatemala and El Salvador and said that he had done antidrug cartel work there with the marines. Of course it had all been very hush-hush and covert in nature.

Daniels vaguely knew about these secret operations. He'd heard of the Iran-Contra Affair and U.S. Marine Corps colonel Oliver North's involvement in it. And he'd heard of other CIA operations that were mostly kept hidden from the public eye. These tales generally concerned covert operations and sometimes assassination missions. Every once in a while stories would filter into the newspapers about some drug operation destroyed or some drug lord killed.

Garton said he'd been so good at his job that the marines had loaned him out to the DEA. If the marine missions had been secretive, the DEA missions were doubly so. He'd done scouting and reconnaissance work. On his recon missions he would spy out the enemy positions and ascertain how many people were there and what kind of weapons and vehicles they had.

Garton also said, "I did missions where I had to destroy drug labs and the like. I was sometimes a sniper and had to take out people."

Garton wove an intricate picture of a shadowy world, where the lines between the "good guys" and the "bad guys" blurred into an ethical haze. Todd said that he had been on these missions until recently. He'd been rappelling from a helicopter when suddenly the copter was fired upon. Knocked off balance, he lost his grip and had fallen from the rappel line and broke both of his legs when he hit the ground. That was the reason he was being rehabilitated back in the States.

Norman Daniels was fascinated by these stories. But they were only a prelude to Garton's next words. Todd related that before he was a marine—in fact, when he was only sixteen years old—he had stolen a credit card and gone to Northern Ireland to help fight with the IRA. To prove it, Garton undid his shirt and showed Daniels an IRA tattoo on one of his shoulders. It displayed a Celtic cross. He said that he had always been sympathetic to the IRA cause and that he was of Irish ancestry himself.

When he landed in Belfast, he had hooked up with a cell of IRA sympathizers. Before long he was showing them how to maintain their weapons. As a boy, Todd Garton had grown up with guns. He knew how to shoot well and how to maintain his weapons. By the time he was seventeen, his services to the IRA went far beyond just cleaning weapons. He was sent out to snipe at British soldiers who patrolled the streets of Belfast.

One particular incident stood out in his memory and he conveyed it to Daniels with the art of a master storyteller. He and an IRA friend were lying in wait in an alley for a squad of British soldiers to pass by. They were hidden behind obstructions and both carried weapons with thirty-round "banana clips." The banana clips were so named because of their distinctive semicircular shape that somewhat resembled a banana. Unfortunately, Todd's friend was not as familiar with weapons as he was. When he jumped into a prone firing position and opened fire on the British soldiers, he bent one of the clips on the ground. This caused it to jam. While he was trying to fix his gun, he was shot and killed.

Todd had made no similar mistake. From his ambush position he opened up on the soldiers. Even though they were wearing helmets and flak jackets, he managed to shoot several of them in the face, killing them instantly. Todd's marksmanship as a boy paid off. He held the British survivors at bay and didn't take off for safety until he'd emptied most of his clip. He escaped down the alley and disappeared from the scene of carnage.

These stories of Northern Ireland really filled Norman Daniels with a thirst for adventure. In comparison to Garton, his stint in the paratroopers had been dull and prosaic. He had been well trained but had never seen real action. It had all been maneuvers and simulated battle field conditions. Before long, he and Garton were meeting over drinks at the American Legion Hall in Anderson and shooting the bull. Garton kept up his stream of war stories and Daniels drank it all in, imagining scenes in the steaming jungles of Central America or of the windswept, rainy streets of Belfast. Daniels knew he had what it took, the same as Garton. But he had never been presented with the opportunity.

Once Garton's legs were better, Daniels and Garton went rappelling off an eighty-foot cliff face near a bridge and waterfall near Shingletown. It was the same area that would look so familiar to Daniels in the photo of Carole Garton near a waterfall. To show how good he was at rappelling, Todd even did it off the bridge, which was a straight shot to the ground below. He may have been inept at computers, but he was good with guns and certain outdoor activities.

As they went on these forays, Todd Garton regaled Daniels with more and more stories. Norman Daniels believed all of them. After all, Garton used certain military terms that weren't common knowledge. And as Daniels said later, "I'm a trusting person. It's a fault, I guess. If someone told me they had a million dollars in the bank, I wouldn't ask to see their bankbook."

But in Todd Garton's case, Daniels should have looked at his "bankbook." In fact, Todd Garton had never been in Central America, never helped on a DEA mission, never been a Navy SEAL and had only been a corporal in the marines, not a lieutenant. He'd hurt his leg in a training exercise and been given an honorable discharge from the marines. He'd never been on a rappelling mission from a helicopter that took enemy fire. And most of all, he'd certainly never been to Northern Ireland as a teenager nor had been anywhere near the Irish Republican Army.

Todd Garton was the biggest con man since P. T. Barnum, and he had Daniels falling for his stories hook, line and sinker. These stories were vivid, exciting and filled with adventure. There was just one flaw—they weren't true.

Yet Todd was so consistent with his lies, so exact in his embellishments, that he had a lot more people than just Norman Daniels fooled. All of this might have added up to no more than good story-telling at the American Legion Hall—except for one thing. Garton's cons weren't ultimately harmless like P. T. Barnum's. Todd Garton's deceptions were about to lead down a road to conspiracy and murder.

Chapter 2

The Hope Chest

The one salient thing about Todd Garton was that from a very early age he could spin a good story. Born Todd Jesse Garton in 1970, he and his brother had an upper-middle-class childhood. Todd lived close enough to a rural area so that he learned how to shoot guns and maintain them. He was bright and articulate, but the "real world" seemed mundane to him. He began to invent a world of his own, and his talent was making others believe in it as well.

Years later, his mother, Pat Garton, would speak of Todd as a very bright child. He had a gift for entertaining himself and others around him. She said he was not a troublemaker, but according to Shannon Colebank, one of Todd's best friends during his late teen years and early twenties, that may not have been entirely true.

Todd told Colebank several stories about his childhood, and these were very revealing. Granted, Todd always had a way of embroidering his tales, but Shannon believed these particular stories to be true. Shannon recalled, "He told me a story of how he accidentally set his clothes on fire as a kid and had to wrap himself in the curtains to put the fire out. His mom was furious that he had ruined the curtains, and had no concern for his burns and no pride in his intelligence for rolling himself up in the curtains to put the fire out, rather than panicking like any other child would have, which would have led to the whole house going up in smoke."

Shannon related another story that Todd told him, which is just as revealing. "Todd was eight years old. His older brother was eleven. Their uncle gave them both bullwhips as presents. Boys of this age of course were delighted with such gifts. One day Todd got his older brother trapped under the bed, holding him there with occasional lashes of the whip. The younger Todd obviously felt the thrill of having power over his older brother. But soon the older brother had enough and started getting angry. This, of course, scared Todd, which made it necessary to keep the older brother at bay. But the longer this event continued, the more angry the older brother got, until he was screaming at Todd in rage, threatening to beat the crap out of him.

"By now Todd's thrill of power had turned into outright fear of retaliation, so he had to keep whipping his older brother to prevent him from getting beat up. Eventually Todd was crying hysterically, picturing the extent of the beating he would inevitably receive once he finally let his brother out. He knew full well that the longer he kept control, the worse the inevitable beating would be, but he was so afraid of any beating at all that he could not stop whipping. He was trapped in his position of power and was too scared to let go of it.

"Wailing hysterically while whipping his brother, Todd provoked an investigation by his father, who came in and yelled, 'What the hell is going on here?'

"Seeing the predicament, the dad took the whips away and told Todd, 'I'm not stepping in.'

"The dad left, and the older brother beat the shit out of Todd."

Shannon added, "I think for Todd, he felt that his father allowed his older brother to beat him to a pulp, which felt like abandonment by Dad. Todd felt betrayed by his dad allowing him to receive a beating, even though he had clearly learned his lesson before the beating. Todd was full of stories about abandonment. It was a big deal for him. Everything he did always involved other people. He always kept himself surrounded by people."

Shannon recalled that Todd resented not being rich and it led to one more of Todd's stories about his childhood. Shannon said, "Todd told me that for a brief time his parents had money, and they used to schmooze with the rich folks on 'snob hill.' But they left him in the car so as not to embarrass them. He felt resentful."

Once again, all these stories were filtered through Todd's understanding of the truth, which was elastic at best. But Shannon believed the essence of the stories were true. Todd had a fear and loathing of abandonment. He needed people around him as a buffer against loneliness and as mirrors to reflect his longed-for attainment of self-worth.

Todd spent his early years in northern California,

but it was when he and his family moved up to Portland, Oregon, when he was sixteen years old, that his full powers of elaboration and fabrication fully blossomed. At that point he had the knack of making others believe his most outrageous tales. Even when people doubted his stories, he wouldn't give up in his allegations that they were true. By sheer persistence and repetition, he could make the most ardent doubting Thomas begin to believe him.

No one knew this better than Todd's friend Collin Colebank, Shannon's brother. Collin was an accomplished drummer and a few years older than seventeen-year-old Todd when they met in 1987. Collin was also a musician in search of a band. Colebank first encountered Todd through Martha Federici, his girlfriend, better known as "Marty." When they first met, Todd could barely play the bass guitar, but the one thing Todd possessed was a powerful dream to become a rock musician. Through sheer persistence, over time, Todd learned to be a very decent bass player, someone that Collin Colebank, an already accomplished drummer, wouldn't take as a wanna-be joke.

But musicianship wasn't Todd's main asset to the band that began to form around him and Collin, a band that took on the name Detente Touch. His main contribution was his drive and energy. The introductory letter that he distributed to local promoters and clubs about Detente Touch clearly indicated how he felt about the band. In it he claimed that his initial vision for the band came in the recording studio. He said he'd spent many a sleepless night laying down tracks. Writing in the third person, he said: *While going through musicians like a*

ghost through a wall, Todd came across excellent studio
drummer Collin Colebank. Two short practices with the
drummer and Todd was ready to go back to the studio.

Todd wrote almost all of the lyrics himself and
sang on the recordings. He had a pleasant voice,
but not a great deal of range. He claimed that he'd
written one song for his girlfriend to sing, but on
the day of the recording she had a virus and couldn't
be at the studio. Out of patience he phoned an old
friend, who had played bass. Her name was Carole
Batchelor, but she would soon take on the stage
name of Ursela Desailles. He asked her to sing, and
it was her vocals that proved to be what the band
needed. With far greater range than Todd, she gave
a strong and memorable performance.

The fourth band member, who was needed to
play lead guitar, remained as elusive as ever. Then
one night, purely by accident, Todd bumped into
Kenny Bergheim. Kenny was a good guitarist. When
he joined the band, Detente Touch was complete.
Todd wrote, *By this time, Todd and Urs had compiled*
ten brilliant, new originals. Everyone was anxious to play.
After a few practices you could see a look in their eye.

Each of the band members wrote a couple of para-
graphs about themselves for a promotion sheet,
and all of it was in the third person. Ursela described
herself as *every mother's nightmare. And every school-*
boy's, too. Domination is her game. Urs loves to wield the
power of controlling the amount of pain or pleasure that
man, woman or children can sustain. However, her true
belief is that all things have a right to be. Ursela always
speaks her mind, but prefers to sing it.

Kenny Bergheim said of himself: *Ken is of a dif-*
ferent breed. Secluded but not impersonal. He is willing

to share a lot with most any female who'll get close enough. Guitar is second nature to this playboy. Everyone finds it difficult to pry it from his hands.

Collin Colebank wrote, *Life through his eyes is only seen one day at a time, but still comprehends tomorrow (even if he is a day late). Collin believes a handshake is the only gentleman's agreement.*

Todd saved the most bombastic hype for himself. He wrote that *Todd is a God-like creature. If you have any doubts, feel free to ask him. Bass player extraordinaire and spokesman for the band, do not ask him his opinion, he'll tell you. His quick wit and sharp tongue will always keep you guessing.*

Shannon Colebank, Collin's brother, also knew Todd very well. He said, "I met up with Todd when he was struggling with his band. I had run sound for my own bands and had all the equipment and know-how. Collin was their drummer and had been exasperated with their amateur sound person and inadequate equipment. Out of sheer frustration Collin called me in to at least help them with their rehearsals. I was such a great influence on them that I was almost adopted as the fifth member of the band."

Shannon had a very interesting insight into Todd's character. According to Shannon, Todd's father was a compulsive gambler. Shannon said that Todd's dad would win a lot of money, only to gamble it away. Shannon recalled that "Todd resented this as an addiction, and thus hated addicts. Todd never smoked or took any kind of drugs. He never even drank coffee, due, I suspect, to his resentment of his dad's addictive personality disorder. Unfortunately, Todd was, in fact, a compulsive gambler himself. He thought that since he never bet on horses or gambled in a casino, that meant he did not have a problem. But the main aspect of Todd's personality was that he was addicted to risk. Everything he did was a gamble of some kind.

"The reason this eventually destroyed him was because Todd was a genius. I had immense respect for his intellect. But because he was so exceptionally intelligent, he always won every time he gambled on something. This, of course, defeats the purpose of a gambling addiction. This kept him in a perpetual state of frustration, in which he would have to come up with weird ways to unconsciously sabotage himself so he could start over with a new risk.

"For Todd, the band was simply a gambler's risk. Everything was required to be at the make-or-break stage. One classic example was when he decided we should go on tour, Seattle to San Francisco, but he wanted to do it in Ursela's car, which was a clunker. He knew the possibility of it breaking down would be hanging over our heads the whole time, which he considered a thrilling risk. I told him flat out that I required him to rent a Ryder truck like any other professionals would do, and that if he did not, then I would not go with them on the trip. He had sense enough to recognize that they could not play without me, and so we never did go on tour. So he decided to become the biggest band in Portland."

To that end, Todd's next bit of hyperbole in a promotion sheet was outlandish to the extreme: *Detente Touch—The Future of Rock. To pass up seeing Detente Touch now would be the same as missing the*

Beatles when they started back in Liverpool. This band in later years will be brought up with the likes of the Doors, Jimi Hendrix, Janis Joplin, Buddy Holly, and Led Zeppelin.

In a way it was too bad that he laid it on so thick. Detente Touch was actually a good band with some interesting material. Todd was a fairly decent bass player and an accomplished songwriter. Many of his songs had elements that compared favorably to other more notable bands of that era. His song "Lost Way" had a sound like that of the English Beat. "This was America" had the sentiments of the Fixx, with a quality strangely reminiscent of the '60s band Quicksilver Messenger Service. "Think of Zebra" contained a lead-in riff like the Red Rockers' song "China." The lyrics to the "zebra" song were memorable and spoke of racial harmony. Todd sang about crying when he thought of all the strife and dying, then he created an image of a zebra, whose black and white stripes complemented each other.

Todd explored the violence of Northern Ireland in a song, "In My Mind." It spoke of little boys growing up to fight and die.

In an almost prophetic coincidence, his last song on the demo tape was "The Never Ending Nightmare." It could very well have been the title for himself and everyone around him in the years to come.

When Todd stepped back from all the hype, he acknowledged the fusion of various elements in the band's early work. He said, "One of the most remarkable things about the group of musicians [Detente Touch] is that everyone who hears them finds different things to like about them, and as a whole is enjoyed by all." In fact, the tunes were catchy, they had good guitar work and the lyrics had some thought-provoking ideas.

To explain the source of all the different styles, Todd said that Ursela's mentors were as diverse as Barbra Streisand, Janis Joplin and Madonna. Collin preferred UFO and the Police. Ken was influenced by Jimi Hendrix and Eddie Van Halen. Of himself, Todd said that his mentors were the rock-and-thrash sounds of the Sex Pistols and Todd Rundgren.

In the Portland area those who listened to Detente Touch did like what they were hearing and word of mouth spread. Comments overheard at concerts by the audience were jotted down by Todd. He noted such quips as: "They got me all riled up and thinking about the way the system really works." "Urs kicks ass on vocals." "Ken just screams." "The drummer was on the side of the stage. It was like the first time I've ever been that close to the drummer."

One comment Todd must have loved was by a young woman who said, "Those guys look edible."

Shannon Colebank had an interesting statement in this regard. "We would go to concerts together. Fifteen minutes after we got to the show, there would be three girls clustered around Todd. I would nod and grin to myself, thinking, 'Yep, that's Todd.' "

Todd waxed philosophical at one point about the band's music and said, "You may think we can't change the world, but we can at least change the world around us." And at another time, "We really don't want to change things, we just want people to become aware of what's happening around them."

But it wasn't long before he was back to the hype. He wrote a broadside: *After listening to some of the questions Detente Touch pose, the nightly news has a tendency to leave a bitter taste in one's mouth. Never before has a band so clearly stated that the propaganda of the world is more prominent now than ever.*

He then said that Detente Touch's rage came in small doses so that they wouldn't preach or lecture onstage, but rather let the listeners start thinking for themselves. Finally he wrote, *This band leads you through political strife, suicide, apartheid, war and inhumanity, yet with sexual overtones that keep you moving, dancing and cheering.*

As Collin said later, "Todd always had a singular vision about what he wanted to be. Lots of guys are good musicians. Technically good, but they lack a vision of what they want their music to be. There is no fire in their music. Nothing beyond its technical precision. Ninety-nine percent of the ideas Todd had were bullshit. But there was always one percent that was a real gem.

"A good promoter, he could talk people into listening to us. We were originally just a garage band looking for places to play. When he started, he could barely play bass at all. But he was diligent and he learned. He wanted to be a rock and roll star. That was his goal. He could take people's ideas and make them work. You could call him our music director. Everyone in the band had things in common musically. We knew what we wanted to hear. Todd would point us in the direction that he felt the band should go. And the rest of us would get excited and throw in suggestions on how that could work to our advantage and success.

"Todd would take all our ideas and give them substance. Bring some order out of chaos. Todd was not modest and he would take credit for what he accomplished. But, hey, he deserved it. We pretty much let him have his way because he seemed to know what he was doing. It's difficult to sell yourself in an artistic environment, but Todd was good at selling himself and us. I believe he could sell a refrigerator to an Eskimo.

"Todd got the band gigs at the Belmont Inn, Satyricon, and the place that would become the Blue Gallery. Detente Touch was making a name for itself in the Portland area."

These were heady times for Collin and Todd. Just up Interstate 5 in Washington State, other garage bands like Nirvana and Pearl Jam were about to explode onto the music scene. There was a new "Norhtwest Sound" being born. Detente Touch deviated from the grunge sound with their glam rock/ heavy metal/gothic approach. It was their inclusion of lead singer Ursela that gave the band a whole new and unique aura.

Ursela had a voice that could emulate Janis Joplin's or Siouxsie's, of Siouxsie and the Banshees, but her style was like Madonna's. Sexual innuendos vibrated from the stage. She knew how to work a crowd and the audience lapped it up. She gave Detente Touch the trademark that it needed. More and more venues in the Portland area opened up to them.

Shannon Colebank said later, "We played assorted small clubs and had a blast doing it. I can honestly say it was the best time of my life. The personalities of all the band members were so totally different. There was constant personal tensions and frustration, but all of us loved the music. There was a lot of potential there. We really were the best band in Portland at that time. But because every time we played, we received nothing but cheers, Todd was frustrated. There was no risk. He decided to do something about it."

Despite Ursela's stage presence, Detente Touch was always Todd Garton's band. Collin recalled, "One day he came up with something really revolutionary. As a matter of fact, he was ahead of his time. He pushed the envelope, where the band's music took off into a scary/sexual/noir/gangster–type mode. He had these ideas coming straight out of *Soldier of Fortune* magazine. It was white guys' gangsta music, before anyone had heard of gangsta rap. It was a concept that Tupac Shakur's Murder Inc. would become later. For Todd it was more like Assassination Inc.

"Some of his ideas came from the band U2's political side. Songs like 'Sunday Bloody Sunday.' Stuff like that. But most of it was pure Todd. Militia mentality. *Soldier of Fortune* craziness. It was all bullshit, but it was entertaining bullshit. There was the whole militia thing going on at that time. Crazy people with guns off in the countryside. Todd tapped into that. It was wild and spooky, but definitely full of energy."

With the advent of this new sound, Collin and the other band members were treated to more and more of Todd's fantasy world of guns, violence and the Irish Republican Army. Collin said, "We used to hang out at Biddy McGraw's Pub in Portland. Drink the best pints with the American wanna-be soldiers of fortune and the beaten-but-never-forgetting Irish illegal immigrants. Portland was passionate about its politics. George Bush Senior once called us 'Little Beirut.' We [Detente Touch] did many shows with an REM-type band called the Killing Fields."

Todd told the band members about his alleged trip to Northern Ireland when he was very young. According to the story he told Collin, Todd had stolen a credit card when he was only twelve years old and somehow made his way to Belfast. At first it was dismissed by Collin as a pure lie. But as he said later, "At first I blew it off. I didn't believe it was possible. But over the years of knowing Todd, the story was consistent enough that I no longer had any reason to doubt it."

In part, Todd had gleaned these stories of Northern Ireland from a man named Bill Parks. Todd had struck up a friendship with Parks in downtown Portland when Garton was fifteen years old. Parks told Garton that he had been a witness to the Bloody Sunday Massacre in 1972 on the streets of Belfast. The incident spurred Parks into becoming a member of Sinn Fein, the political arm of the Irish Republican Army. He told young Garton countless tales of the "Troubles" and his role in them. Todd absorbed Parks's stories until they became his own. He elaborated on them wherever he fancied they should go. Todd would confess years later, "I felt extremely sympathetic to the IRA cause and wired up." It was the stories of gun battles and secret missions that wired him up. They were the fodder of his *Soldier of Fortune* daydreams come to life.

Parks told Todd how the Garton name was steeped in Irish history. He added that he should be proud of his Irish ancestry. Before long, Todd was reading everything he could lay his hands on concerning Northern Ireland and the insurrection there. The information he gleaned added authenticity to the stories he told to fellow band members in Detente Touch.

According to Collin Colebank, Todd said that once he was in Ireland he managed to hook up with a group of IRA supporters. Colebank said, "Todd was in a group of people and he showed them how to take care of their guns. He was a country kid and familiar with guns. He found himself in a situation teaching other people about guns and how they work. Basically how to maintain their weapons. He didn't set up a class and teach people about shooting soldiers from rooftops, but these people ended up being snipers later."

In these tales that Todd told Collin, he said that he'd stayed in Ireland for about a year. Then according to Colebank, "At that time he realized where he was and what he was doing. Realized he was making a mistake and had to get home. That was the scary challenge."

Todd wove all these tales of Ireland into the band's general discussion of the music of U2. During these sessions he liked to show off his "IRA tattoo"— the one he had supposedly earned while in Belfast. The members were taken with U2's political songs. Collin remembered that U2 was very popular in Portland at the time.

So far, Todd's stories had been harmless enough, a strange but effective bit of self-promotion. But somewhere along the line Todd began to weave in more sinister tales. One of his most fantastic stories was the tale that he had been paid to kill two men in the Portland area. He said he had bound their arms and legs and then decapitated them. He supposedly did this when he was only sixteen years old. He threw their bodies into the Columbia River. He said, "These were really bad men. Fewer people would get hurt because I killed them. I did it professionally."

Todd had several *Soldier of Fortune* magazines lying around his room, and he loved their stories of high adventure and danger. He also enjoyed the advertisements in the back of the magazine that allegedly offered jobs to mercenaries. There were various shadowy companies or organizations that would hire mercenaries to do jobs in various hot spots around the world. All you had to do was contact the PO box or phone number listed.

One day Todd told Collin how easy it would be to set up an assassination company. This may have started out as a lark, but Todd was dead serious about it before long. According to Colebank, "On several occasions we talked about how easy it would be to put together an assassination company. I regarded *Soldier of Fortune* magazine like a comic book. You open up the back of this magazine and you look at all these ridiculous companies that people are advertising. They're actually advertising in a national publication. How simple it would be to set up a company, put an ad out and take people's money. You set up a business, you have an eight hundred number and you start making an income. Todd said we could scam them and who were they gonna complain to? It would be like complaining about your Sea Monkeys or your secret decoder ring.

"Todd always believed that if you leaped, there

would be a net waiting underneath. The fun part was the emotional crush at the end. You know, the classic story of the frog and the scorpion. The scorpion was Todd."

(The story goes that a scorpion couldn't swim a stream and asked a frog to take him to the other side. The frog said, "No, you'll sting me." The scorpion answered, "I wouldn't do that. I'd drown." So the frog agreed to take the scorpion to the other side. Halfway across, the scorpion suddenly stung the frog. "Why did you do that?" the frog asked. "Now we're both going to die." The scorpion answered, "I couldn't help myself. I'm a scorpion.")

Collin continued, "Todd always had a bigger, better plan than the last one. In the end, you just knew you would be paying for it when it was over."

Collin may have looked upon *Soldier of Fortune* as a kind of adult comic book, but Todd Garton apparently did not. Many of his later acts would lead right back to this concept of a company that contracted hits. He never grew out of this fantasy life.

If Collin Colebank and the other members of Detente Touch were willing to listen to all of Todd Garton's fabrications about his secret life in Ireland, then as an assassin, there was one more person in Portland who was absolutely enthralled by him and his tales. She was young, impressionable and deeply intoxicated by Todd Garton. She was sixteen-year-old Lynn Aasen.

Unlike Todd, Lynn was a Portland native. Lynn would recall years later the exact moment she laid eyes on Todd Garton: "I was at Park Rose High School. I was standing at my locker with four of my real close friends. And there was a rumor going around about a new guy from California. And none of us had seen him yet. So we were just standing in the hall, and just talking about him. And I remember looking over and he was walking down the hallway."

Lynn Aasen was smitten by Todd Garton right from the start. She soon asked another girl, who already knew Todd, to introduce her to him. Lynn said, "I was in band at that time in the percussion section. I played drums. And there was a girl also in that class that had met him before. So through the band class, we were formally introduced."

Lynn soon found out that Todd was part of a rock and roll band. It added to his luster in her eyes. About a month after their first meeting, they were in a boyfriend/girlfriend relationship. Not long thereafter, Lynn recalled that they had their first sex. Todd's thoughts on this haven't survived, but Lynn thought it was wonderful.

Lynn was enthralled with Todd's status in Detente Touch. She called it "his band." And for all intents and purposes, it was. She said later, "Todd sang. He wrote songs. He played instruments. He did everything."

From a distance this could have been any teenager's relationship, but Todd was not a typical teenager. With Lynn Aasen as his admiring listener, his fabrications of his adventures grew to amazing heights. And Lynn lapped up every word without question. Todd gave her his copy of *The Anarchist Cookbook*. It depicted clandestine ways to kill people and make bombs. Todd indicated that he was proficient in making Molotov cocktails. He said Lynn needed to hide it for him, because if it was ever discovered in his room by certain people, he might be killed. He didn't specify who the people were.

Todd stuffed newspaper and magazine articles on Northern Ireland into the book. He told Lynn that he had been there as an operative with the IRA. His tales to her differed a little from the ones he had told band members. He announced to Lynn he had made more than one trip to Ireland. And these trips had been when he was fifteen and sixteen years of age, not twelve as he had told Collin Colebank. Even these fantastic assertions did not sway Lynn in her belief of his stories. She was too much in love with Todd.

Todd had so much knowledge about Northern Ireland that Lynn readily believed what he had to say. He recounted the stories with such sincerity and detail that it drove away any lingering doubts she might have harbored. Todd gave her a short history lesson on the Troubles and about the factions in Northern Ireland. *The Anarchist Cookbook* became her most prized possession—her Holy Grail of all that was Todd. Lynn Aasen became Todd's most devoted worshiper.

Todd continued to give her articles and photographs to keep within the pages of *The Anarchist Cookbook*. With some articles he would point to them and say, "I participated in that." There was even a photo of the Irish countryside with an individual whose face was not distinct. Todd said that it was him.

The Anarchist Cookbook became full of Todd memorabilia. Besides articles on Northern Ireland, she stuffed photos of Todd with his band members between its pages. She had one prized photo of him leaning against a wall. She thought it might be of him in Ireland. He gave her a quote in Latin to hide within its pages. She didn't know Latin. He said it referred to the Fatherland, in other words, Ireland. He gave her a drawing he had made of a flaming cross with lettering, CHURCHES ON FIRE. He told her, "It's because the fight over there isn't just political. It's religious, too."

Eventually Todd altered the front of *The Anarchist Cookbook* to reflect his passion for Northern Ireland. Originally the cover had just been a plain front with the title on the top portion. Todd covered over this title and replaced it with SINN FEIN. Then he added, *The kids are not all right.* This was in reference to a song with the lyrics, "The kids are all right." Todd said in the case of Northern Ireland the kids were not all right. They had to grow up with strife and bloodshed. They were in constant danger of being killed in a cross fire.

Right in the center of the book cover, Todd added a logo from *Soldier of Fortune.* It displayed two knives and a beret. Within the pages of the book he managed to combine his passion for U2 and the IRA cause. It was a compilation photo he constructed of eyes, which were portrayed on a U2 album cover, looking over a Belfast skyline. The eyes seemed to be hovering over everything, spying on the people below. It suited his ideas of intrigue and danger.

Todd also turned Lynn on to the books he enjoyed. She was already a devotee of Anne Rice novels. She especially liked *Interview with the Vampire.* But Todd took her down a different road with novels of suspense, assassinations and covert operations. These were titles like *The Day of the Jackal* and *The Eagle Has Landed.* Jack Higgins was his favorite author. He told Lynn that Higgins's novels portrayed the kind of life he had led. Lynn began to read them.

The one political/semimilitary organization that Todd didn't like was the Palestine Liberation Organization (PLO). He talked about their methods and compared them to the methods used by the IRA. He agreed that some of the methods were similar, but he told Lynn he really didn't care much for people from the Middle East. It was not his cause. What he liked was the Irish cause, through and through.

What Todd liked, Lynn liked as well. To show her affection for him and his beliefs, she went to Catherine O'Connelly's Irish Shop in downtown Portland to buy him a gift. As she stated later, "I like jewelry. I wanted something special for him and myself. And since rings weren't really appropriate, a cross was something we both could wear. They both had silver chains on them. They had Celtic artwork and were kind of trendy at that time. Since Todd was really into that, I wanted to be into anything that he was into. It was a symbol of love. They both had love knots, sort of a symbol that they wouldn't ever end."

But silver crosses alone weren't enough for Lynn to show her devotion to Todd. One day she took a razor blade and carved a heart into her flesh on her upper thigh. In the middle of the heart she carved the letter *T.* It, of course, stood for Todd.

At this point Todd seemed to be enamored as much with Lynn as she was with him. He gave her

the nickname Malichi (in some spellings Maliki).
He told her it came from the Bible and also from
an ancient Irish myth. He said the Bible reference
referred to an angel. But in fact, there is no verifi-
cation that "Malichi" or "Maliki" are either in the
Bible or ancient Irish myths. It may have been one
more of Todd's fabrications. There is a Maliki that
refers to an eighth-century Medina scholar named
Malik ibn Anas. Maliki is one of the four Islamic
schools of law pertaining to the Koran in the Sunni
tradition. Whether Todd ever knew about this is
unknown. Perhaps he liked the word and molded
it to his own myths. Lynn apparently was so in love
with him, she never checked it out. If he told her it
meant angel, then she was "his angel."

But more than anything Lynn was drawn to Todd
because of his connection with the band Detente
Touch. It was exciting to be around him and the
others as they improved with their music. More
and more venues were opening up for them. They
practiced in a "band house" in downtown Portland.
It was chaotic, it was energetic; it was intoxicating.
It was a version of sex, drugs and rock and roll.
Drugs may not have been a factor of Detente
Touch's existence, but sex was always hovering in
their lifestyles and lyrics. And Lynn was anything
but coy on the matter of sex. She admitted later to
having sex with Todd in a motel's hot tub after a
band practice.

Official documents would also point to another
hot-tub episode later, one that Lynn would not verify. Another teenaged boy named Bill Johnson was
in the hot tub with his girlfriend. So were Todd and
Lynn. According to the document, they all had sex

at the same time in the hot tub. There was even talk of switching partners.

Lynn had a very sexual nature and she was fairly up front about it. She desired Todd and had sex with him as much as she could. Yet it might have astounded Todd to know at the time that he was being cheated on by Lynn. And not with another boy. According to her, she was also having sex with a girlfriend. As Lynn said later, "I'm a typically very huggy, kissy person. And she and I had been through a lot together." The closeness eventually led to sexual encounters, which Lynn referred to as "sixty-nine" in nature. This entailed mutual oral copulation.

Lynn was anything but circumspect about her use of the term sixty-nine. In fact, she used it a lot as a teenager and it became kind of a code word with her. As an adult, Lynn would combine the word Pandoora and 69 to form an e-mail address. For some reason, she would add an extra "o" to Pandora, making it Pandoora 69. Basically, Lynn Aasen was bisexual with the major stress on the heterosexual side. She wanted sex with Todd Garton more than with anyone else.

Being with Todd, hanging out with his band, tattooing and scarifying herself, Lynn Aasen was a handful by her sophomore year. She repeatedly skipped school and was rebellious. Her parents had divorced and her home life was in an uproar. She caused such a commotion at school, she was suspended. Undisciplined at home, she took off for a runaway center. After she left the center, she stayed in the homes of various friends, eventually settling down at one home. But her rebelliousness had an undesired effect as far as Todd was concerned. She lost contact with him at school, since she was denied access to campus. They both may still have had their Celtic crosses with the inseparable love knots attached, but Lynn was soon to discover that Todd was anything but undyingly loyal. In fact, in her absence he had found himself another girl. Her name was Carole Holman.

Carole Holman was born on June 14, 1969, in Oregon. There were already three boys in the family and everyone was praying for a girl. When Carole arrived, she was named after her paternal grandmother. Carole's mother, Virginia, recalled that at the age of two her daughter could draw well and make up songs. She loved the color pink and everything in her room was soon pink. Her father, Jim, thought it looked like the inside of a Pepto-Bismol bottle.

Carole loved her big brothers, Scott, Mike and Donald. Even though each one of them was temperamentally different, they all got along well. The boys doted on their sister, and she called them "my boys."

Carole's favorite movie as a girl was *The Wizard of Oz*. Her father, Jim, related, "As a child it was a very special occasion to get a bunch of pillows and lay flat on the floor and watch the movie with me. She knew it all by heart but, even so, would get all scared when she saw the Wicked Witch. I would tease her by singing, 'We're off to see the Gizzard. The wonderful Gizzard of Oz.' She would say, 'Daaad!' "

Carole loved Halloween and Jim had a lot of fun taking her around the neighborhood trick-or-treating. He particularly remembered one costume she loved. It was a Raggedy Ann outfit made by her grandmother. Carole also dressed up in costume as an angel. Her mother recalled that Carole's favorite baseball team was the Angels. She often wore their baseball cap.

There was excitement in the area in 1980 when Mount Saint Helens began to erupt. Carole would take her binoculars out and look at the eruptions right from her backyard. She was fascinated by the plumes of smoke and ash that spiraled upward from the peak. It was a vivid reminder that they all lived in volcano country.

Even though Carole was accomplished at "girl" activities—such as dancing classes, playing the cello and cheerleading—she also thrived on sports. Tennis was her favorite. She played doubles in high school, and Virginia recalled some amusing incidents on the tennis court: "Carole played doubles with a skinny girl named Lisa. Whenever there was a tough shot, Lisa would watch it go by and then call out, 'Carole, it's yours.' "

Carole enjoyed going on camping trips with the family and especially being around water. Her father recalled, "She loved the water and never wanted to get out. When camping at the lake, she would spend all day long in the water and I'd have to force her to get out and come back to camp. As an infant, her favorite thing was her bath. Her love for the water started at an early age. Our main vacation activity was boating and camping at the Cove Palisades in eastern Oregon. Carole had no fear in the boat. We decided to sell our boat after a few years of camping and take our children to Disneyland.

Carole never forgave us for selling our boat just when she was of an age to water-ski."

Carole wasn't afraid of new challenges. Her mom remembered the first time Carole tried golf. She had never swung at a golf ball in her life, but she stepped right up to the ball and knocked it down the fairway. Virginia said, "She kept hitting it straight all day long. She didn't duff it once. She just had natural ability when it came to sports."

This carried over to rafting as well. Carole went on a rafting expedition and fell out of the raft. She came up spluttering from the river, but she was eager to go again. She even tried skydiving.

Carole Holman was basically a happy, family-oriented kid. But unfortunately, the Holman family was beginning to unravel. Jim and Virginia had their problems and it eventually led to divorce in 1987. Carole took it hard and it led to some rebelliousness. She wanted to drop out of school. She started staying out late. And she took a job at an Arby's, where she met an older girl named Marty. It was Collin Colebank's girlfriend, Martha Federici. The job at Arby's brought her right into contact with Todd Garton.

Marty had known Todd since a curious incident at a community college, where Marty was a student and worked at the college's radio station. One day a teenager walked in and introduced himself as Todd Garton. He wanted to be a disc jockey on the station. This was highly unusual, since he was underage and not even a student on campus. Yet somehow he convinced the radio station's manager to let him have a try. Soon he was doing a shift right after Marty. All of it was against the rules, but Todd was never one to let rules stand in his way. He conned the manager into giving him the job.

Because of his ties to Marty, Todd got a job at Arby's, the same restaurant where Carole had started to work. The moment she showed up, Todd was immediately attracted to her. She had a cute page-boy haircut and very green eyes. And she was outgoing and funny. Before long she was attracted to him as well. Todd forgot all about another girl to whom he had pledged undying devotion, Lynn Aasen.

There was a huge difference in personality between Carole and Lynn. Lynn Aasen swallowed every lie Todd told without question. But according to Collin Colebank, "Carole was the one person who could see right through Todd's bullshit. It amused her to see how he pulled the wool over other people's eyes. She thought it was funny. She liked to see how far he could go with his outrageous stories. He was always going full tilt. There was no shy side to Todd. Whenever he tried it on her, she called him on it. He couldn't get one past Carole."

Even though Carole knew that Todd was the grand master of BS, she still liked him. He had style, he wasn't shy and he was fun to be around. His leadership in Detente Touch made him even more attractive.

Carole had style as well. She was musically gifted and could sing. Marty remembered, "Carole had a sly sense of humor. Very dry. She could zing them out before you hardly knew what was going on. Very quick wit. She was fun to be around."

Eventually Todd, Carole, Ursela, Shannon and one more male all moved into a band house on Thirty-ninth Avenue in Portland. Shannon recalled: "I built a recording studio/rehearsal space in the basement for them and recorded all their practice sessions, which was a tremendous growth experience for them, having good recordings of themselves to critique."

But five was hardly the maximum number of people in the house. There were always band members moving in and moving out. Teenagers and twenty-year-olds looking for a place to party or to crash at night. Carole's father got wind of the setup and didn't like it. He didn't like Todd's influence on Carole as well. But in a confrontation Todd told Jim that if he interfered, he would never see his daughter again. Jim believed him and backed off.

Virginia Griffiths, married again, recalled how "we met Todd and Carole for breakfast to try and come to a compromise on their relationship. My husband was very angry and told Todd at one time that he could be arrested for contributing to the delinquency of a minor. We found out later that Todd was a few months younger than Carole. We thought he was twenty-one by the way he looked and acted.

"My husband thought Carole needed to see a doctor at this time because he felt she was not thinking clearly. After a few sessions with the doctor, he told us that he had never talked to a teenager that was so pleasant and levelheaded. He told us that she did not do anything irresponsible and she was working and finishing school."

Even if Carole was levelheaded, many of the other people who came to the band house were not. Collin Colebank remembered the frenetic anarchy of that band house. He said later, "Musicians were always coming and going. Todd was like a ringmaster. It was a real zoo. Todd loved the atmosphere. The band would practice there, but after a while it would dissolve into drunken debauchery. That's when Marty and I would take off. We weren't into that scene. But Todd ate it up."

Shannon Colebank recalled Carole from this time period. "She seemed very generous. She was built like a fertility goddess. Her eyes were huge; her lashes were amazingly thick; she had full lips and was very curvy. She had a very healthy sexiness about her. She was very loyal and supportive. I think lots of guys wanted to take her away from Todd. I would overhear random boys saying to each other, 'She's too good for that jerk.' "

Apparently, though, Carole enjoyed Todd's brash and clever remarks. They were young, apparently in love, and Todd was the king of a musical "Animal House" in downtown Portland. But into this rock and roll scene another girl walked straight into their relationship. The girl was Lynn Aasen.

Lynn had never lost her obsession with Todd. She still wore the Celtic cross around her neck to remind her of Todd. Somehow she discovered that he was working at an Arby's. When she went there and asked for him, the girls behind the counter acted strangely. According to one version, he wasn't there at the time. But the girls told her to ask Carole about him. Suspicious of what Carole's connection was with Todd, Lynn followed up on her. She discovered that Carole was not only dating Todd, she was living with him. Carole was obviously Todd's new girlfriend. It made Lynn furious, but not so much at Todd. It was directed mostly at Carole. She felt that Carole had stolen what should have been hers. After all, she was the one with a heart-shaped scar on her thigh with the letter T in its center. She was the one who kept his precious tome, *The Anarchist Cookbook*. As far as she was concerned, Carole Holman was just an interloper. Lynn was certain that when she introduced herself into Todd's life again, he would choose her over Carole.

But that's not the way things played out. Collin Colebank, who liked Carole, did not like Lynn Aasen. In fact, he said that none of the other band members did, either. He would recall later, "Lynn was a bubblehead. There was nothing upstairs. She was obsessed with Todd. Lynn was a hanger-on and a groupie. I think that Todd tolerated her. She began to come to band practice again. Todd tolerated her because she was there. No one else in the band would. Everybody else wished she would just go away. Todd and Carole were obviously an item. They lived together. And Lynn continued to come to band practice and hang around. She wasn't a part of the creative process. Carole had talent. Nobody would give Lynn the time of day. I mean, we never had an out-and-out discussion of it with Todd. We never told him, 'Get rid of this person. She's really disrupting our creative process.' I think he just took advantage of her. She would make up excuses to be there. She'd come to Todd with some stupid problem for him to solve. It was all bullshit. She just wanted to be around him. It must have been hard on Carole. They didn't like each other. But Todd never asked Lynn to go away."

Perhaps Todd never asked Lynn to go away for

one reason—why only have one admirer when he could have two?

An important incident happened around that time that had a profound effect upon Carole. As Shannon Colebank remembered it, "Carole got an ectopic pregnancy. A fertilized egg got stuck in one of her tubes. She got a fever and threw up constantly. Todd thought she had gotten poisoned and he really freaked out. He had this clutching possessiveness of her. I suppose any man would freak out like this over the woman he loved, but I thought it was an overreaction, like he was more afraid of her abandoning him by dying, than he was afraid for her. He was truly scared.

"I drove them to the hospital, and when she found out it was an almost-pregnancy, she became desperate to keep it. They told her it was not a pregnancy, it was an abnormal growth that had to be removed to save her life.

"This changed her. After that, she was a different person. I guess it made her grow up real fast. She was no longer a serious, silent observer; now she was more flippant and talkative. She was no longer just a horny teenager; she was now a potential mother. Emotionally she was a much more mature person after that."

On top of all of this, Todd Garton's rock and roll dreamworld suddenly came crashing down in flames. According to Collin, "One day Ursela announced she had more compassion for animal rights than human rights. She quit the band and that was the end of Detente Touch. Todd was so furious with Ursela, the focal point of the project, he said she wasn't worthy of the air we were breathing. If Todd was in a killing mood, he would have killed Ursela then and there."

Interesting enough, Shannon had a very different reason for the band's demise. He attributed it to Todd's sociopathic need for risk taking. Shannon said, "Todd decided to be the Marilyn Manson of the '80s and try to get publicity in the most asinine ways. He would constantly try to invent ways of inciting riots or getting arrested onstage. But since the rest of the band was seriously interested in their music careers, as opposed to the risk of disaster, it always came off as pointless and prankish. The people who respected our music were embarrassed by our stupid show, and the creeps who wanted a riot were frustrated by the professionalism of the rest of the band who always tried to quell trouble.

"Todd purposefully destroyed it all so he could start over with a new risk. At the time Key Largo was the hottest club in town. It would only book bands that could guarantee that five hundred people would show up. Todd lied to Tony Di Micoli, the owner of Key Largo, and guaranteed him we could pull a crowd of five hundred people. Todd was able to weasel his way into booking two Saturday nights in a row at Key Largo. I wish I could have heard the magic words he must have used to scam someone as jaded as Tony.

"To assure disaster, Todd refused to advertise the show; I'm sure he conjured up some bizarre reasoning in his head as to why this would be necessary. But this is the cliché gambler's behavior. Obviously, no one showed up and Tony was pissed as hell. Detente Touch was effectively over in Portland."

Whatever the reason, Detente Touch was indeed through, and the band members went their separate ways. Todd and Carole eventually moved into Todd's parents home in a section of Portland. Yet in some ways this arrangement was even more chaotic than the band house. Todd and Carole began to get into more fights there. They would break up to make up. The one thing the move did accomplish was that Lynn Aasen no longer came around. She may not have known where they were living at the time. And even if she did know, she was not welcome there.

Shannon still kept in touch with Todd and Carole, and he noted Todd's increasing hostility toward people who had money. Shannon recalled, "Todd had taken up the crossbow. He had a little crossbow pistol and he would drive around at night shooting new Camaros with it. The new Camaros represented the wealth he resented not having. Immediately after the band days, he took to this childish expression of his anger. He said to me, 'I don't know why anyone would buy those cars.' And I said, 'The only reason they buy those cars is to purposefully antagonize *you!*'

"At that, Carole burst into extremely nervous laughter. She was very uncomfortable with me teasing Todd like that."

But Shannon persisted and said, " 'It's true, Carole. It's National Antagonize Todd Month!' And that's when Todd started smiling at the whole stupid situation."

The chaos in the Garton household was symptomatic of everything else that was happening in Todd's life at the time, but Todd Garton still had grand dreams, and a very curious incident happened around this time. Either he went through with it, or it was just one more of his elaborate lies. According to Shannon, "Todd got some friend of his to steal a blank high-school diploma from a local school, which Todd forged and used to scam his way into the police academy. What a thrill it must have been to him to risk getting caught lying on his police application, and then have it hanging over him all while he was there that they might do an accurate background check and catch him. But once again Todd was a genius. He sailed through the academy with flying colors. He eventually became too disgusted with it because the first thing you do every morning at the academy is salute a garbage can. The whole system was like the military, designed to break you of all ego. Add to this was the fact that he was just too plain intelligent for the police department."

Since there is no corroboration of this, it was probably one more of Todd's elaborate lies. The thrill for him was probably in making Shannon Colebank believe something so outrageous was actually true. If Todd was a genius, he was a genius in that regard. He could make almost anyone believe in his lies. The more bizarre they were, the better.

However, his next step was not a lie. He decided to make a clean break from his bygone rock and roll days. If music wouldn't save him, then he would turn to his one other love—military adventure. He decided to join the U.S. Marines.

An odd incident occurred at this juncture, and the only reference to it comes from Lynn Aasen. She said that before going into the marines, she and Todd spent a weekend together at Portland's Imperial Hotel. After he returned to California in the Anderson area, where his parents now lived, she said he sent her a cardboard box full of items. According to Lynn, "He sent me my brown leather bomber jacket that I let him wear back to California. Some letters. And an engagement ring."

Lynn is the only one who ever mentioned this ring. Todd would not verify it later. But if Todd did actually send it, his timing was off. Lynn was now in a relationship with a guy named Chris. Chris knew Todd from high school and didn't like him. In fact, he made Lynn remove the letter *T* from her self-inflicted tattoo. She did so by crossing it out with a razor slash. But there was one thing she didn't do. She never told Chris that the Celtic cross she constantly wore around her neck was to remind her of Todd.

Another story also surfaced later through Lynn. She said that when Todd went down to the San Diego area to join the marines, he phoned her. Chris answered the phone. Once he heard Todd's voice, he cursed and hung up. He told Lynn, "I think that was your ex-boyfriend." Lynn would claim later that Todd was calling her to ask her to marry him.

On August 21, 1990, Todd Garton's marine days began. He went into active service at the Marine Corps Recruiting Depot in San Diego, California. But he was either clumsy or just plain unlucky. During basic training he severely injured his leg during a training exercise. This pulled him out of his class and into medical rehabilitation and physical reconditioning.

On January 15, 1991, Todd was well enough to

be reassigned to Platoon 1125. Ten days later he earned an expert rifle badge. Because he was in the military during the time of the Gulf War, he also earned a National Defense Service Medal. On March 15, 1991, Todd completed boot camp and was assigned to Camp Pendleton, where he enrolled in the infantry school. After completing this course he even took a diving course at Coronado. But the injury he had sustained to his leg in boot camp was still giving him problems. It was supposed to be a three-week class, but he only completed one week.

Todd was in the Schools Battalion at Camp Pendleton when his leg finally became too much of a problem. On September 13, 1991, he received an honorable discharge from the marines. He had been a marine for exactly one year and twenty-three days. He ended at the rank of an E-3 lance corporal. He never was a lieutenant, as he would later claim. Nor did he receive a Purple Heart medal, combat medal, or SEALs diving-bubble pin.

Washed out of the military, his rock and roll dreams up in smoke, Todd was a sullen, unhappy individual in the fall of 1991. Something very murky happened during his last days with the marines, and dates are not clear. Once again the only reference to what happened came from Lynn Aasen. According to her, he proposed marriage to her once again sometime during the period he was at Camp Pendleton. This time she got the message. Lynn was ready to accept and phoned him back, but the person who answered the call was Carole Holman. Lynn told Carole that Todd had just proposed to her. Momentarily taken aback, Carole recovered enough to say,

"Imagine that! Because he's just proposed to me, too!"

Todd would not verify this story later, but it was not out of character for him; one letter from Todd to Lynn around this time adds credence to her claim. It began by telling Lynn that eyes were the window of the soul, and his eyes were now worn and tired from the troubles of the world. He said that he saw a world of pain all around him. He still felt pain in his leg. He spoke of horror killings going on all around the world, bringing strife and misery. Then he called out to her to lend him a hand to help bind the pieces of a broken man.

Todd once again called her Maliki. His angel. He asked who cared for her. He said that he did. Then the letter really got maudlin. Todd wrote: *I adore you, O Lynn. I count myself as nothing before your divine majesty. You are life, truth, beauty and goodness. I glorify you. I give thanks for your existence. I desire to serve, obey and love you.*

By this time Lynn had a hope chest. She kept Todd's copy of *The Anarchist Cookbook* there. She put this letter, and other ones like it from him, within the pages of the book. Lynn's hope chest was a reliquary for everything Todd ever gave her. It held all her hopes that one day they would be together forever. But what Todd gave her more than anything else were lies. While he said he adored Lynn, he was in the process of making wedding plans with Carole.

Lynn somehow found out. In anger and desperation she shipped overnight to Carole some of Todd's lovelorn letters. She wantede Carole to be so angry with him that she would cancel the marriage. Whatever Lynn hoped to gain from this, it didn't work. Todd and Carole went ahead with their plans to get married.

There was another woman in the Holman household by now, and her name was Victoria. She went by the name Vicki and she began dating Carole's father in 1989. Vicki related later, "Jim was so anxious for me to meet his beautiful daughter. And she was beautiful, inside and out. We hit it off right away. There remained a sort of impasse between Jim and Todd. Jim didn't want to lose his daughter, so he kept many things to himself. She also kept many things from us. But the one thing we always believed, whether we understood it or not, was that she and Todd loved each other."

Jim and Vicki were married in 1990 and Carole never seemed to resent that fact. In fact, she got along with her new stepmom very well. As the wedding day for Todd and Carole approached, scheduled for St. Patrick's Day, 1991, Vicki said, "Carole was excited. We talked about their plans. They wanted to get married in Reno, and we said that we would pay for whatever they wanted. Her dream was to have a traditional wedding dress with a long train, and I was determined she was going to have exactly what she wanted. She came home for a visit and we went to every wedding shop we could find. Late in the day we found it. It was perfect. Exactly what she dreamed of. It was frilly and feminine and had a long, flowing train. And it fit perfectly, requiring no alterations at all, which we took as a good omen."

The actual wedding in Reno was a nice affair, according to Vicki Holman. She and Jim met Todd's parents and everyone seemed to have a good time. Todd wore his dress blue marine uniform and smiled for the camera. And Carole looked radiant in her frilly white wedding gown. As Vicki said later, "They seemed like any young couple just starting out in life. We didn't know then that Lynn was in the picture."

But Lynn Aasen was always somewhere in the picture as far as Todd Garton was concerned, even while she dated or lived with other men. She lived with Chris for a while and then began to date a man named Dean Noyes. They met while she was working at a pizza place.

Incredibly, even though Todd was now married to Carole, he still sent mementos to Lynn to place in her scrapbook. He knew on one level that he would always have an admirer in her. He sent her a copy of his enlistment papers. He sent her half of his dog tags. He didn't let her know that he was now out of the marines for good. He strung her along with the story that he was still active with them. Even more incredibly, he didn't let Lynn know that he was now married to Carole. Apparently, he and Lynn still phoned each other on the sly.

When Todd found out that Lynn was dating Dean Noyes, he wrote her a letter filled with more fabrications about his present life. He said that he wrote letters to her, for her and about her. He hoped that she would keep these and not put them in a box to send to anyone. He asked how her life was going and commented on her new boyfriend. He said that she sounded happy and then he wrote, *That's all that matters, isn't it? I'm mixed up and messed up. My body's in deep pain. I tried running again. I got half a mile before my leg gave out. I've got to heal fast. I've got some business to take care of.*

Lynn understood that business meant going on a job to kill someone. She assumed he was doing this for the marines. Lynn later said, "Business was always to run off, go play soldier boy and kill people. Just kind of a package plan." She wasn't horrified that he was doing this. It was what gave Todd such an allure.

Todd went on to say that he was thinking of buying a motorcycle. It was a former Los Angeles Police Department bike. He wanted to modify it and take it down to Mexico, but then he surmised a Jeep might be better for Mexico. He alluded to the fact that there might be "business" down that way.

In his letter Todd signed off by saying, *Keep me in your thoughts and prayers, for you're always in mine. Love, Todd.*

Todd and Lynn constantly communicated by phone behind Carole's back. During these phone calls he would never give her a straight answer about whether he was married or not. How he got around this fact is not exactly clear. The one thing that was clear was that by the spring of 1992, Lynn was pregnant by Dean Noyes. In a rush they planned a wedding for May. When Todd got word of this, Lynn later told of his feelings: "He said that there wasn't anybody who could love me as much as he did. He wasn't very fond of Dean. And I said, 'Well, if you don't want me to do this, if you come up here, I will leave a whole church full of people. I'll leave with you.' "

Todd did not go up to Oregon and on May 25, 1992, Lynn Aasen became Mrs. Dean Noyes. Later she asked Todd why he didn't come. The answer he gave her was cryptic. He said, "I want you to be strong enough for yourself."

Incredibly, Lynn Noyes didn't find out for certain that Todd was married to Carole until after her son, Jordan, was born on November 9, 1992. She phoned the Garton household and wanted Todd to be Jordan's godfather. Instead of talking to Todd, she got Todd's mom on the line. For the first time she discovered that Todd had been married to Carole for over a year.

Even with this information, even with all the double-dealing Todd had been doing behind her back, Lynn still wanted him to be Jordan's godfather. He never showed up for the ceremony.

But Todd still sent Lynn more and more mementos of his life. She placed them in the scrapbook of Todd that she kept in her hope chest. Layer by layer *The Anarchist Cookbook* grew; it took on almost a mystical quality for her. She never lost hope that she and Todd would one day be together for good.

Chapter 3

World of Chaos

Right from the start Carole Garton was the bread-winner in the family; meanwhile Todd chased his pie-in-the-sky fantasies. While they lived in Anderson, California, Carole took a job with a hotel chain named Oxford Suites in nearby Redding. She started out at the desk and worked her way up. She was a very good worker and a quick study. Along with these qualities she was conscientious and friendly. The people there liked her enough to offer her a job training others to become motel managers. This took her as far away as Portland, Oregon, and San Luis Obispo, California, on training programs. Todd usually stayed behind pursuing his pipe dreams. It wasn't often he would do any work that would be considered a nine-to-five job. It was also during this period that he attended Shasta College, where he met Norman Daniels and told him all the lies about being a sniper for the marines and having been in Northern Ireland.

Carole excelled in her training activities, and the chain offered her a chance to manage two motels in Bend, Oregon. This was in central Oregon and Carole jumped at the chance. Todd was equally willing to move. Central Oregon offered a variety of hunting and fishing activities, and he was always an outdoor person. Once they moved there, Carole buckled down to her new managerial duties. These included running the Cimarron Motor Inn and the Maverick Motel in Bend. She even helped them improve their computer systems. During Carole's tenure the motels ran smoothly and efficiently.

Todd didn't mind all of Carole's duties with the motels. He was busy with his own schemes, which again concerned rock and roll. Todd started a business he called Emerald Productions. It was a promotions company that attempted to book rock acts into local venues. According to Collin Colebank, who still kept in touch with Todd, Emerald Productions tried to book out-of-town acts all over central Oregon. Collin recalled, "These were bands with a few days of downtime between gigs in San Francisco and Seattle. Todd would try to get them booked in Bend, Medford and Ashland. He even claimed to have booked Peter Gabriel in a two-hundred-seat venue in Medford. I never saw anything to confirm this, but didn't doubt he could have done it. He had a way of talking people into a lot of things."

Todd even talked Collin's new band, the Willies, into playing in Bend. The Willies at the time had a great reputation in the Portland area. One of the local papers named them the best local band of the year. Collin later said of the Bend trip, "Emerald Productions booked the Willies and set us up at the Oxford Suites and paid us well. Todd wanted to book us regionally, but he could never provide solid proof of any guaranteed backing. We were not excited about letting Todd run our finances while we were on the road. The numbers never added up. The Bend show was a flop. Maybe seventy-five people at a roller rink. Ticket prices and the overhead were clearly not in line.

"Todd reminded me of the promoter in the movie *Spinal Tap*. He always had these big ideas. Todd told me later he took cash advances on his American Express card. I was pretty sure he was getting cards under false business names, with no intention of ever paying them back."

Todd at least had one side project in the Bend area that was fun for him and Carole, if not particularly lucrative. He helped form a band called Forbidden Fruit. Carole was even the lead singer in the band. And by all accounts she had a good voice. Perhaps not as strong as Ursela in Todd's old band, but nonetheless competent with good range. The concept of the band was akin to U2's *The Joshua Tree* album with Sinéad O'Connor vocals. As Collin said, "It was a good idea. It worked for the Cranberries. Forbidden Fruit had more testosterone. A driving sound. They even did a cover of one of the Sex Pistols' songs. They came to my place in Portland once to record an album. We recorded twelve songs and completed the project. Although it was unoriginal, it was very passionately performed."

Shannon Colebank also recalled Forbidden Fruit. He said, "It was a novelty act. It was not about the music. I think it was an excuse for Todd and Carole to work together on a project. In Forbidden Fruit Todd played drums, something he was not very good at. Carole played guitar, something she had only done for a year or so, and this other guy, George, was their bassist. Carole sang.

"I liked the project, actually. They were just trying to have fun with it. In Detente Touch we were all so deadly serious about it. But Forbidden Fruit had a sense of humor about themselves. Most of the songs had a joking nature to them. Not actually funny, but at least tongue in cheek. Very simple compositions, considering Todd was a beginner drummer and Carole was a beginner guitarist. There was a good crafting of songs."

Carole may have had fun with Forbidden Fruit, but otherwise life in Bend with Todd became a struggle. While he was fooling around with Emerald Productions, she was making the bulk of their income. As Vicki Holman said later, "The only time Carole seemed unhappy and disillusioned with their marriage was while living in Bend. She called me one day and told me she didn't think the marriage was going to work. I'm not sure what happened at the motels. I know that they had a problem with Todd, and I think it eventually led to Carole quitting."

Once again Shannon Colebank had a different view of why Todd and Carole left Bend, Oregon. He knew Todd very well during this period. Shannon was the professional soundman with Emerald Productions. He said, "Emerald had become the second largest promoter in the whole area after Monqui. After Todd had that tremendous success, he decided to open his own nightclub. He leased the skating rink in Bend and hired me to be the sound tech. It was his most thrilling risk in that every show was so close to the make-or-break point that he would almost have a nervous breakdown every time. His addiction was catching up with him and he was a strung-out risk junkie, constantly freaking and very high strung."

Apparently, Carole had either become addicted to some of this risk taking as well, or had been cajoled into it by Todd. Collin Colebank remembered, "Todd and Carole would show up on the Harley and ask me to go rappelling off the I-205 bridge at midnight (the bridge over the Columbia River between Portland and Vancouver). I told him I wasn't that bored yet and didn't want to call Marty from jail. They laughed, called me a wimp and roared off to their next adventure."

But all of the adventures around Bend were finally catching up with Todd. And in 1995 Emerald Productions came crashing down around him. According to Shannon Colebank, "The Grateful Dead came to Eugene the same weekend Emerald Productions had one of its most expensive shows at the skating rink in Bend. All the concert goers went to Eugene and Todd lost his shirt. He was not able to pay the bands or make the rent on the rink. The whole thing collapsed. Todd had a nervous breakdown and ran home to his parents in California."

Carole soon followed. Todd began to help his father in a fence construction business. They called it G and G Fencing, for Garton and Garton. Carole got a job with the Bell Insurance Agency, and as in all her other jobs she worked very hard and made her mark. Grace Bell, a part owner, was very impressed with Carole. She said later, "Carole had big, expressive eyes and was very kindhearted. She was a dependable and lovely lady. She was competent, very professional, and people liked her. It was great having her there. Carole became almost like a family member to me."

Grace Bell's assessment of Todd Garton was not as flattering. In fact, she said, "He, on the other hand, was a braggart. Everything was all about him. He had the most outrageous stories. I knew most of them were lies. They were just too outlandish to be real. I thought, 'What a jerk.' I didn't like him, but then I thought, 'Well, if Carole loves him, he must have some redeeming qualities.'"

Carole wrote her friend Krista about this time, and many of her complaints were the same ones she always had about Todd and the marriage: *We were up in Portland recently, but Todd and I got in a fight on the way over to see you and decided not to come. It would be nice to have a steady paycheck. This is what we seem to fight about most—money.*

Carole said that Todd couldn't sleep well at nights because of financial problems. As for herself she said, this was nothing new and she was doing the best she could: *I'm kinda needing to work out some feelings of being resentful because of all the years I've been concerned about money and supporting us.*

After this she said that both she and Todd had acquired bad habits and were trying to be nicer to each other. Then she said how much she liked working for Grace and Kenneth Bell at the insurance agency. Carole said that Grace and Kenneth weren't the typical stereotype of insurance agents. They never pushed anyone into buying more than they

needed and they were very low-key. She said that
Grace encouraged her to apply for her license so
that she could handle auto insurance. Grace was
always very positive and supportive of Carole's abilities. Carole wrote that Grace was a woman who had
come up in a generation where she had to prove
that she could be a businesswoman in a world full
of men.

Then Carole mentioned Todd's latest scheme.
He wanted to be a counselor at a camp working with
troubled teenagers. It was these teenagers' last
chance before being incarcerated. She thought
Todd would be good at it. She said he was missing
the military, and the discipline would be good for
him and the teenagers.

Carole added one more telling comment to the
letter: *Is life a constant struggle, or do things eventually
get smooth only to find ourselves bored out of our minds?*

Apparently, Todd's job as a troubled-youth counselor did not work out and he was, indeed, bored
out of his mind. Bored with his life and bored with
Carole. This was not the life of adventure he had
dreamed of. He wanted action and romance. He
dreamed of survival skills and adventure. Perhaps
he even thought of the ultimate survivor who had
lived just up the hill from where they now lived in
Anderson. In the last part of the nineteenth century and early part of the twentieth, a man named
Ishi lived in the nearby canyons and mountains and
became the truly last "wild Indian" in America. He
had hidden from the whites and lived with a dwin-
dling band of Yahi Indians until they died off, one
by one, and he was all alone. He made all his own
weapons, caught his own game and lived secretly

in caves and wherever he could be without being detected. He occasionally swiped some of the white man's food or gear, but he was never discovered doing it. After all his other tribe members died, he lived alone for many years; tired of his solitary life, he walked one day into Oroville in 1911, certain that the whites would kill him. Instead, he became a celebrity. Professor A. L. Kroeber, of the University of California, took him under his wing and studied everything he could about Ishi and his way of life. He and Ishi became friends. Ishi went to live on the campus in San Francisco, but the weather and white man's diseases were not beneficial to him. In March 1916, just before dying, he told Kroeber, "You stay, I go."

Here was a local who exemplified stealth, cunning and an ability to live off the land. Todd wanted that life as well, and he remembered one admirer in Portland who believed he already lived it. The admirer was, of course, Lynn Noyes. If he couldn't lead a real life of adventure, he would keep on inventing one and tell her all the details.

Just as Todd had not told Lynn that he was married to Carole, until forced into admitting it, he lied about his continued involvement with the marines. She thought he still did special operations for them once in a while. Todd told her that the fencing business with his father was just a front for his more clandestine activities. He gave her the lie that he'd told Norman Daniels, that he was a lieutenant in the marines and he'd earned the rank while being in the field. He indicated that he was still going on special operations to South America.

Lynn recalled, "I saw pictures of his medals. There

was a Purple Heart in the pictures. It's when some-body gets hurt in combat." What he didn't tell her was that he was able to purchase the Purple Heart somehow, even though it is one medal that is never supposed to be sold.

Lynn added, "He also had been a diver down at Coronado. He had a dive-bubble pin to prove it." How he obtained the pin remains a mystery.

Todd told her about rappelling out of helicopters into the jungle and going on secret missions. Sup-posedly his leg was good enough now to do these kind of operations. Lynn said later, "It was part of his job. He wasn't specific as who the job was for. He briefly mentioned killing people. It wasn't some-thing he talked about often. He was on some sort of reconnaissance team. And he was a sniper. He mentioned he'd done these things in South America and Nicaragua. He said he was always on call to do a mission. One time he mentioned the name of a colonel he worked for out of Quantico (a marine base in Virginia). The last name was kind of a tongue twister. Something like Seminole or Simonelli. This colonel was the head of a Black Ops group. Todd said these were people who went in and did things and came back out, and nobody even knew they were there. He wasn't very specific, other than it wasn't very savory."

And then Todd brought up a new and interesting twist on the theme of secret operations. For the first time he mentioned to Lynn a shadowy organi-zation called "The Company." Lynn could not be specific as to the date he first mentioned the name. But it appears to have been in late 1995 or 1996. Todd said in effect that The Company was a pay-for-hire assassination organization. Anyone could route money to them to have someone killed. It didn't matter who the target was. Given enough money, a member of The Company would be sent out to kill the individual.

Lynn said later, "They took people out. They killed people for money. It was all just business."

Over time Todd became more specific about The Company. He told Lynn it was not part of the government, but ex-CIA operatives and others would sometimes freelance for it. He said that he was such a freelancer. They trusted him because he was a professional and always got the job done. He indicated that he had already killed several people while working for The Company.

As if all of this weren't enough to impress Lynn Noyes, Todd said that he occasionally helped the Butte County Sheriff's Department on drug raids. He sent her a photo of someone ready to break down a door during a raid. The man's face was turned away from the camera. Todd titled the photo, "Guess who?" He then answered the question. He said the individual was him, though in fact he never worked for the Butte County Sheriff's Department.

On top of all these stories, Todd told her one more, which took the cake. He mentioned the name George Korum, who was a band member of Forbidden Fruit. Lynn knew George when he used to live in Portland. According to Lynn, "One day Todd told me he had killed George. It was because he [Korum] stole a bunch of things from him. Musical equipment and whatnot. One thing was a guitar. He didn't say how he killed him."

This was one more instance of Lynn taking Todd at his word. In fact, George Korum was alive and well. It was just one more lie in a mountain of lies.

Asked later why she never checked up on this story, Lynn said, "I always believed everything Todd said. When I first met him, the relationship that continued over this whole time frame, things that happened in my life, Todd was always there for me. He always supported me. He was always someone I could count on. At a couple of the lowest points in my life, Todd was there."

At some point the silver chain on Lynn's Celtic cross broke. She already knew that Todd wore his cross with a black rope instead of a chain. He told her he added two copper-type beads to the rope. He said he had picked them up on a mission in Belize. When Lynn had her Celtic cross fixed, she added a black rope instead of a silver chain. Then she added two silver beads to the rope. They stood for her and Todd being together.

Lynn Noyes had not seen Carole Garton since her days in the band house in Portland when they were teenagers. For some reason, though, Todd took Carole with him on a trip up to Portland in 1996 and they stopped by the Noyes residence. Dean wasn't there at the time, but Lynn and Jordan, her son, were. Lynn was pregnant with her second child. Carole brought her puppy, KD, with her, and that may have helped ease the tension with Lynn. While Jordan played with the puppy, the adults talked. Lynn remembered the visit as being amicable. They talked of old times in Portland and how much fun the band had been.

But one thing caught Lynn's eye and made her

jealous all over again. She noticed the bomber
jacket Carole was wearing was Todd's. There were
two crossed flags on the back, one Irish and one
American. It had the name Patriot emblazoned
near the flags. Lynn knew that was one of Todd's
code names. There was also the word *"Eins"* printed
on the jacket. Todd told her this was Gaelic for the
word "one." One, of course, had special significance
for Lynn. It was a U2 song that Todd loved. It was
"their" song. She felt that Carole had no right to
be wearing that jacket.

According to Lynn, the song "One" by U2 was
explained to her by Todd. She said that he had
told her, "It's a love song and it pertains to you and
me."

Todd, at the time, was also sporting a new tattoo
on his arm. It portrayed a Celtic cross and American
flag and Irish flag. It was similar in some respects
to the jacket emblems. Beneath the Celtic cross and
flags was written, ONE BUT NOT THE SAME. All of it
was further proof of Todd's devotion to the Irish
cause.

The visit ended well enough, but Lynn could
not forget the jacket or the word "Eins." More than
ever she felt that Carole was an interloper in their
lives. If she hadn't been kicked out of high school
at a critical time, she felt it was she, not Carole, who
would be together with Todd now. Todd did not
dissuade her that there was no chance of that ever
happening. He still phoned her on occasion and
began to paint a very negative picture of Carole.
Like many of the other things he said, these por-
trayals were filled with lies. According to Lynn,
"The marriage he portrayed to me about her wasn't

very pleasant. He was miserable. He said she was cheating on him and it hurt him. [This was a lie.] I resented her for making him feel that way because I cared for him."

Lynn was very paranoid about anyone cheating in general. She feared that Dean might try it and she told him early on in the marriage, "If you want to cheat, don't do it. I'd rather you brought the woman home and did it right in front of me. I'd rather know about it than having you lie about it and cheat on me because it will devastate me."

Lynn put her money where her mouth was in this regard. She didn't have extramarital sex behind Dean's back. She came right out front and told him she occasionally still had sex with Natalya. She claimed later that Dean was okay with it. Whether he was or not, Lynn took several trips to New York to visit Natalya where she now lived. They had sexual encounters while she was visiting.

For Lynn Noyes's twenty-fifth birthday, Natalya said she would pay for a new tattoo. She and Lynn went to a tattoo parlor run by Lynn's girlfriend "Needles." He inscribed a tattoo on Lynn's left upper bicep. The tattoo he made for her depicted a yin and yang symbol. As Lynn explained later, "Yin and yang are two parts that make a whole person. The male sign and female sign, when you are together with someone, you are one and the same." She even added the word "ONE" above the yin and yang symbol. It complemented Todd's tattoo of ONE BUT NOT THE SAME. It referred to the U2 love song, "One." It symbolized Lynn and Todd's devotion to each other.

Dean Noyes was not fond of the tattoo. And he

was even less fond of Todd Garton's continual contacting of his wife. As 1996 progressed, Lynn was increasingly irritated by Dean as well. She felt restless and trapped in her marriage. She wanted a way out. Todd began to give her ideas that did not include divorce.

At first it was just wishful thinking. Lynn remembered both of them saying, "Wouldn't it be nice if Dean was out of the picture? The same about Carole. I remember Todd saying, 'What if something happened to Dean? What if something happened to Carole?'"

Originally it was along the lines of wishing either Dean or Carole might have an accident. Life would be better with them out of the picture. Then sometime in the fall of 1996, after Lynn had her daughter, Amanda, the wishful thinking took a deadlier turn, prodded onward by Todd. For the first time Todd mentioned the word "murder." The plan was very vague in the beginning. Sometimes he spoke of killing Carole. At other times he spoke of killing Dean. Lynn listened to his musings, but she made no comments either way.

But by 1997 Todd had a more definite plan in mind. He was a keen observer of human nature and saw that the very thought of Dean cheating on her drove Lynn into a frenzy. It was the perfect excuse to bring her on board for killing Dean. Todd took a trip up to Portland, Oregon, that year and followed Dean around. For once, he really was on a covert operation, albeit one of his own devising. As Todd snooped on Dean near his place of work, Dean had no idea he was being followed. And what Todd discovered could not have been more helpful to his plan. He discovered that Dean really was cheating on his wife.

Once he discovered this fact, Todd told Lynn and said that he had proof. He gave a description of the woman and said that she was one of Dean's coworkers. They appeared to be carrying on the affair in the downtown area. But strangely, for once, Lynn did not fully believe him. Perhaps on some level she knew that Todd often elaborated on the truth. She said later, "Part of me believed him. Part of me didn't. I didn't want to believe that Dean was cheating on me. I wanted confirmation."

She got it soon enough. The husband of the woman with whom Dean was cheating called Lynn that summer and told her of the affair. His description of the woman matched the one Todd had given her. When Lynn confronted Dean with this information, he admitted that he had been cheating on her. Lynn was furious.

The next time Todd contacted her about killing Dean, she was more than willing. She said later, "After this conversation I had with Todd, I said, 'Go ahead, take him out.'"

There was a $125,000 life insurance policy in place on Dean, and Lynn was the beneficiary. She not only looked forward to having the money after Dean was killed, she also indicated that part of it could be used to have him killed. Todd had already told her that The Company would hire someone to kill for a price. Lynn decided no one was better suited for doing the job than someone from The Company, especially Todd.

She recalled, "I didn't get very specific with him about it at that point. I kind of left it up to him. I said that I didn't want anything to happen in my home, because that's where the children were and it was our home."

As far as going ahead with a murder instead of divorce, Lynn said, "At that time I was so hurt and really full of anger. And then there was my relationship with Todd. My parents early on went through a really bitter divorce. And my line of thinking at the time was this might be easier in the long run for the kids, because they were so little. They could deal with a loss as opposed to going through a bitter custody battle."

Soon after the decision to go ahead, Todd informed Lynn that he had spoken with The Company and they would make this hit a "freebie." In other words, they wouldn't charge anything and would let him do it without their guidance or control. If he gained financially later from any insurance money, that was okay with them. They trusted him to be the hit man.

Lynn recalled, "He would do it. It was personal. It was a favor for me."

In the fall of 1997 Todd Garton began to make preparation for the murder of Dean Noyes. Yet for all his lone-wolf talk over the years, he decided not to go it alone. Instead, he would take on a partner. He had to look no farther than someone he knew very well, twenty-seven-year-old Dale Gordon.

Northern California resident Dale Gordon was an ex-marine, just like Todd Garton. He joined the corps and became a mechanic. He was good at his job and moved up through the ranks. He even served time overseas. By the time Dale was honorably discharged, he held the rank of lance corporal.

Because of the expertise in mechanics that he learned while in the marines, Dale bought a wheel alignment shop in Redding called Continental Alignment. It mainly serviced big rig trucks and Dale built up a steady clientele. Unfortunately for him, a mutual friend introduced him to Todd Garton one day in either 1994 or 1995. They discovered they were both marines and struck up a friendship. It wasn't long before Todd was telling Dale all his lies of adventure and glory.

Gordon recalled how "he told me he was a lieutenant in the marine corps. I believed him because I didn't believe a marine would lie. *Semper Fi*—always faithful and all that. He told me he was in force reconnaissance. Like an elite military unit. He went to navy dive school. He even had a diving-bubble pin to prove it. He had four other medals. He talked to me about them very much and how he earned them. One was a Purple Heart with a star and also a navy citation. It was a Purple Heart with a star because he had been wounded twice in combat.

"I went over to his house and he had these medals by a green wall, next to the fireplace. And there was, like, a gun rack, which could hold the guns. He had marine corps emblems and an officer's medal. Like the marine corps globe."

Gordon knew that an enlisted man's U.S. Marine Corps emblem looked different from an officer's. The Eagle Globe and Anchor for an enlisted man was plain, while the officer's had braids that resembled ropes sticking out from the side. Somehow Todd had obtained one of these so he could "prove" that he had been a lieutenant.

Garton always had objects and mementos to back up his stories. He showed Gordon a scar on his arm. He said it came from being hit by an AK-47 bullet. He told of his antidrug missions in El Salvador and Nicaragua. He told how he had even gone to para-trooper school. Todd said that he had become proficient with the M-40 sniper rifle and also the M-15-82 H Bar. This was a heavy-barrel weapon.

Asked later if he believed all these stories, Gordon said, "Yes, I did because of *Semper Fi*. Marines are always faithful to one another. I had some very good friends in the marine corps. I didn't believe one marine could lie to another."

Dale was so impressed by Todd's stories that he gave him a glass mug with the marine corps logo on the side. It was so Todd could put some of his medals in it and display them on the mantelpiece of his home.

Todd's lies to Gordon soon escalated. He said that he had a B.A. degree and he was trained as an emergency medical technician (EMT). And he said that he sometimes helped the Butte County Sheriff's Department on drug raids in their county. But most of all, he had stories about killing people. He had so many, in fact, that Dale Gordon could hardly keep up with them. Gordon said later, "He did it a whole bunch of times in the marine corps. A whole bunch of times as an assassin. Several times in Ireland. He even talked about killing someone as a child. He told me he was out in the woods with his rifle and he saw some older men raping some little girl. So he shot the men. And then he told me how scared he was.

"One time Todd got a package from the CIA. Some pictures came in the mail along with a bunch of money, like five thousand cash. And Carole accidentally opened it and she saw it. She got all scared. And he told me he never wanted Carole to touch his mail ever again. His mail was a very private thing for him.

"I believed him because the stories were very real stories. He would give you smells, sights, everything. He would give you names. Very real stories."

Two of the "very real stories" included episodes close to home rather than off in some foreign country. Dale recalled, "Todd said that if you kill a certain way, you'll never get caught. For example, in a store he got into a fight with another guy. He rammed his head through one of the refrigerators and killed him inside the store. He ran, trying to get away from the police. He hid inside a Dumpster underneath all the garbage. He talked about the food smelling just terrible and all the stuff in the garbage. The cops looked inside the Dumpster, but they never found him.

"He told me another story. He and his wife were at a bar. He and Carole were on his Harley-Davidson. Someone was trying to pick up Carole, so he took the guy out behind the bar. He got into a fight with him and killed him. He told Carole, 'We've got to get out of here.' So they took off.

"He said another time that someone who lived out in the countryside—he was paid five thousand to kill him. He used a really cheap pistol. A little cheap twenty-two. He drove up to the guy and said, 'Hi, are you so-and-so?' He said, 'Yes.' Then Todd shot and killed him."

Just like Norman Daniels, Dale Gordon felt that his military career as a mechanic was nothing compared to Todd's adventures in and out of the U.S. Marines. He wanted to live a life like that. Todd brought his 10/22 rifle to Dale's alignment shop and actually fired it in there. Dale could see that Todd was a very good marksman with a rifle. It was obvious he knew quite a lot about firearms. Gordon said later, "He had a Remington three-oh-eight rifle. It was a sniper rifle. Very similar to the marine corps M-Forty. He knew how to set it up real good. We went out to fire the rifle. We were sighting it in. What we did—there is a scope, to where you could turn the knobs on the scope. And you use a laser range finder. You could point the laser range finder at something, get the range, then turn the scope so many clicks to get that range. There is even on the eyepiece a little chart. It told you the range and how many clicks to turn it. Say the target's at four hundred yards. You shoot it. The bullet would hit the bull's-eye exactly.

"That's what we were firing for, because you would shoot one time at four hundred yards, another time at eight hundred yards. We were trying to get a bullet to hit the targets exactly, because the bullet drops after so far.

"Todd had plans for this rifle. One plan was to set it up as a sniper rifle. He was going to sell it at gun shows. The other plan was to keep it. He liked it because it was a three-oh-eight, which was the same as military use. He was talking about going back down to Nicaragua. The cost of the rifle was about twelve hundred dollars. The ammunition was real expensive, too."

Todd grew so attached to this modified rifle, he didn't sell it. But he talked to Dale Gordon about making more and selling them at gun shows. He wanted Dale to help him in their production. He touted the .308's excellence as a deer rifle. Dale said, "Todd talked about selling it for any purpose. If somebody wanted to buy it for assassination, that's fine. If somebody wanted to buy it for deer hunting, that's fine, too."

All of these grand plans and target practice out in the field were fine and Dale enjoyed Todd as a companion. But being around Todd was always a dangerous proposition, and often a costly one. According to Grace Bell, Shannan Hawkins was Continental Alignment's bookkeeper and Dale Gordon's girlfriend as well. Shannan indicated to Grace that Todd spent a lot of time around the shop and it really bugged her. What bugged her even more was that Todd would sometimes talk Dale into doing work in exchange for guns instead of money. This made Shannan mad because they needed the income. There was always something underhanded going on when Todd was around, as far as Shannan was concerned.

Dale found out just how dangerous Todd could be in October 1996. Todd went to visit the alignment shop one day while Dale was working on a Freightliner truck. This happened about the time that Todd and Lynn were talking about getting rid of their respective spouses. Dale had an ironclad rule in his shop, only he or one of his mechanics was to drive the big rigs off the rack. No drivers were to do this on their own.

On that particular day, Dale remembered, "I finished the alignment. I went to go wash my hands. Todd motioned for the driver to get into the vehicle. The driver started in gear, clutch out, and it took a nosedive into the pit."

This incident ruined Dale Gordon. He was not only sued but lost valuable equipment in the accident. Before long he lost even more than that. Dale was forced to declare bankruptcy and the business went under.

Whether Todd waved the driver on as an accident or sabotage, only he knows. But from that point forward, Dale Gordon began to rely more and more on Todd Garton for his livelihood.

Without a business bringing him income, Dale began to do odd jobs for Garton. He didn't blame Todd at the time for wrecking his business. He still looked up to Todd as a paragon of what a man of action should be. Dale helped Todd and his father in their business, G and G Fencing. According to Dale, "When I declared bankruptcy, I lied in the bankruptcy court. I stated that I had more money than what I had. I declared bankruptcy for around fifty thousand. And I lied in court. I lied about the distribution of money. So I channeled some of the money to Todd. It was sixty-two hundred that I bought into the G and G Fencing business."

Around this time Todd cajoled Dale into another shady business venture. Just when this happened isn't clear, though it appears to have been in the spring of 1997. This incident concerned Todd's Bronco being stolen from Main Street in Cottonwood. It was later found out in the country with bullet holes in it and Todd collected insurance money for its destruction. But Dale later confessed to Shannan that he was the one who had taken the Bronco and filled it full of holes so that Todd could collect the insurance money. He told her that Todd had threatened him if he didn't do it. But she didn't believe him. She knew that Dale worshiped Todd and would do almost anything he said at this point. She was so upset by this latest escapade, she broke up with Dale.

Just how far Dale would go is evident about how he viewed himself in the early summer of 1997. He talked about the loss of his business and said, "What this did to me was make me bitter. It made me hateful. It was just enough to pull my strings into terrible stuff. I had severe depression. Suicidal thoughts. Alcoholism. I felt so inferior compared to Todd. He was all this great stuff. And I looked at myself and I was so terrible next to him. I was only a corporal next to him being a lieutenant. I just had an A.A. degree compared to his B.A. degree [a lie]. He said he got it at Chico State University [another lie]. He also had teacher's credentials [one more lie]. I felt like a complete failure."

With Dale Gordon in such a state of mind, he was a perfect candidate for Todd's plans to kill Dean Noyes. Dale was already under Todd's spell, and this only increased when he, financially ruined, went to live in Todd's house along with his wife, Carole. Dale lived in a room in return for helping Todd on fence-building projects. Todd began a character assassination tirade against Dean Noyes. He told Dale that Dean Noyes was married to a friend of his named Lynn. He had known Lynn since his days in Northern Ireland. She had helped the IRA in their cause against the British (all lies). Now she was living with this tyrant Dean in Portland, Oregon. Todd told him that Dean abused and beat her. He said that Dean threatened to kill her if she ever tried to leave him. He was a drunkard and a bully. A real scumbag.

Dale recalled, "Todd said it would be a better place if he were killed. He said he ought to kill Dean himself. He asked if I wanted to come along. There was a lot of mind manipulation. He told me how God was a killer, so by killing people, you were doing the work of God."

An angry, bitter and confused Dale Gordon considered the assassination job that Todd presented to him. The idea percolated aimlessly along until the summer of 1997, the same summer that Lynn Noyes discovered that Dean was cheating on her. Once she gave the go-ahead to have him eliminated, the planning by Todd went into a higher gear.

Lynn's first piece of advice to Todd was that Dean was soon going to a conference in San Francisco. She said it would be a good place to kill him and Todd agreed. To Dale Gordon, who was now agreeing to go along, Todd gave the same story he had given Lynn Noyes that The Company was allowing him to kill Dean as a "freebie." In other words, they weren't going to pay him to do it, but that Todd and Dale could benefit from the life insurance money Lynn would collect after Dean was dead. Todd told Dale he would receive $25,000 for his help in the murder. (Later this amount was reduced to $10,000, according to Dale.)

For the prospective hit, Todd and Dale bought some latex gloves to use so as not to leave any fingerprints at the scene. They also bought a San Francisco city map. Dale recalled, "We talked about what we would do. The person working at the motel—we would say we were Dean Noyes and we forgot our key. We would get the key, go to his room, unlock the door. I would stand cover in the hallway and Todd would shoot him in the room."

Just what would happen if the motel clerk remembered the real Dean Noyes, Todd never told Dale of a contingency plan. But in the end this was academic—for some reason the planned hit in San Francisco never came off.

So, Todd decided to shift his plans northward to Portland, Oregon. Sometime around Halloween, 1997, he and Dale Gordon drove up I-5 and stayed at a Hampton Inn in the Portland area. This served a dual purpose for Todd. He could scope out the area and, more important, be with Lynn Noyes again. He had to bring her thoroughly into the scheme if it was going to work.

Dale remembered the trip's purpose: "It was to set things up and talk to Lynn. We were going through Dean's house. [He was at work.] Just checking it out, because we thought we might have to kill him in his house. It was around Halloween, so there was a spider-type thing hanging from the ceiling. We talked a bit with Lynn and went into the kids' room and looked around. There was some *Star Wars* stuff. We talked about that and Lynn showed us some toys she had bought for her son."

Todd and Dale walked through the entire house and even into the yard. They noticed a sliding-glass

door and Todd thought they could pop it and
enter the house if they had to. At some point Lynn
opened her hope chest and showed them *The Anarchist Cookbook* that she had been saving for many
years. By now it was stuffed with Todd memorabilia. It had photos of him in his band days. There
were photos of him supposedly working with the
Butte County Sheriff's Department. And there were
photos and articles especially pertaining to Todd's
adventures in Northern Ireland.

Dale recalled: "We flipped through the pages. I
particularly remember one picture in the book.
There was a man standing, like in between two
buildings. He had a black ski mask on and, I believe, camouflage utilities. He was carrying what
looked like an M-sixteen. Todd said it was him. He
didn't say what he was doing, but I kind of got the
idea he was up to killing someone."

Dale also remembered that Todd wanted *The
Anarchist Cookbook* back. He said, "Todd wanted to
get it back from Lynn because it had all the stuff
about making bombs and killing people. But Lynn
treasured it."

There was a verbal tug-of-war between Lynn and
Todd over the book. He wanted it because it did
have concrete ideas about killing people. She wanted
it because it stood for everything he was. Lynn won
out in the end. There was no way she was going to
part with her precious book of Todd Garton.

Yet, as it turned out that evening, she didn't need
to have Todd just in photos. Lynn went with Todd
and Dale to the Hampton Inn. While Dale stayed
in his own room, Lynn went to Todd's. For the first
time since they were teenagers, Lynn had sex with

Todd once more. She said later, "Todd and I hadn't had a physical relationship for a number of years. I was really hurt by the fact that Dean had been cheating on me. I was under the impression that Todd wasn't together with his wife at the time, since that's what he told me. I thought it would make me feel better if I went out and did the same. We had sex in the room at the Hampton Inn."

Lynn and Todd and Dale went to breakfast the next morning at a restaurant in Portland called the Grotto. Afterward, they dropped her off at a woman friend's house. As Lynn recalled, "They dropped me there because I had to come up with an extravagant reason. I had to lie to Dean. I said I was out with my friend that evening and had spent the night there."

After dropping Lynn at her friend's home, Todd and Dale went to Dean's place of business in downtown Portland. Todd talked of getting bugging devices from a friend of his in the CIA and bugging Dean's phone. This led to a half-baked plan of somehow extorting money from Dean rather than killing him. Todd didn't elaborate to Dale, and this plan never got off the ground.

Basically, the Halloween trip to Oregon was termed a "reconnaissance mission" by Todd. There was no attempt made on Dean's life, and the same could be said for another trip to Oregon in January 1998. Todd, who had enjoyed sex with Lynn, wanted to see her again. They made plans to meet halfway in the Eugene-Springfield area of central Oregon. Since Lynn had some problem with her driver's license at the time, she got a girlfriend to drive her there. This worked out well for the girlfriend, since she had lived in Springfield and wanted to go there anyway and visit old friends.

The trip almost went awry before it began. The weather was very bad in January and Lynn phoned the Garton household, wondering if Todd was still on for the journey. She hoped to reach him, but Carole picked up the phone instead. Somehow Lynn was able to mask the real intention of her phone call. This call could have scuttled Todd's intentions of being with Lynn as well. She was under the impression that Carole was no longer living with Todd. But foreseeing this contingency, Todd had told Lynn that sometimes Carole went over to the house to watch the dog when he was away.

Todd and Dale did journey up to Eugene as planned. They met Lynn and her friend Keri and went out to dinner. Then Keri went out dancing with friends and decided to stay over someone's house for the night. Todd, Lynn and Dale all got rooms at the local Marriott. Dale had to stay in a room by himself once more, while Lynn and Todd shared the same bed. Lynn indicated later that she and Todd had sex again.

But this trip wasn't all about sex. As Dale said later, "We were all in the room together talking about the hit on Dean Noyes. We had brought our guns along. There was a Rossi three-fifty-seven. There was a Colt forty-five. There was a little pistol and the ten/twenty-two sniper rifle. There were plastic knives. They were plastic knives so we could go through a metal detector. There were latex gloves. And a bunch of ammo. We had all these to show Lynn we were really going to do this."

But they didn't do it then, and Todd was starting to get cold feet about having Dale Gordon as his principal partner in this. According to him, Dale would act "flaky" at times. He wanted another partner to back him up and keep an eye on Dale. He remembered his old friend from Shasta College, his sometime rappelling partner, Norman Daniels. He decided to reestablish contact with Daniels.

Norman Daniels was certainly no stranger to Todd Garton's fascination with assassins and special ops. There had been a whole period around 1993 and early 1994 when he had been intrigued by these kinds of stories. Then over the next few years he had lost contact with Todd. Daniels, who was one year older than Todd, had gone to high school in Alameda, California. Alameda is a large island in San Francisco Bay, just west of Oakland. Through much of the twentieth century it was dominated by the naval air station that accounted for much of its employment. But it also had a core of one of the largest collections of Victorian homes in the state of California, harkening back to a stately, simple nineteenth-century upper-middle-class life.

Norman went to Alameda High School in the central portion of the island. The student body was an incredible mix of white Europeans, African Americans, Chinese, Filipinos, East Indians and a polyglot of people from all over the world. And as the 1986 yearbook stated (the year Daniels graduated), *What do you get when you cross a jock, a prep, a new waver, a rocker, and an academic achiever? A top box office hit called* The Breakfast Club, *right? Wrong. You get Alameda High School.*

Yet Norman didn't really fit into any of these categories. If anything, he was the "quiet, nice guy" on campus that the others were barely aware of. He didn't belong to the science club, art club, drama club, video club or any of the other numerous clubs on campus. Unlike Todd Garton, who always wanted to be in the spotlight and was the centerpiece of a rock band, Norman ghosted through high school and graduated without fanfare.

After he graduated, he enlisted in the army and joined one of its most elite units, the U.S. Army airborne infantry. He learned how to parachute and also how to fight as an infantryman. He was a member of the airborne infantry from 1987 through 1989. As he described his role in army life later, "I was in the muscle of the army. I jumped out of aircraft. I did infantry work. My work was combat."

Little did Norman Daniels know at the time, but his life in the army was much more exotic than Todd Garton's true marine experience. Norman was stationed at Fort Wainwright, Alaska, near Fairbanks. It was the largest and coldest maneuvertraining area in the world, encompassing 1.5 million acres. Just how extreme the weather could be is indicated by the usual summers of 80 degrees Fahrenheit that dip to minus 50 Farenheit during the winter.

The base was instrumental during World War II and the battles against Japan, as well as during the Cold War. The Soviet Union was just across the narrow Bering Straits from Alaska. Though later records didn't reflect for sure, Daniels may have been part of Task Force Geronimo. This was an elite force of highly trained airborne infantry, the kind that Todd

Garton only dreamed about. They were always on call for immediate action.

Just how rugged an area Daniels trained in can be seen by one anecdote. During a training exercise one battalion of soldiers was set upon by grizzly bears. By the time the bears were through, they had ripped apart twenty-eight soldiers' packs in search of food. Norman Daniels's army experience may not have been assassinating drug lords in South America, but neither was it a stroll through New York's Central Park.

After the U.S. Army, Daniels returned to California and married a woman named Andriah Praiter. The marriage did not last long, but Andriah later made one very telling remark about Norman: "He is naive, always too-trusting and giving in to people. He would believe almost anything." This naive side of Norman was one factor in their eventual divorce.

Norman had a son named Justin by another woman, but apparently he never married her. This woman left Justin in Norman's care, and he raised the boy the best he could. Norman later married a woman named Carole, who was not Justin's mother. Life was not easy for Norman, Carole and Justin during the mid-1990s. Norman and Carole both worked at Round Table Pizza for a while in 1995 and 1996. At some point they had to supplement their income with food stamps. Eventually Carole left Norman as well. Yet it always seemed that Norman was the one who picked up the pieces and struggled on, taking care of himself and his son. Basically, he was a hard worker who did his best, but his "too-trusting nature" was always there to trip him up.

Norm took on a second job at the Kickin' Mule Feed and Fuel Store in Cottonwood. It was a combination convenience store and gas station. Coworkers there liked Norman. He was friendly, conscientious, and polite. The employer also thought Norm was a good worker. Norman did the best he could to give his son a good home life.

But Norm was still having troubles making ends meet. He had bills to pay and a young son to support. Then one day in July 1997 a fateful meeting occurred. As Daniels recalled, "I was working at the Kickin' Mule when Todd and his wife came in to purchase some items at the store. And he wrote a check. I told him that I had a family and that I was working pretty hard, and times were tough. I was barely meeting my bills, and still slipping a little, and I needed an extra job. He explained to me that he had a fencing business, and was I interested in some part-time work. He handed me his business card and told me to give him a call."

Daniels did give Todd a call, and he began working part-time for him in August 1997. He started building fences, mixing cement, hauling cement and carrying posts. And as was so typical of Todd, he paid Daniels under the table in cash. In fact, he even paid him in more exotic items than cash on one occasion. As Daniels said later, "I wasn't specifically paid for the days I worked. I was given money equal to some of the hours worked, and in other areas he took me to lunch and stuff like that. Helped me out with a bow—an expensive compound archery bow."

But just like Dale Gordon before him, Daniels had an "accident" while being around Todd that would change his life. It was only on the second day of the job that Daniels injured his foot while working. It became swollen and tender. Before long he was hobbling around, barely able to work.

Daniels's injury was perfect for Todd's schemes. He knew that Norm was in need of money. He began to tell him that there might be an easier way to make it than carrying around cement and digging post holes. "My foot was injured. We had gone back to his house after we had done some work," Daniels recalled. "As we got back, he just all of a sudden asked the question, 'Do you want to be an assassin? I know you need the money. I'm an assassin.'

"Todd said he had been approached by some people in the government at Langley (CIA headquarters in Virginia). And that these people were covert people and took care of him. Over the last four years he had done thirteen hits. And these people were taking care of him. If I was to become involved, they would take care of me the same way."

Daniels didn't decide right away, but by now Todd had him hooked on shooting his new compound bow. Norm enjoyed archery and he said later, "Archery became our tie. It was September 1997. We did target practice. We would go to the Bow Rack, which was an indoor range. I'd see him maybe once or twice a week."

Because of all this contact with archery, Daniels paid another visit to Todd's house in Anderson. He admired all the guns that Todd had there and the medals above the mantelpiece. Just like Dale Gordon before him, Daniels was very impressed by Todd's Purple Heart and navy diving-bubble pin.

Todd controlled him with new and more outrageous stories of missions in South America. As Daniels recalled, "He went into more detail of missions and things that he had done during his time in South America. He explained to me about the men he was in control of. He went into great detail about his life and career."

In October, the same month that Todd and Dale went on their first visit to see Lynn Noyes, Todd approached Daniels again about the assassination organization, and for the first time he mentioned the name Dean Noyes to Norm. He connected the name to someone who might be the target of a hit.

After the Eugene-Springfield trip of January 1998, Todd's character assassination of Dean Noyes went into high gear. He told Norman Daniels that Dean was an evil man. Daniels recalled, "He said this man was a dirtbag. He was embezzling money from the Mercy Hospital. He specifically said there were several contracts out on this man for his embezzlements. He also said he was mistreating his wife. He was cheating on her. He was basically just a lowlife." (The only part of this that might have been true was Dean cheating on Lynn.)

Finally, due to all the stresses of being a single parent and his financial woes, Norman Daniels agreed to join Todd Garton on a mission to assassinate Dean Noyes. Todd assured him that he wouldn't actually have to shoot Dean. Norm would be there as backup. This agreement to join the plan placed Daniels into close contact with Dale Gordon, who was now living in the Garton residence. This association led down a new and strange path, for both men had already invented military/assassin games. Dale Gordon had invented a role-playing game that used a booklet and dice. Daniels invented a computer game.

Gordon's role-playing game was called World of Chaos. He'd started developing it as a teenager and kept refining it through his marine days. It was so popular with some of his fellow marines that they all played it right through their time in the service. By 1997 World of Chaos had gone through several versions and Gordon was even thinking of putting it on the market to try and earn an income from it.

Basically, it was a multiplayer game with individual players taking on different roles such as an ex-military person, a driver, an assassin or a cop. Gordon said, "It was a really violent game. You drove around. Ran people off the road. Shot at them. You had various weapons. You could gain experience and your abilities went up. You used dice to see if your abilities went up. I considered myself an expert at writing role-playing games."

As far as where he obtained information about the various weapons used in the game, he said, he asked Todd's advice for some. Gordon recalled, "I did a lot of work on it. Sometimes I would spend the whole weekend working on it. Hours on end. I made changes to all the stuff."

Norman Daniels also had developed a couple of games for computers. Daniels said, "One game was a two-player game. It wasn't really a strategy game, but an action game. You had two guys with two screens, and two people could run around a maze-like area, pick up weapons and ammo and shoot at each other until they expended all their lives.

"The other I was going to develop for the Internet. It's a large-scale strategy game. Had twenty-one different combat pieces and ten different ground pieces. I made a topographical map and you were able to manipulate all these pieces. The purpose of the game was to take over all the cities on the game board."

Dale Gordon was so impressed with Daniels's computer-programming abilities, he had him help create a character-generating program for World of Chaos. Gordon said later, "You roll up the characteristics; the higher the number, the better your abilities were. You'd roll for the type of character you were. Road rebel, assassin, ex-military, cop, whatever. It would determine their strength, dexterity, speed and looks.

"Some of the shooting stuff I learned from Todd and used that. Especially stuff on long-range shooting. I talked to Norm about doing a Web site for me. He helped on the programming. He was writing it on Basic, so all you had to do was just write it into the programs. The computer figured out what your statistics are."

After the Eugene-Springfield trip of January 1998, Todd began to wean Gordon and Daniels away from role-playing and computer-assassin games and toward practicing for the real thing. They had nearby fields in which to practice with live ammo, and the bull's-eye of their target was Dean Noyes. The reconnaissance trips were over. The assassination mission was scheduled for February.

Chapter 4

Plan A

It was mid-January 1998 and Todd Garton was serious about the hit on Dean Noyes. To prepare Dale Gordon and Norman Daniels for the bloodshed, he made them watch videos of assassination movies. Dale recalled these movies: "There were a lot of videos we used to watch. It would just be movies—superviolent movies. And Todd was showing me, this was the way you kill. There were movies like *Sniper*. He made a certain point in that movie. There was like another sniper in the movie, and when he went to kill somebody, he purposefully missed the person he was shooting at. Todd made a big deal about that. He was very concerned that when it came time to kill that I would not kill for him."

Todd also had Dale and Norman watch the movie *Bound*. This was essentially about two women who ended up killing the abusive boyfriend of one of the women. Afterwards, they got rid of the evidence so no one knew that it had occurred. Todd stressed the point of not leaving a trace. He also had them watch *The Jackal* and *The Day of the Jackal*. Dale said later, "There's two versions. We watched both of them. Also *La Femme Nikita*."

Todd was especially keen on movies that depicted snipers killing from ambush. He said it was the best way of not being detected. Stealth and cunning were key ingredients. Why kill someone in a blaze of loud gunfire when you could do it from cover? He indicated that's the way he had done things in Northern Ireland and in South America.

Along with the assassin movies, Dale said they also watched a lot of satanic movies. Todd's point in this was that there was nothing ethically wrong about killing. Especially killing a man as despicable as the version of Dean Noyes that he presented to Dale and Norman. Todd was very concerned about Dale's attitude for the upcoming mission to Oregon. He wasn't sure that Dale had what it took to be a cold-blooded killer. He kept on drilling into him that Dean Noyes was a scumbag. He said he was stealing money from a hospital group and beating up his wife. He emphasized that the world would be a better place without him; Todd and Dale and Norman were doing society a service by getting rid of Dean.

"Todd said that Lynn wanted out of the marriage, but Dean said he would kill her if she ever tried," Dale remembered.

In an attempt to see just how loyal Dale really was, Todd tried to set up a scenario for Dale to kill someone in the Anderson area. Dale remembered that "he wanted me to kill some drug addict or innocent bum. Something like that. There was also this person who bought my shop [Continental Alignment] and he wanted me to go kill him. He told me just walk in there and shoot him and walk out. And he planned to shoot him from a different angle. He [the owner] was in one building and we went to another building on the opposite side of the street. I remember there was a Dumpster there. We talked about sitting up on top of the Dumpster and taking a shot with the Ruger ten/twenty-two."

The two men actually went there and Todd wanted Dale to take the shot. Dale didn't and they walked away with the owner of the shop never knowing how close he came to being gunned down.

With Dale's attitude still under suspicion, Todd turned to his other partner, Norman Daniels. He gave him the same spiel about what a horrible person Dean Noyes was. He mentioned there were several contracts out on Dean's life, and they might as well be the ones who cashed in on it. This whole contract business took on a new twist when Todd remembered the name of Lynn's friend in New York—Natalya. The name itself had a kind of exotic allure, straight out of a movie of intrigue. Todd told Daniels that Natalya was a broker in New York who dealt with assassins. She took information from people who wanted others killed and passed it on to the paid assassins. "He mentioned this woman who lived in New York," Daniels recalled. "He explained she was an information broker. In an assassination business the broker is someone who picks up contracts or hits on people and trades black-market information. Underground type of information. I believe he also mentioned she was an assassin at one time and in the IRA."

There was also another twist about how he was going to collect money for the hit that he told Daniels. This differed from what he had told Lynn Noyes and Dale Gordon. Daniels said, "Todd was independently going to hit Dean Noyes and then collect the contracts. Independent of what other people were doing." In other words, Todd and his buddies would kill Dean first and beat the other assassins to the punch. Then they would collect the contract money that the others missed by moving too slowly on their target.

As far as his own role in the upcoming mission went, Daniels recalled, "I was there to watch Todd's back. Anything that required other hands than himself. I was a support person. I would go up there and help him out with things that he could not do, such as a lookout if trouble was coming around a corner. I was also to provide him with an alibi if it was needed."

Interestingly enough, Todd had one more job for Norman Daniels to perform. Norm was to watch his back against Dale Gordon. Daniels said later, "He let me know that Dale Gordon was involved and that he did not trust Dale. He asked me to help watch Dale Gordon, because Dale might do something crazy. Dale was very paranoid and Todd didn't trust him. I was to watch his (Todd's) back."

The trio of gunmen started stockpiling a cache of weapons for the upcoming trip. All of these men already owned several guns, but they also went to Jones Fort, a gun supply shop in Redding, to look at more guns and ammo. Daniels remembered one trip with Todd. "We took a trip to Jones Fort— an armory filled with firearms, black powder, semi-automatics, rifles, shotguns. Different kinds of ammunition." They eventually put together a cache of several rifles and pistols, including a semiautomatic Tech 9.

Daniels recalled that they added one more pistol to the list. "It was, like, for personal protection. It was really small [like a derringer]. The barrel had a breach, and to remove the bullet and casing from it, you broke it instead of charging it. The barrel would open like a shotgun."

About the Tech 9 he said, "It's like a submachine gun. It's a nine millimeter and holds a twenty-five-round magazine. We took along four or five magazines for it. This gun was Dale Gordon's."

Dale spoke of other equipment besides guns that was being collected for the trip. "There were some latex gloves and plastic knives. I had a butterfly knife. I also had a Leatherman Knife. And a little first-aid kit. And flexy cuffs like handcuffs. So you could handcuff somebody if you needed to. If you wanted to transport somebody, and didn't want them to get away, you could cuff their feet and hands. This included Dean Noyes."

Todd also bought two-way radios for communication purposes. "We had little two-way radios. There was an earpiece and a piece you talked through," Dale recalled. "The radio was about six inches tall, three inches wide and an inch thick. It ran on four AA batteries. They were black [with] a little antenna on it and volume control."

As far as use of the radios, Norman Daniels remembered, "It was so we could stay in contact with each other when we were out of sight. And also for silence. When you were in an observation post hidden from view, you would be able to signal quietly in the communication device instead of yelling, 'Look out!' He [Todd] could be warned ahead of time if somebody was coming up from behind him.

Besides the guns and communication devices, Todd also had his team buy "appropriate clothing for Oregon," but his taste for attire ran to the bizarre. Norman Daniels remembered, "We went to the Factory Outlet stores looking for shoes. We got ties, button-up shirts, pairs of slacks, belts and wool caps. It was meant as a disguise. It was explained to me by Todd that this is the type of clothing that Oregonians wear."

In this choice of disguise, it was as if Todd were outfitting his crew to look somewhat like a cross between the Blues Brothers and Ninja warriors.

To ensure a "quiet hit" on Dean Noyes in Oregon, Todd began to manufacture homemade silencers for the guns. Even though he didn't thoroughly trust Dale Gordon, he brought him in on the project because of Dale's expertise with weapons. Dale recalled, "He used PVC pipe. There was some of that around the house. There was some that was two inches in diameter. And that's what we used for the silencers. There was an adapter on the barrel of the gun. That was a metal adapter. And there was a PVC adapter. It took it down from two inches in diameter to one inch in size. And that's so you could screw it onto the pistol or rifle."

The silencers were adapted to be used on both a Ram-Line .22 pistol and the 10/22 rifle. Todd and

Dale took foam from a large amount of material used for archery targets. The foam was self-healing. In other words, an arrow could be shot into the target, and when it was pulled out, there was no hole to show where it had been. It was very soft and spongy.

Dale remembered the material and said, "We tore off pieces of the foam and it's real spongy. You could compress it with your fingers. It was more like a plastic-type foam. Real soft. You took off pieces, put it inside the silencers from the end that screws into the barrel. You fill a whole bunch of it in there. As you shot through the silencer, the stuff would want to come out. It would sort of squeeze to the side, then start flying out the side. So you had to tape the end of it with black electrical tape. And you could get, like, a hundred-rounds shot before you had to put some more self-healing stuff in there."

The 10/22 was somewhat different from the pistol. Dale remembered that it had a metal insert, somewhat like baffles. There was also a foresight on that silencer to line up with the rifle's rear sight. Todd made two silencers himself, and Gordon helped him with the third.

Along with the silencers, Norman Daniels remembered that Todd Garton had bought special ammunition to be used on the operation. He said, "Todd bought subsonic ammunition. The idea was that it traveled under the speed of sound. The 10/22 would generally make a loud noise when fired. Not so with the silencer and subsonic ammo."

Norman recalled one more thing about the modified 10/22 rifle. He said that it had a point sight attached. When the red dot of the laser on the point sight beamed on a target, all the gunman had to do was fire the rifle at the target. It made the 10/22 very accurate.

It was one thing to make plans, collect clothing, ammo and weapons, but Todd wanted them to do more than that. He wanted actual hands-on firing of the weapons with silencers. Dale recalled a field just off I-5, near Red Bluff, where they went to fire the pistols and rifle. Norman Daniels didn't even have to go that far. He and Todd walked to the back edge of Todd's property on Adobe Road and fired out toward the woods. This wasn't exactly in a city, but it wasn't in the wilderness, either. Norman test-fired not only the 10/22 but the Tech 9 as well. He tested the 10/22 for calibration of the point sight. Daniels recalled, "Todd Garton's backyard was pretty much all open. It's a large field area and the backyard actually looked out over Bureau of Land Management land (often called BLM), near Reading Island. There was no problem about firing there."

During this training regimen, perhaps the most bizarre incident occurred with Dale Gordon. Whether Todd told him to do it or he thought it up on his own, Gordon decided to hunt and kill cats with the silencer-enhanced pistol. He roamed the area shooting every cat he could lay his sights on. Dale remembered, "We killed just about every cat in the neighborhood. Lots and lots of cats."

In the last week of January 1998 the pace picked up even more. After every gunfire session, Todd met with the others at the Anderson Moose Lodge to discuss strategy. Daniels recalled, "We sat away from everybody else and discussed the area around

Gresham (a suburb of Portland where Dean and Lynn Noyes lived). We discussed which way the streets ran, the rail line, and he started pointing stuff out. He didn't have a map, but he explained the area. He also discussed what alibi Dale and I should have for being up there."

The first alibi that Todd would tell Carole Garton was that he and the others were going to try and sell camouflage gear up in the Portland area, but somewhere along the line the story would change.

Todd told Dale and Norm one more important thing. He said that Lynn Noyes was not only aware of the plan to kill Dean, but she was helping it by providing valuable information and material. Lynn said later, "Dean had tons and tons of family photos, and a few of himself. I sent Todd one of these. Also a scrap of paper about where Dean parked after he got off work. A couple of after-hour pubs he went to. The gym where he had a membership and worked out. These were all the things Todd knew about but wanted me to specifically write down."

One of the most important things Lynn sent to Todd was a set of keys to the house and vehicle. Lynn remembered, "I sent him a whole key ring. I was always losing my keys and we had several sets. There were keys to all our vehicles. And we had one key to our home that unlocked all the doors."

Lynn also gave Todd a list of the garages where Dean parked his car when he went to work in downtown Portland. This was invaluable information for Todd. His top priority was to kill Dean in one of the parking garages. They could make it look like a mugging or a carjacking gone bad. They could get in and out of there fast.

Todd originally told Lynn he would need $10,000 to conduct this hit. He said it wasn't a direct payment for the hit, but rather it would cover expenses for him and Dale and Norman. But Lynn balked at the $10,000 figure. She said, "I was a stay-at-home mother. I needed the money for the kids. So, I told him if we end up together, the insurance money would be split fifty-fifty. If not, I really didn't think he needed the ten thousand. But he insisted and it was basically something we agreed to disagree on. Todd never came out and said we would be together afterward. It was always, what if, what if. But there was also, could I handle being with him, knowing that he was responsible for killing my husband. I said I wasn't sure."

Sure or not, Lynn did nothing to stop the plan and kept on giving Todd information that would help eliminate Dean. In fact, she gave information on all the vehicles that Dean and she owned. They had a 1977 Jeep Levi's Edition CJ-5. It was in the garage more often than not. They had an older classic Mercedes. Dean generally drove back and forth to work in a little black two-door Fiero. And they also had a Bronco, which Lynn generally drove.

All this information, a photo and the key ring, Lynn sent to Todd in a small cardboard box. Daniels recalled, "He physically showed me the set of keys. And a photo of Dean Noyes. She also gave Todd schedules of his day-to-day activities. About the keys, he said they were keys to the front door of Lynn Noyes's house and to the vehicles. We discussed what was going to take place during the crime in question. That it was a backup plan. The original plan was to hit Dean away from his house when he was at work. [In the alternate plan] we would remove Dean from the house and kill him. Todd said that in case something went wrong with any plan, that if there was an opportunity to hit Dean Noyes at the house, then that's what the keys were for, so there would be no breaking and entering."

Todd Garton ran even more ideas by Dale Gordon. Dale recalled, "I remember there was a house key and there was one for the full-size Bronco. We talked about killing Dean at his house. The style Todd said would be like cowboy style. Get in there, kill him sloppy and get out. Sloppy just meant get in there and do it. Do it quick. We also talked about taking him from the house, and take him someplace where there was nobody around and kill him in the car. We also had two lock-pick sets. One to go through a window. Todd had all this stuff and a picture of Dean in a marine corps green pouch. Something from when he went to sniper school."

On February 6, 1998, the waiting and planning and practicing were over. Todd phoned Dale Gordon at Redding Four Wheel Drive, a place where he was working part-time. He told him to tell his boss that his mother just had a heart attack and he needed to go to the hospital immediately. With Norman Daniels, there didn't need to be an excuse to get off work at the Kickin' Mule. Todd already had instructed him to take the weekend off. Todd picked Daniels up at his residence on Gas Point Road in Cottonwood and took him to his home on Adobe Road. They began stuffing the Jeep with guns, ammo, clothing, silencers, latex gloves and all the equipment they would need.

Daniels recalled that the firearms they loaded included a .357 Rossi pistol, 10/22 rifle, Tech 9 and two .22 pistols. There were boxes of ammo and the communications devices as well. He said, "We took nine-millimeter full-jacket ammo for the Tech nine. A couple of boxes of twenty-two shells."

When Dale Gordon joined them, he would bring along his Colt .45 1911 model pistol as well. Dale also remembered taking a speed loader for the .357 Rossi. It was an awful lot of firepower to kill one man.

The Jeep was all loaded by the time Dale Gordon arrived from work. Garton was very antsy to get on the road. Dale remembered, "He was all upset. It was 'We need to get there right away. We're fighting time. We're fighting the weather.' So I jumped right in the Jeep and we took off."

The trip to Oregon from Anderson, California, in the wintertime isn't always a smooth ride. It snows heavily on I-5 as the road rises past Mount Shasta. By the time it reaches Siskiyou Summit, at 4,300 feet, it can be slow going with passenger cars and big rigs reduced to driving with chains. The time would be a little faster with a Jeep, but not exactly a racecourse. And it wasn't a straight-through shot for the team. Todd wanted to pick up one more item. They only had two walkie-talkies. He determined each member of the team needed one, just in case.

Todd stopped at a Circuit City electronics store in Eugene. While Todd went to buy another radio, Dale walked over to a Sears store, and Norm guarded the Jeep. Someone had to stay there and guard the cache. Dale Gordon walked around in Sears and contemplated buying Norman Daniels a watch. For something that might depend on timing, it was incredible that Daniels didn't have one.

While Gordon was wandering around in Sears, Todd phoned Lynn Noyes on his cell phone. He told her that he and Dale and Norman were on their way up to Portland. He didn't tell her what they planned, but she could guess. Lynn said later, "He called and said he was on his way up to Oregon for business, and that I should know what he was referring to. I shouldn't see him. If I did see him, there was a problem."

Todd hung up his cell phone, thinking everything was now going according to plan. Tomorrow they would find Dean Noyes in his parking garage, kill him—hopefully without being seen—and split. But his phone call to Lynn Noyes had repercussions that he couldn't have imagined. As Lynn said later, "This call put it all into real perspective for me. I got really scared. I panicked."

Her sudden panic attack had ramifications that would put them all in danger.

The first thing the trio of gunmen did when they reached Gresham, Oregon, was to drive by Dean and Lynn Noyes's house on Burnside Road. It was already late and fairly dark outside, but all three could plainly see a Bronco and Fiero parked in the Noyes driveway. After their trip to the Noyes residence, Todd drove to downtown Portland where they checked out the two parking garages near Dean's place of employment. Daniels recalled, "We stopped in there [the first garage] and scouted out the stairwell and the elevator. We were looking over the layout and for escape routes."

They went into both garages and looked around. Gordon recalled, "We scoped it out. We went all the way from the bottom to the top. I remember Norman walking through the staircase and I was, like, at the top of the stairway. I had a radio. I was talking to Norman, seeing how the radios were working. Also, looking how we could get away from this place."

After the scouting of the garages, Todd drove to a Quality Inn on the corner of Burnside Road and Hogan. He booked one room for all three of them and made sure the room was on the ground floor. Not wanting to draw attention to themselves and all the guns they were carrying in dark plastic cases, Todd pulled the Jeep around to the window of their room. But what he did next could have hardly been more conspicuous than if he'd drawn a large bull's-eye on all of them. Todd went inside, lifted up the window and took off the screen. Then he had the others pass the guns and equipment directly from the Jeep through the window and into the room. Luckily for them it was late, and no one saw them.

Crowded into a motel room with guns, ammo and equipment, Todd gave them a final briefing about their alibis for being there. Instead of the alibi about selling camouflage clothing at a gun show in Portland, he told Dale and Norm to say, if ever asked, they were up there seeking out bids for G and G Fencing contracts. Each one of them was to stick to this story. He also told them what their individual roles would be the next day. Dale Gordon was to be his main backup in killing Dean at the garage. Norman Daniels's role was more complicated. Daniels said, "I had the Tech nine. If anything went wrong, such as being pursued by the police, I was to shoot at them to keep their heads down while we made our escape. I was not to shoot to kill."

Todd gave them the rundown on the area in case they somehow got separated. They were to get to the rail system and make their way back to its end near Gresham. Todd indicated a little park near there. That's where they would congregate and he would pick them up.

There was one more duty to be done before lights out. Norman Daniels stood near the edge of the Quality Inn while Todd and Dale took off in the Jeep. They kept in constant communication by the radios so Norm could tell what the maximum distance was for their use. After determining this, Todd and Dale came back and everyone went to bed. But it was not a restful night for either Dale or Norm. These two were wound up and had a hard time sleeping. The only one in the group who seemed relaxed was Todd.

It wasn't daylight yet when Todd got the others up. According to Norman Daniels, Garton made them put on their "Oregonian disguises." These included a button-up shirt, tie, socks, shoes, slacks and raincoat. This last item was a curious one. It wasn't raining outside.

Once again Todd had the others help him pass the guns and equipment directly out the window and into the back of the Jeep. And once again they were lucky. No one saw them do this in the early-morning hours. Loaded up and ready to go, Todd Garton drove them all by the Noyes residence on one last scouting expedition. But he must not have gone directly by the house or he would have noticed one disturbing thing. Dale didn't see it, either, but Norman Daniels did. He recalled later, "It was still dark. As I glanced over, it didn't register at the time, but there was one vehicle missing. The Fiero was still there. The Bronco was gone."

Not having registered this fact at the time, in part from lack of sleep and jangled nerves, Norm didn't mention this to Todd or Dale. Instead, they all went to a local Denny's and Todd bought them breakfast.

Breakfast over, it was time to go and kill Dean Noyes. Todd drove about fifteen miles to downtown Portland and parked across from the entrance of the parking lot where Lynn said Dean normally parked his Fiero. It was still early, and Todd was sure that it would be easy to spot Dean's car when it went into the parking lot. Even though it was a Saturday morning, Dean had to work that day. There weren't many people around at that hour and his Fiero should have been very conspicuous as it drove up. Daniels remembered, "It was Lynn's plan to tell Dean to take the Fiero that day. She was to say that the heater in the Bronco wasn't working. So he wouldn't take that vehicle. He would take the Fiero which had a heater. Our plan was to follow him. Then when he parked, we were going to take care of him in the parking lot."

But the minutes ticked by and there was no Fiero. The men fidgeted and looked nervously at their watches in the crowded Jeep. More than an hour went by and there was no sign of Dean. Frustrated and angry, Todd started the Jeep and they slowly cruised through both parking lots, looking for the Fiero. It was at this point that Daniels suddenly remembered what he had seen on their drive by the Noyes house that morning. He had seen the Fiero sitting in the driveway and the Bronco was gone. There was no reason that Lynn Noyes should have taken the Bronco anywhere that early in the morning. Dean must have taken it.

Daniels told Garton what he had witnessed, and Todd was extremely angry. They searched the garages for the Bronco and couldn't find it. There was a good reason neither vehicle was there. On Friday night, about the time that Todd, Dale and Norm drove into Portland, Lynn Noyes had a tremendous loss of nerve. She related later, "I knew that Todd and Norman Daniels and Dale Gordon were in town and they were going to try and attempt to kill Dean. I got scared. I specifically asked him, pleaded with him, to take the Bronco to work. By him taking the Bronco—the parking structure he normally would have parked at, the Bronco wouldn't fit in the parking structure. So he would have to park near a loading dock at work. Somebody has to clear him in, clear him out. And they didn't know about that."

Dean eventually agreed to take the Bronco. It probably saved his life that morning. But the day was far from over. Todd Garton, furious about the missed chance to kill Dean in the parking lot, drove across town to another motel and began to put Plan B into action.

Chapter 5

Plan B

After the debacle at the garage Todd Garton drove to a Hampton Inn across town. Norman Daniels recalled, "Todd said that it was the best motel he had stayed at. Every time he's been up here, he always went to that motel." Part of the reason may have been his good memories of having sex there with Lynn Noyes.

There would be no repeat of passing guns and ammo through a window at the Hampton Inn. Todd was assigned room 218 on the second floor, but he still wasn't above doing a bit of chicanery. He only booked the room for himself and Dale Gordon. Daniels secreted himself into the room later when no one was watching. Bit by bit, the men brought the guns and ammo into the room from the Jeep. Because some of the guns were in large black carrying cases, which looked somewhat like briefcases, they were easily concealed.

One of the first acts Garton did in the new room

was to phone Lynn Noyes. He wanted to know what went wrong at the parking garage. Daniels remembered him being very upset on the phone. He'd seen Todd mad before, but rarely like this.

Lynn Noyes also recalled just how angry Todd was. She said later, "Todd called and said there was a problem and I needed to meet up with him. He didn't say what the problem was on the phone."

But Lynn Noyes knew very well what the problem was. Her actions of the night before had sent Dean off in the Bronco instead of the Fiero, so he could not park in either one of the garages. She was afraid to go and meet Todd at the Hampton Inn, but she was even more afraid of what might happen if she didn't. The last thing she wanted was Todd and the others to show up with guns on her doorstep.

Getting up her nerve, Lynn drove to the Hampton Inn and walked to room 218. She briefly met Dale Gordon and Norman Daniels there. Since she hadn't met Daniels before, Todd introduced her to Norman. They spoke only briefly and then Daniels and Gordon left. As soon as they did, the fireworks began.

Garton was extremely angry. Lynn recalled, "He asked how come Dean wasn't in the parking structure he was supposed to be at. They had been up all night. Waited for Dean to show up and he never did. He was furious.

"I lied to him and said, 'I don't know what happened. He should have been there. He took the Bronco. He parked someplace else.'

"We ended up arguing about it. He was really mad. I said, 'Well, why don't you go home.' But he was very hotheaded. We just kept arguing. He said there were other people involved and there was a lot of time and money invested into it and something needed to be done. It was out of his control to a point because there were so many other people involved. The whole situation with Dean, it put him in an awkward position with The Company. He said whether I wanted to be involved or not, I now was in way over my head. My family's lives would be in jeopardy. He said he could be killed. I could be, even my children.

"At this point he threw me up against a wall. I was really scared.

"Then he said, 'We're going to try again.' I said, 'Well, I don't really want you to.' "

It didn't matter what Lynn Noyes wanted at this point. Todd was going to go through with the hit on Dean, come hell or high water. He told her so and said to brace herself for it.

It was a very rattled Lynn Noyes who left the Hampton Inn that afternoon. As she crossed the parking lot toward her vehicle, she caught just a glimpse of Norman Daniels and Dale Gordon as they approached the building. But she was too distraught even to acknowledge them. Lynn said, "I was crying when I left. Out of the corner of my eye I noticed Dale Gordon and Norman Daniels. I didn't even say hi to them or anything. I sat in my truck for a few minutes, kind of put myself back together. Then I stopped at a grocery store and went home."

Dale and Norman had been out of the room for nearly an hour. They went to have lunch and give Todd time to "talk" to Lynn. When they got back, Todd told them about the argument he'd had with

Lynn. He said that she didn't want them to go through with the hit, but it was too late for that now. Since they were here, they were going to do it. Daniels noticed that Lynn had been crying. He asked Garton about this. Todd said, "I yelled at her that there was a lot of time and effort put into this. There's no going back."

Once Lynn reached her home, she also realized that there was no going back. If she didn't come up with something, the gunmen would surely show up at her door, intent on killing Dean. She fretted and worried and finally came up with a plan she hoped would satisfy Todd. She phoned him at the Hampton Inn in the late afternoon. She recalled later, "I stated my position. I didn't want anything to happen in my home. I said, 'Well, I'll see if I can get him to go out to a movie. Down at the big Cineplex thirteen theater. It's in the general area where we used to live. If I can get him to go to a movie theater, maybe you can get him there.'"

Lynn also indicated that Dean's brother was coming over that evening. She mentioned that Dean might go to the movies with his brother. But just what Todd and the others were supposed to do about Dean's brother, she didn't say. She was still hedging her bets. In reality, she had no intention of sending Dean and his brother off to the movies. She hoped that Todd, Norm and Dale would go to the theater, wait around and eventually leave the area out of sheer frustration when Dean didn't show. But Lynn's wavering would have the absolute opposite effect of what she had hoped. Todd had plans of his own, and after this phone call they would lead him and the others right to her doorstep.

In a scene straight out of the movie *Traffic*, where two U.S. federal agents and a Mexican policeman discussed strategy in a swimming pool, Todd took Norm and Dale to the Hampton's pool. He deemed it safe there to discuss his new plans. Nobody could bug them in a swimming pool while he formulated Plan B.

Daniels recalled, "We discussed several possibilities of how to assassinate Dean Noyes, since the parking-garage incident failed. We talked about this in the pool. One idea was to take care of Dean when he went to the movies with his brother that night. Todd would use his rifle, since it was silenced. He said it was a cheap rifle. It could be thrown away later."

They also bandied about another idea, one that could not have been to Lynn Noyes's liking, and she had unwittingly helped them in their planning. When she sent the key ring, with all the vehicle keys on it, to Todd, it also contained one key that opened up all the house doors. Daniels continued, "We were going to take him away from the house and kill him. Make it look like it was a carjacking or the like. We were going to take Dean's brother's Suburban and take both Dean and his brother and kill them. We were going to remove them from the house so nothing would lead back to the house. Todd said if one plan fails, there's other plans to follow. If Lynn Noyes is away from the house, there may be opportunity to kill them in the house."

Todd didn't want to conduct the hit until it was good and dark. So in the meantime he decided to do a little target practice. But the location he chose defied description. He decided to fire his silenced rifle right through the screened window onto the street below. It didn't matter that traffic was moving up and down the street all the time. He was determined to test the silencer then and there. He picked up the 10/22 with the homemade silencer, pointed it down at the street below and fired. It was just as good as anticipated. The silenced rifle made hardly any sound at all. Todd fired off a few more rounds at a Styrofoam cup lying on the other side of the street. But even with the point sight, he missed every time.

Daniels recalled, "Todd had fired a few rounds through the window while I was there. But he was finding that the point sight wasn't being accurate. I went outside the room and stood down by a road sign. And there was a Styrofoam cup out there he was aiming at. He was attempting to hit it with the rifle. The Styrofoam cup was between bushes that ran along the edge of the property and the road sign. In a tan bark area. I'd just set it up and was observing the cup while Todd was shooting at it. We were using the communication devices. And he would shoot. He would ask if it struck the cup or not. Or if I could see where the round had hit. It was off. I saw some sparks at times."

Finally Dale Gordon went outside as well. Daniels continued, "Dale stood at the north side of the parking lot, and I was standing at the south side, near the road sign. We were watching for traffic to make sure that there was no traffic when Todd was shooting out the window. He was using subsonic rounds. It sounded like the snapping of fingers. It didn't sound loud at all. Like a snap."

Garton eventually became frustrated with the

point sight and firing out the motel window. He wanted to go someplace that was more open with no traffic around. He told Gordon and Daniels to come back up to the room. When they did, Gordon looked at the screen and was surprised by the small size of the holes in the screen. He commented to Todd, "Look, you can barely notice those holes."

While they still had time, Todd, Dale and Norm took a rifle down to the Jeep and headed across town to a more suitable target practice area. Daniels recalled, "We went north over the bridge, over a river, and into an industrial area. We drove through the industrial area, turned around, and on our way back Todd told us to stop. He jumped out and went down into a field area, where he was going to test-fire the twenty-two."

Gordon remembered, "I was driving the Jeep and Norman was in the back. We continued to drive. We just did circles. All three of us had communication equipment. Suddenly Norman said something about a homeless man walking along the side of the road. I don't remember seeing him, but we drove past."

Gordon may not have seen the homeless man, but Daniels certainly did. And from where he was sitting, the man was heading straight toward Garton down in the field. Daniels said, "Gordon and I continued to drive around in an oval. We were doing that to stay close to Todd so that if he needed to be picked up at any time, we could be there. I saw what I believed to be a transient person. He was wearing a rain gear and carrying something like a large plastic bag. I warned Todd over the communication device, 'Be advised that there is a person in the area.' He didn't hear me well, so I had to repeat it. I didn't remain in eye contact with the transient because we were in the vehicle and we were heading in the opposite direction of the person. I lost contact with him.

"We continued to do a racetrack. At some point Todd got back on the communication device. He said, 'Hot LZ [landing zone]. Extract! Extract!' It's a military term for stating he was in trouble and that he needed to be extracted. We continued to circle around. Todd told us he would be at a certain area to pick him up alongside the road. We actually had to do a few racetracks to finally pick him up. We weren't supposed to pick him up with another vehicle in sight. It took three more tries before we were finally able to pick him up.

"When we picked him up, he said a couple of things. One, he lost one of the magazines to the ten/twenty-two. And second was about the bum. He said the transient had come up on him when he was out there testing. He said that he had to kill him. He explained that the transient walked up to where he was laying as he was test-firing the rifle. He hit the transient in the chest first. And then when the transient was unaware of what was going on, he walked up on him and unloaded the rest of the magazine into the transient's eye. Then he said he had to scrape his brains up with a spoon. That was a very vivid thing he said. I think he covered him with some sort of Visqueen out there. Visqueen is a thick plastic used to lay down for doing landscaping."

The truth of the matter was that Todd Garton probably did not kill the transient in the industrial park (may not have even seen him). Police never did find a body in the area, and no one reported a gunman in the area. But he had both Daniels and Gordon believing this tale. Asked about the incident later, Daniels said, "I believed him. Because the transient was in the area and when we had done the racetrack again, the transient was no longer visible along the side of the road. So it was my assumption the transient had gone off the road somewhere."

Gordon and Daniels may have believed this story, but then again they never went down into the field to see if there really was a dead man there.

After this harrowing incident they all went back to the Hampton Inn to try and relax. But by now they were all wound up. The room seemed cramped and too small to contain all their nervous energy. Before long they went out to eat and then Garton drove them all to Burnside Road. It was time to go and try to kill Dean Noyes once again.

But nothing worked smoothly that day for Todd Garton. He was right in one respect—it had been wise to bring Norman Daniels along to watch Dale Gordon. After the incident with the transient, Dale was nearly out of his mind with worry. Dale admitted later about their drive to the Noyes neighborhood, "I was extremely scared. I was totally out of control of everything. I had no say in anything. I couldn't give orders. Todd was in control."

Todd may have been in control when they got to the corner of Burnside and 212th Street, but not for long. He wanted to park the Jeep there only a half block away from the Noyes residence. It was right next to an unoccupied house. But Dale Gordon was so fidgety, he practically jumped out of the Jeep as if he were going to walk away. He and Todd had words. Daniels couldn't hear what they were saying, but he recalled, "I observed Todd and Dale having a conversation. Dale did something to make Todd paranoid."

Frustrated with what looked like Dale's insubordination, Todd drove about a quarter mile away and parked behind a strip bar known as the 505 Club. In some ways this was a better place to park. The Jeep fit right in with all the rest of the vehicles in the parking lot.

"We had parked the Jeep in the parking lot at the rear of the place. The 505 Club," Daniels remembered. "We loaded up all the equipment that we were going to use. We walked down the street toward Dean's house. We were going in to get Dean Noyes and take him out of his house if possible. We were to take both of them, him and his brother. Todd said he had regrets about having to do that, but he was going to do it. We were going to take Dean's brother's vehicle and drive away. We were going to dump it somewhere and make it look like it was a carjacking. Or a robbery."

Apparently Garton lied about the next part of the plan. He told Daniels and Gordon that Lynn knew they were coming to the house to get Dean. The fact of the matter was she didn't. Daniel's continued, "Todd said she was going to be up in her room with both the children. They [Todd and Dale] were going to go in and grab them quiet and leave."

After the three men collected their guns and ammo out of the Jeep, they began walking down the quiet, residential street. It must have been an incredible sight, if anyone had been there to see them. They were all dressed in dark clothing, concealing weapons under their coats, and carrying plastic gun cases and communication devices. Norman Daniels had the Tech 9, a .22 rifle and the small Beretta. He also carried one hundred rounds of ammunition. With the Tech 9 he was ready for almost anything. He said, "It would fire as fast as you pulled the trigger. It was an assault weapon. Used for attacking an enemy by suppressing their ability to fire back." His enemy that night was anyone who interfered with the operation. This included police officers, according to Todd's plans.

Dale Gordon carried his .45 Colt pistol and the silencer-enhanced 10/22 rifle. The rifle was so long it had to be carried in his arms wrapped up in a coat. Both weapons were fully loaded. Todd had his .357 Rossi pistol and a .22 target pistol. According to the present plan, he was to be the main gunman, who actually shot Dean Noyes and possibly his brother.

All of their hearts were pounding as they walked the nearly quarter mile to the Noyes residence. It was about eleven o'clock at night when suddenly they were standing in front of their target. Only one door separated them from their quarry—Dean Noyes and his brother. Daniels recalled, "We stopped outside the residence in front. Both Dale and Todd moved forward. Todd had the keys that Lynn had given him in his possession. We all had the radios. I was nervous. Extremely nervous. Todd went up to the front door."

What happened next took Norman Daniels completely by surprise. He recalled, "At that moment Dale Gordon dove under a vehicle. He was extremely skittish. I whispered to Dale, 'Hey, you need to get up there and help Todd.' It was kind of surreal."

Dale reluctantly climbed out from underneath Lynn Noyes's Bronco and went up to help Todd at the front door, while Daniels observed the street from behind a tree. As he did, Gordon started attaching the silencer to his rifle. Todd slipped the key that Lynn had given him into the top lock of the door. It opened smoothly. He radioed Daniels, "I'm going in." Then he turned to Gordon and said quietly, "Come on. Let's go. I've got it open."

But it wasn't quite open yet. There was still the door handle to unlock. Gordon took a few steps forward as Garton slipped the key into the door handle's lock. Suddenly Garton turned around and hissed at Gordon, "I can't get the door open. The key won't work."

Totally paranoid now, Gordon took off toward the street and Garton was right behind him. Gordon was close enough to hear Todd Garton say, "The cops were called. We got to go!" (In truth, no cops had been called.)

Daniels was crouching behind a tree with his weapon at the ready when a voice suddenly came over his communication device. It was Todd's voice. The message was, "Abort! Abort! Mission scrubbed!"

Daniels looked up in amazement to see a panicked Dale Gordon zip right by him, followed by Todd Garton. He wanted to ask them what happened, but they were moving too quickly. It was all he could do to keep up.

Bewildered, Norman Daniels watched incredulously as the other two practically ran down the street with an armload of guns, ammo and equipment. The next fifteen minutes could have been straight out of a Keystone Kops farce, if the situation wasn't so deadly serious. Daniels recalled, "We headed east back down Burnside toward the Jeep. Both Dale and Todd were fast walking. Almost to the point of a jog. I was trying to walk normally. I did not want to look suspicious. Somebody walking fast, obviously, will draw more attention than somebody walking slowly. A few cars went by. As we walked toward the 505 Club, Todd stopped and tossed his silencer over a wall."

What happened next differed according to who was telling the story. Todd had just thrown his silencer over a wall and into some bushes when, to Daniels's astonished eyes, Gordon took off by himself northward away from the Jeep. Daniels surmised that Gordon had completely flipped out and was now like a loose cannon.

But Gordon had a very different take on his actions. He said later, "Todd told me he didn't want to get caught with the weapons. He handed me the Ram twenty-two pistol. He told me to take off in that direction. He could go one way in the Jeep and I would go the other way. Todd wouldn't get caught with the guns with the barrels off and silencers."

Scared as he was, Dale was too browbeaten by now to argue with Todd. He not only grabbed Todd's weapons, but he had his own and took off into a residential neighborhood. Daniels was not privy to their conversation, and he was speechless as he saw Gordon disappearing into the night with an armful of guns. For his own part, Norman still carried the Tech 9, .22 pistol and Beretta, and he followed Todd willingly back toward the Jeep to deposit them there. The weapons felt like hot irons in Norman's hands, and the sooner he could cover them up in the Jeep, the better.

Once they arrived at the 505 Club, Daniels deposited his weapons in the back, but their wild adventures were far from over. Daniels said, "As he [Todd] was leaving the parking lot, he went across the street and made a left turn, where there was no left turn, and ran over the island. He drove over the divider in the middle of the road. I was concerned. I mean, if a police officer was around, that's something he would want to check out. Especially coming from a place that serves alcohol.

"He went north and west into the residential area. We were looking for Dale. As we were driving around, Todd suspected a vehicle that was across the street of Eastman. He thought he saw a police cruiser. But I said, 'No, it's not a police cruiser. It's a taxi, with the taxi light on the top.' But he professed it to be a police car."

Thoroughly rattled now, Todd Garton's next actions were just as bizarre as Dale Gordon's. Daniels said, "He was going rather fast and suddenly he turned off his headlights. I don't know why. He wouldn't say."

So, now they were driving too fast on a Saturday night, with no headlights, near a place that served liquor. When they finally pulled over, Daniels thought their nightmare might be at an end. He was wrong. Todd—against all logic—drove right up to the front yard of an occupied residence and started pulling guns out of the back of the Jeep. All

Daniels could do was watch in wide-eyed disbelief as Todd began pulling the weapons out and deposited them into the bushes. The only thing that saved them at this point was that Dale Gordon picked this particular moment to reemerge from the darkness.

Once he did, Todd picked up all the guns that he had just deposited into the bushes and placed them back into the Jeep. All three men climbed into the Jeep, their adventures for the night almost over. It took only a few more wrong turns and wandering around before they were finally back at the Hampton Inn. They all stumbled into room 218, exhausted, disillusioned and with jangled nerves. They'd been up nearly forty-eight hours, with hardly any sleep, and their assassination mission had been a huge and humiliating flop.

Unbeknownst to Todd, Norm and Dale as they tried to unwind from their ordeal, Dean Noyes's life had been saved by the most improbable of means. Dean had worked on the front-door knob a few months previously, but he had botched the job. Lynn Noyes said later, "The door had a dead bolt and bottom lock. You just had to jiggle the bottom lock a little bit to get it to open. Not all the time, just sometimes."

But for that little jiggle on the night of February 7, Dean Noyes and his brother would have been dead.

Things were not peaceful behind that locked door in the Noyes residence on Burnside as well. Lynn knew that Todd still intended to kill Dean after the failed parking-lot attempt. Whether she really intended for Dean and his brother to go to the movies or not, only she knows. The fact of the matter was that Dean and his brother stayed in the house. And for every hour they did, it put her and her family in deeper jeopardy. She knew that Todd was extremely angry earlier in the day. Todd had promised he wouldn't do anything at the house, but she never had seen him that angry before. She half-expected to see him and Norm and Dale come barging in, guns drawn at any time.

It wasn't even much of a relief when Dean's brother left. Todd and the others could still be coming over to the house. Yet despite her anxiety that they would arrive, she took no new precautions to secure her home. She locked the doors, but that was of little consequence. Todd had the key. Lynn had no idea until much later that Todd and the two other men had actually been at her front door trying to get in. But she knew Todd well enough to know that there was reason to worry. She even said later, "I thought he might come in and kill us all."

By 2:00 A.M. on Sunday, the tension was finally too much for Lynn. In effect, she had a nervous breakdown. She told Dean she needed to be taken to the hospital right away. He said that he would take her, and Lynn phoned her parents to come over to the house and watch the children while they were gone. As Lynn and Dean took off, she left behind a completely vulnerable house with her parents and children inside, having no idea that there were armed gunmen in town. Just what might have happened if Todd had decided to take one more crack at the house is anybody's guess.

Lynn's excuse for her action was lame at best.

She said later, "I was hoping at that point if Dean and I weren't there, it would deter Todd from actually coming into the house. Our Bronco would be gone. He knew that was our family vehicle. I was under the assumption if Dean and I weren't there, they wouldn't have any reason to come in the house."

But Todd could have just as easily surmised that only she was gone in the Bronco. A lone Fiero in the driveway might have been an invitation for them to commit a home invasion. They were certainly primed to do this earlier.

In the end, it didn't matter what Lynn thought. Todd Garton had had enough of trying to kill Dean Noyes in the Portland area. He and the others loaded up the Jeep on Sunday morning and, once it was light enough, went back to the industrial area to search for the lost ammo magazine that he had dropped when Daniels spotted the transient. At least in this they were lucky. Todd found it exactly where he had dropped it. He was also lucky that neither Dale nor Norman asked to see the body of the transient that he had supposedly killed. Even though he was adept at lying, he might have had a hard time explaining about the lack of a body in the area.

He was less lucky in another matter. He didn't go back to pick up the silencer that he had thrown over the wall after running away from the Noyes house. There it would sit for many months until a police officer discovered it.

Disillusioned and dispirited, the trio of gunmen made their way back down I-5 toward California. But Todd could not stay that way for long. He was an optimist by nature. The grass was always greener on the other side of the hill. If Lynn's spouse couldn't be eliminated, there was always one other spouse, his.

Chapter 6

Colonel Sean and Company

There was even more incentive for Todd Garton to make Carole Garton a target by the winter of 1998. At that point she knew that she was pregnant and had told Todd. She was very excited about the prospect of a baby, and he pretended that he was as well. But, in truth, Todd did not want a baby and couldn't stand small children. A baby in the house was the last thing he wanted, especially one with Carole.

If Todd did not look forward to a baby, the same thing could not be said for Carole or the rest of her family. Vicki Holman said, "Ever since they were married, I teased her about having a baby. I began almost every phone conversation with, 'Are we pregnant yet?' She would laugh and say, 'No, not yet.' She was taking the Pill, so she wasn't going to get pregnant. In 1997 she told me that she was going off the Pill and wanted to have a baby. She said the doctor warned her it could take a year.

"One time she called and I didn't ask her if she was pregnant. We talked a little while and finally she asked, 'Aren't you going to ask me if we're pregnant yet?' I screamed and she laughed and we both cried. Our first grandchild was on the way.

"The first thing we did was to send them a video camera so we could have movies of her during the pregnancy. We knew we wouldn't get to see them much. But we talked often. Todd seemed excited and admitted he was a little scared about having a baby. He had definite ideas about the way things would be. Carole wanted to name the baby Connor, but Todd said his name would be Jesse [for his dad]. His middle name would be James [for Carole's dad]. He said there would be no nicknames, like J.J."

Todd might have acted excited about the baby for Vicki's benefit, but he began spreading vicious lies behind Carole's back to Dale Gordon, Norman Daniels and Lynn Noyes. He indicated that Carole had been sleeping around and that the baby wasn't his. (Later, DNA tests would prove that it was.) Gordon remembered, "He always sort of would say, 'The baby's not mine. It's somebody else's.' He kind of joked about it and made fun of it."

Carole, on the other hand, looked forward to having a baby. And so did her employer, Grace Bell. Grace helped Carole set up a room in the insurance agency so that Carole would be able to bring the baby to work. Todd and Norm went in one day and helped Grace move some furniture around, and in front of Grace, Todd pretended to be happy about Carole's pregnancy. But Grace Bell was appalled when Todd told her he planned to name the child, who was going to be a boy, Jesse James Garton. She said, "It was just like him to do something like that. Give a baby the name of an outlaw."

Interestingly enough, the baby's due date, June 14, 1998, was also Carole's birthday.

Carole wanted to see her parents in person and show them how her pregnancy was progressing. Easter Week, 1998, was coming up and she talked Todd into going with her up to the Portland area. Vicki Holman remembered, "Around the first of April, Carole called on a Friday afternoon and asked if we'd like to have company for the weekend. We were thrilled. They were leaving as soon as she got off work and were driving straight through. It's about an eight-hour drive. They got here about midnight. She was so beautiful. We spent the whole day talking about the baby and planning our trip down. We wanted to be there for the birth. She said she would like me to be in the delivery room with her. Todd wanted no part of that. We sat together on the sofa and I laid my head on her tummy and felt the baby kick. It was wonderful."

Carole also went to visit her mom, Virginia, and stepdad, Gary Griffiths. Virginia said, "When Carole became pregnant, she was very excited. She would ask a million questions about what to do about this or that. I told her to take it as it came and to relax. I told her she would know what to do when the time came. I planned on coming down after the baby was born and spend a couple of weeks with her. Krista was planning on coming down before the baby was born at the end of May."

Todd and Carole also went by the apartment of Carole's friend Krista while they were visiting in the area. They went out shopping with her and stopped by a store that sold Guinness products from Ireland. Todd bought several items, including a hat that had the name Guinness and its logo on the front. When Krista's husband came home, he and Krista went to Biddy McGraw's, an Irish pub, with Todd. Carole was not feeling well and stayed in Krista's apartment.

While they were at the pub, Todd made a series of phone calls. He told Krista he was trying to contact his old buddy Collin Colebank. In fact, he was trying to reach Lynn Noyes. He eventually contacted her and Lynn remembered, "It was late, after I put my kids to sleep. He said he wanted to see me and he was at this bar. Would it be possible for me to come down and see him. Well, at first I said I didn't think I was going to be able to leave because it was late in the evening. Dean was home. Todd said he was with Krista and her husband at one point. But her husband left and just Krista was there. She was at the bar with him. If I didn't come down to visit him, then he would end up going back to her apartment and basically spending the evening with her. I really didn't want him to do that. I was afraid they would have something intimate at some point during the evening. And I didn't want that to happen, so I found a reason to leave."

At that time Lynn had no idea that Carole was even in Portland. Todd had told her that he and Carole were separated and she thought Carole was back in California. There was also no way that Krista and Todd were going to have "something intimate" that night. Krista didn't like Todd and only put up with him for Carole's sake. But Todd was very good at manipulating people and knew which buttons to push into making Lynn come see him. By the time Lynn got to Biddy McGraw's, both Krista and her husband were gone.

What happened next, Lynn recalled, "He was kind of happy. Lightly buzzed. We walked around for a while. Then we drove in my Bronco for a little bit. And there's a park that's fairly close to that area, and we stopped there for a while. Initially just to talk. Then at some point we ended up having intercourse in my Bronco."

Afterward, Lynn told Todd that she liked his Guinness hat. He gave it to her. She took him back to Krista's neighborhood and let him off a block away. Todd told Carole that he had been visiting a friend. He didn't say who the friend was. Lynn wore Todd's hat home and made up some lie to Dean as to where she had been.

When Todd and Carole returned home to California, he turned to Norman Daniels in his quest to get rid of Carole. Todd no longer trusted Dale Gordon after his antics in Oregon during the failed hit on Dean Noyes. He knew that Norm was more trustworthy. All he had to do was somehow con him into the scheme. And the plan Todd came up with was elaborate, complicated and inventive. He knew he still had a possible candidate in Daniels because of his financial woes. As Daniels said later, "After we got back from Oregon, I was still financially distraught. Todd told me I could make $25,000 on a different hit. It was discussed at my mobile home on Gas Point Road. It was in the first week of April."

For the first time Todd actually mentioned The Company to Daniels. Before that, he had just alluded to some shadowy organization of assassins.

Daniels recalled, "He said these people were a collection of assassins, people that have been doing work for the government and personal contracts. He said he and Natalya, who lived in New York, had affiliation with The Company. If I wanted in, he could get ahold of them by various means—e-mail, phone and, I guess, pager. He also handed me a business card. It had the word 'Patriot' on it. He told me that was this assassination ring's code name for him. And it had his one-eight-hundred pager number on it."

Todd told Daniels he would have to perform one assassination before he was officially allowed to join The Company. He warned him that it would have to be someone he knew and he would have to do it up close and personal. Todd also told him he would have to pass a physical before being allowed to join. A travel nurse would come to his home and take a blood sample and do a physical. (This never occurred.)

Daniels said he was interested in joining The Company. He said later, "I was pretty much dejected about my life and the way things were going. And yet I was unsure if I really could do something like that."

Todd told Daniels that The Company was headed up by a shadowy individual known as Colonel Sean. This colonel sometimes dealt with Natalya in New York. Daniels recalled, "I was not given a lot of details other than that he was a colonel in the military. I wasn't given which branch of the military but that he was out of Langley. He had operations of covert stuff. Todd didn't go into detail and expound on the day-to-day operations of what he did. Just that he was heading an assassin ring."

As far as contracts went, Daniels said, "Todd said anybody could take a contract out on anybody." Todd went on to say that if Daniels decided to join, he would receive a package from The Company.

Daniels didn't say yes or no right away. He left things hanging with the implication that he was interested.

Both Todd and Carole Garton applied for life insurance policies at about this time. The policies amounted to $125,000 each in case of death. Nurse Angie Williams of Corda Medic gave them both exams and they passed. The policies were issued to the Gartons, and now Todd had a financial incentive to have Carole killed.

This incentive was upped by an incident that happened that put Todd Garton into bad financial straits as far as G and G Fencing went. He entered into a contract with a man named Rick Clark to install thirty-three hundred feet of Legend Ranch Rail Fence on Clark's property. But for some reason the job was botched and Clark sued Todd. This only added fuel to the fire on Todd's part to get rid of Carole and collect the life insurance money.

Todd Garton decided to bring in Lynn Noyes on the project. Her main role would be to help convince Daniels to go through with it and make sure Daniels would not flake out the way Dale Gordon had. In his terminology Lynn would become an "operator." And Todd used a new lie to draw Lynn into the scheme. Lynn recalled, "Todd said that Carole was always just kind of in the background of The Company. At one point she had gone to Ireland with him or something. And she had really irritated the person that was a supervisor of his and that she had actually shot somebody in the leg. All he said was that that person's name was Sean. So, this person, Sean, had a personal vendetta against Carole. He [Todd] sort of knew there was a contract out on her. And that was why somebody would want to kill her. Also, she had done something that was in opposition to this company he was working for and that it was out of his control."

As to why Carole had shot Sean in the leg, Lynn added, "He said at one point, in the whole (Ireland) movement, there's a more Catholic side and a more Protestant side. And she had been a traitor to that side [the Catholic side] and was doing something for the Orange [Protestant] movement for money."

Todd did not tell Lynn at this point that he wanted Carole killed. He let her think that others did. Then he added there wasn't anything he could do about it. He also said that he had discovered this "contract" by mere chance. Lynn recalled, "At first he thought he was the target. He discovered someone was supposedly following him around and that Carole had taken out a life insurance policy on him. He thought she might have wanted him dead. As far as a reason why, he had gotten really out of shape and they [The Company] were kind of irritated that he wasn't able to do a lot of jobs that he was supposed to do at the time. But I remember at one point it clearly appeared that it wasn't Todd. And I remember him saying, 'I think it's Carole, and there's nothing I can do about it.' It was around then that he told me about the altercation in Ireland between Carole and this Sean person."

This had supposedly happened sometime in the 1990s. Lynn said, "Carole's connection with The Company—she helped out when needed. The Company and the Irish Republican Army were just friends and acquaintances that Todd had known. And at that point he'd been involved with both."

Eventually Todd filled Lynn in on the fact that Norman Daniels was trying to join The Company. He told Lynn that early on he was worried that Daniels might be trying to target him. But as time went on, he said, it became more apparent that Daniels's target would be Carole.

Even though Daniels was not yet 100 percent sure that he was going to join The Company, all throughout April 1998, he was certainly tilting that way. And in preparation for the chance that he might join, he went with Todd to a gun store in Redding known as Jones Fort. The name was a play on words of a regional town called Fort Jones. Jones Fort was owned by Todd Garton's good friend Marshall Jones. In an even more strange coincidence, Marshall's wife, Tracie, was one of Carole's best friends, and Tracie's sister, Sara Mann, was Dale Gordon's girlfriend. Todd often accompanied Marshall to gun shows, where he displayed camouflage gear manufactured by Rancho Safari.

Daniels said of their trip to Jones Fort, "Both Todd and I went there, and Todd did not have enough money to pick up a pistol, so he brought a twenty-gauge woman's shotgun to offset the price of the pistol. The shotgun was a bird gun. It was Carole's.

"We looked around at pistols. At an Armando Rossi forty-four magnum. It's a five-shot revolver handgun. My choice—I wanted a forty-five semiautomatic. Todd suggested the Rossi was a better weapon to own. I just happen to like the forty-five semiautomatic. There are more shots. The kick of the weapon isn't as great. So when you fire a forty-four, it has more power in it. It will kick your hand back. But Todd said a semiautomatic has a tendency to jam, where a revolver won't jam."

In the end, Todd won the argument and talked Daniels into getting the Rossi .44. Marshall agreed to the price of the sale, and it was agreed that Daniels would be the official purchaser. Norman did the initial paperwork so that a fifteen-day background check could be performed on him. No money was exchanged at the time and Daniels was scheduled to pick up the Rossi on April 27, 1998.

Norman Daniels passed the background check, and on April 27 he and Todd went to Jones Fort to pick up the Rossi .44. Todd brought along $150 in cash, and since that wasn't enough for the total price, he again brought the .20-gauge shotgun as well as part of the deal. Todd told Daniels that The Company had provided the $150. He did not say why they had not provided enough money for the whole deal.

Daniels recalled about the actual exchange, "Both he and Marshall were talking as I was filling out the document for the pistol. When it came time to settle the account, Todd placed both cash and the twenty-gauge shotgun in exchange for the Rossi. Besides receiving the pistol, there was other equipment purchased, such as cleaning equipment, a holster and two boxes of ammo. It was a black nylon right-handed holster. [This was even though Daniels was left-handed.] He bought fifty rounds of silvertip hollow points. It's a type of ammunition. The hollow point, it causes the round to mushroom and it can cause a severe wound. Anyway, I handed the money to Marshall Jones. Todd stated to me in front of Marshall Jones that this was money from a job that he owed me, of being in the fencing business."

Todd was smart enough to know that if the police ever traced the .44 Rossi back from a crime, it would lead straight through the paperwork to Norman Daniels and not him.

Daniels recalled he and Todd went to test-fire the Rossi that very afternoon. Daniels said, "We went to take it out by the Jelly's Ferry target range and break the barrel in. Just shoot rounds through it and break the barrel in to get it working. A brand-new pistol isn't as accurate, from what I understand, until several rounds have passed through it."

Daniels compared firing the gun to breaking in a new car. He said that a car will run better after it has put on a few miles. Todd also practiced with a .308 rifle while they were at the range. And he tried impressing Daniels with the specifications of this particular rifle. Todd said that the .308 had a floating barrel. Daniels explained, "He said to me this made it more accurate. I didn't understand the specifics of that, but it's supposedly more accurate than a stock rifle. The barrel is not anchored to the stock."

This may only have been more gobbledygook on Todd's part to try and convince Norman he knew about high-powered sniper rifles.

Dale Gordon also remembered Todd and Norm bringing the .44 Rossi into Garton's house. He said, "They were in Todd's house and I remember being in the living room. I saw two people [Todd and Norman] holding the gun. A forty-four Rossi special with a three-inch barrel."

He also recalled Todd and Norman going down to a field behind the house and firing it back into Bureau of Land Management land. "They took the forty-four special and they went down into the field below the house. I was in the house. There were gunshots. You could hear it. I remember them talking about shooting it."

Not long after test-firing the pistol, Norman Daniels agreed to join The Company. Todd said that he would be receiving a package from them.

Todd decided to construct the package with no writing on it or in it that could be traced back to him. Instead, he decided to use labeling tape. To this end he went to the OfficeMax store in Redding and purchased a Casio KL 750 E-Z Label Printer. With this device he could do all the lettering on the envelope as well as the instruction sheet to Daniels. Todd also bought two Casio label tape cartridges to be used in the label maker. He bought eight Duracell AA batteries, a Care Mail bubble-lined envelope and a Motorola Express Xtra Pager, which was to be given to Daniels to activate.

Strangely enough, after being so careful not to leave a trace, he paid for all these items with a G and G Fencing check, #6105. The total came to $172.90.

When he returned home, he made up the instructions and outside labeling on the package and sealed the envelope with wax from a jar that Dale Gordon owned. If this wax was discovered later, it would lead back to Gordon, not him. But then he made an impression in the wax with his U.S. Navy SEAL diving-bubble pin.

The end of April 27 brought Todd Garton right to Norman Daniels's front door with a package in his hand from The Company. At exactly 12:01 A.M., April 28, 1998, Garton handed him the envelope with the inscription NEWBIE RECRUIT, PATRIOT RECRUIT on the front. He was sure that the articles, the photos, the pager and the instructions would be enough to convince Norman Daniels of their authenticity. And eventually he was right. But Daniels did not buy it all right away.

Daniels said later, "When I first got the package and found out who it was [to be killed], I thought he, Todd Garton, wanted his wife dead. He just set it all up. I was sure I'd seen the photo of Carole before. And the articles were just general. He led me to believe she was a part of the IRA. There was a bomb found in a bookstore in Britain and Todd suggested that she had done that. And she [Carole] and Lynn would lead potential victims into a place where they could be assassinated. Carole had changed her affiliation from Green to Orange. Carole was on one side and went to the other. That's why she was being taken out.

"I thought it might be a hoax, but I quickly disregarded that. Because of all the other information that I received from him. And I was taking him on his word. I was just thinking that he put too much detail to it for it to be a hoax."

Todd left Norman Daniels's residence in the early-morning hours of April 28. Garton believed that Daniels would follow through on all the instructions, including the demand that all materials related to the package should be destroyed. However, he would have been appalled at Daniels's next actions. For the most part Daniels followed through in destroying the evidence. He shredded the photos of Carole and flushed them down his toilet. He also burned the other document and the outside of the envelope in his barbecue pit. But he didn't watch this closely and not all the material turned into illegible ash. Daniels also kept the wax seal that looked like a ram's head, but was actually an imprint of Todd Garton's SEAL diving-bubble pin.

As to why he kept this, Daniels said, "The wax seal was removed from the package the moment I opened it. I put it in the only drawer of my nightstand. I just knew I would need it. If I was ever caught, I would be able to show proof. I just knew to keep the seal and it would help. After that night I knew that something would go wrong. When I opened the package, I objected to the person [to be killed]. I said I couldn't do this because I was going to get caught. From what I understood, eighty-six percent of all homicides are domestic in nature. That means the victim knew the murderer. So, I had a very bad feeling of what was happening.

"It had been impressed upon me by Todd that I needed to get rid of the stuff so I wouldn't have any evidence leading back to me. So if any circumstantial comes up and I got my place raided, there would be no evidence. But I kept the wax seal."

Daniels also inadvertently kept one other piece of "circumstantial." These were two pages of instructions on how to activate his pager. It concerned his pager cap code, the pager serial number and the phone number for the pager. Daniels activated this pager on the morning of April 28. He called the 800 number and talked to a customer representative; that person activated it for him. Daniels eventually gave this pager number to Todd Garton and Lynn Noyes.

As far as contacting Garton by pager, Daniels said, "First I called the one-eight-hundred number, an operator would answer and they would ask the name or the extension of the person I was trying to page. After giving them the name Patriot, they would then prompt me for the message I would like to leave and they would repeat the message and say, 'It's sent.' "

Daniels could leave a worded message or a series of numbers. Basically, he used the pager just to contact Todd to call him back, but he could also leave a coded message.

It's not obvious why Todd told Dale Gordon about the upcoming hit on Carole. Dale was not part of the plan, since Todd didn't trust him. Perhaps he did so, because he was afraid Norman Daniels might mention something to Dale and he wanted to beat him to the punch. For whatever reason, he gave Dale a synopsis of why he thought Carole was a target. And he added some new twists to the story. Dale recalled, "The reason, some of the things that Todd was telling me, I thought she had enemies. One was The Company. Todd's CIA friends. There was also a tagger. A person from the CIA that was following him at work. He told me to carry a gun and be careful."

Another enemy was even more bizarre. Gordon continued, "There was the Clarks. The people Todd and I did a fencing job for. He told me Rick Clark came by his house. He told me he was checking up on him. Todd told me he was in the house. Todd was going to shoot Rick Clark when he walked in the door. Then he was going to get one of my guns, grind the serial numbers off and place it in his [Clark's] hand. But when Rick Clark was outside, Carole came home, and when she did, that scared him off. It was because of a fencing job that went all wrong. They owed us money. They didn't want to pay. Todd said he went out to their place one time with his attorney, and Todd and the Clarks got into a fight out there on his property."

Gordon believed Todd and didn't even object to his gun being used in a murder. In fact, he followed Todd out to the Clark residence with murder in mind. Gordon said, "We drove out to Clark's house because we were going to kill him. I had my forty-five. Todd had his three-fifty-seven. But he wasn't there."

While this separate vendetta was taking place, Norman Daniels was struggling and sweating over his upcoming assignment to kill Carole Garton. The only relief from this came in the form of an archery tournament on May 3 and May 4 in which he and Todd participated. It was the Western Classic Trail Shoot, one of the largest competitions of its kind in the United States. People came from all over the world to Redding to participate for cash and prizes. In fact, there was a special prize of $50,000 if anyone could hit a one-inch target twice from one hundred yards.

Perhaps Garton wanted to impress Daniels with his archery skills in the shoot—one more reason to make Daniels believe he was a deadly assassin with all types of weapons. It nearly backfired on him, though. By the end of the day, Todd Garton looked more like one of the Three Stooges than Robin Hood.

Charles "Chuck" Hawkins, of Redding, who was on the same team as Garton and Daniels, was an accomplished bowman; he remembered Garton's antics that day very well. What he recalled certainly did not put Todd Garton in a good light. Hawkins said that even before the shoot, "I loaned Mr. Garton a couple of videos, *Pro Sniper* and *Ultra Sniper.* I do a lot of hunting and long-range shooting. And I wanted to learn more about it and to be more accurate for purposes of hunting. When I loaned him the tapes, he came with Norm Daniels."

Todd showed Daniels an individual in one of the videos—an expert named Carlos Hathcock. Hawkins continued, "Todd told Norm, 'This is the guy that I was telling you about.' He was going on, showing Norm this was his mentor or whatever. He acted like he'd trained under him down in southern California. For sniping. He acted like he had been a long-range sniper. Marine sniper. The way he acted was that he had just gotten out [of the marines]. I questioned that. Just the shape he was in. It would be like me saying I just got out of being a marine sniper. I'm way overweight. I don't fit the part. He was overweight. Probably forty pounds. Didn't look like a marine sniper to me.

"He wanted me to wear one of the shaggy outfits at the archery shoot. I did. As far as selling the suits, he did a good job. One of the things he was doing was going around hitting up vendors. Trying to push the product. He said that he was interested in buying the Bow Rack [an archery store in Redding] and that he was buying part of the Moore Ranch. A fairly large ranch off Adobe Road."

This was at a time when Todd and Carole were barely making payments on their rental home on Adobe Road. Carole even had to borrow money from her parents to help buy baby clothes.

Hawkins continued, "Our team, Team Shaggy, was put together about a week before the shoot. I noticed at the shoot he [Todd] put his quiver upside down on the bow. He and Norm both had their quivers on upside down. The feathers were up. When you draw your bow, feathers are normally down. I poked some fun at him. I teased him about it. He got a little hot and didn't like it. He said that's the way he did it for turkey hunting, so he could kneel down and shoot so his feathers wouldn't hit the ground. It didn't make any sense. I turkey hunt with a bow. My feathers don't touch the ground. I shoot a longer arrow than him."

One incident in particular made Charles Hawkins double over with laughter. He said, "Todd was trying to shoot a long ways with a recurve bow. He missed the whole target and hit a truck. We made more fun of him on that one. He kind of had to laugh that one off. He just wasn't a very good shot. He talked himself as to being a good shot, all these big bucks.

"When you shoot a bow and arrow, you hold your hand open on the bow. You hold so that your thumb and your fingers are open. You wouldn't put your finger on the arrow itself. That's a bad habit. When you draw, if you have razor blades on

there, or broadheads on there, you can cut your
finger. A lot of people cut their finger real bad."
Apparently, Todd put his finger on the arrow and
was lucky not to rip it to shreds.

Hawkins said, "I just mainly stayed away from him.
I knew he was full of it. Just in general, he had a
long line of BS. I didn't want to listen to it."

After having made a fool of himself by hitting a
pickup truck in the parking lot, instead of the target, the wonder of it was that Todd Garton could
still represent himself as a skilled assassin in Norman
Daniels's eyes. But as Charles Hawkins said, "He
had a long line of BS." Somehow this BS worked
on Daniels.

At least in this he had the aid of Lynn Noyes,
who was doing all she could to keep Daniels on
track in the hit of Carole Garton. Todd gave Lynn a
general idea of how Daniels received the package
from The Company. Lynn said later, "He [Daniels]
was delivered a package of pertinent information,
pictures, orders of what he was supposed to do, the
person he was supposed to kill. The first time that
somebody was to be killed, it was to be done a certain way. He had the option of—when he received
the package—not opening it. If he, in fact, opened
this package, that would mean he would have to
go through with what was inside the package, or
they and their family would be killed.

"At a point [Todd] said usually for the person
that was wanting to get involved in this company,
that the first hit had to be somebody close to them.
And being that it was Norm Daniels's first package, that is how it was supposed to be done."

Lynn believed that Carole would be the target because of stories Todd had told her about Colonel Sean. He said that Carole had gotten into an argument with Sean and shot him in the leg. She had also turned her allegiance from the Catholic cause to the Protestant one. As a substrata to all of this, Lynn believed that Todd was somehow involved in the hit as well. He didn't want her to believe that, but she knew that he didn't want the baby that Carole was going to have and he didn't like children. Lynn had thoughts that somehow he was helping The Company fund the hit on Carole because of this baby.

Lynn said later, "The front that he put up at the time that he was a happy, bubbling father-to-be, he didn't like doing it. It made him sick, but he did it anyway. He didn't believe he was the father. He said that they [he and Carole] had been separated off and on. It would have been some sort of immaculate conception because he hadn't been with her. He gave a couple of different options of who the father would have been. He told me specifically that it was either one of the hotel chains she worked for—the son of one of the people that owned or managed one of the hotels. Or just a local person. A local breeder, actually. Meaning somebody who just likes to get women pregnant and not take any responsibility.

"He even had said that it would be better if she was killed. It would be better if she died from an unfortunate accident." He also made a curious comment that it would be better for her reputation. Just how having her murdered would be better for her reputation than divorce, he didn't say. Perhaps he meant it would be better for his reputation.

Todd did not tell her directly that he was setting up the unfortunate accident. But Lynn surmised that this could very well be the case. She didn't like Carole anyway, and she took no steps to warn her.

Todd told Lynn that she was to be "Norman's friend." She was to listen to his concerns and guide him. But most of all she was to prod him to carry out the hit before the deadline of May 20.

Lynn said, "Todd told me that his friend Norman was a single parent who had a son. The mother of the child was very irresponsible and that Norman was really kind of down on his luck and didn't have a lot of money and he was having problems raising his son. I felt really bad about the fact that this child was living in adverse living conditions. Todd said there were times when Norman had to leave the kid home by himself and he was little at that point. Todd had taken care of him for a few days and it was a sad situation.

"And that really appealed to me. I felt bad for him and I said, 'Well, is there anything I can do to help this guy with his kid? If he's a friend of yours, I trust your word on that.' "

Todd told her to be friendly with Daniels. Talk to him every chance she could. Listen to his concerns. Try to ease his mind. And help him carry through on the hit. Otherwise, Norm would be the target of an irate bureau.

Lynn did as Todd suggested and recalled her first conversation over the phone with Daniels. "He told me a little about his life, the situation he was in, his child. He said he was just a gas station guy. It kind of progressed from there. It went from his life to talking about The Company. He told me he received a package." (This is something she already knew through Todd.)

Daniels gave her some details about the contents of the package, but not who the intended victim was at this point (although she already knew this as well). In some ways he thought that Lynn was the one who had paid for the hit. He knew that Lynn did not like Carole. Daniels said later, "It was explained to me by Todd that Lynn Noyes was my profiler. A profiler is someone that is to psychologically evaluate a person and their capability as far as doing something. To watch them and make sure they don't become wild and unstable.

"I suspected her involvement with The Company. Lynn had stated to me on a few occasions that she really hated Carole Garton. I think, coupled with Todd Garton telling me that anybody could put out a hit on anybody and that her vehemence, this hatred, it was an assumption on my part that she wanted Carole dead.

"[Todd and Lynn] go way back to their teens and they have both worked together before. They were in the IRA when they were in their teens, and that her and Carole had worked together to lure people into situations where they could be assassinated. Todd and Lynn hd been on the run in Ireland. And they slept in a safe house. They were the best of friends. He also said that Lynn worked for The Company and she had tried backing out. Then he stated, 'Once you're in, you are in.' "

Todd's luck with all these lies held. If Daniels had asked Lynn only once about Northern Ireland, he would have found out that she had never been there, and certainly had not been a member of the IRA.

As time went on, Garton told Daniels he would need a code name. Todd already had a code name with The Company. He was Patriot. Lynn Noyes was "Josephine." The code name for her had been lifted from the movie *La Femme Nikita*. Daniels said, "Todd had said that I'm going to have to come up with a name for my code name. I was throwing stuff out like 'Hamlet.'"

Subconsciously, Daniels had stumbled on the perfect code name for himself. Just like Shakespeare's tragic character, Daniels fretted and worried about performing a task that he did not want to do. His anguish and torment became a constant factor of his life. He worried that there were Company snipers in the neighborhood who would kill him if he did anything wrong. He also worried that a hit man from The Company would kill him if he waited too long to complete his mission. He wanted help for a way to extricate himself from the predicament he found himself in. But he didn't know whom he could trust.

Todd Garton did not like Hamlet as a code name. He wanted something more Irish. Something more decisive. Daniels said, "Todd kept suggesting certain names. And 'Devlin' was one of them he was really pushing for me. We were coming back from the Visalia archery shoot, and I gave in on his request.

"He said there was a book by Jack Higgins, *The Eagle Has Landed*. What he told me was that there was this German officer named Sean Devlin, and that he was disguised as a British commando. And he had his German uniform underneath. They were trying to capture Churchill. And this soldier saw this little girl fall into a creek and was drowning. And the soldier pulled off his British uniform. Obviously, the people saw the German uniform as he was stripping that off. He [Todd] said that I fit the character's persona and that's why he wanted me to take that name. But Todd plagiarized [*sic*] the character; because after I read the book, I found out that what he told me and what actually happened in the book were different."

Had Daniels looked more closely at a lot of situations, he would have found that there often was a discrepancy between what was fact and what Todd Garton presented as fact.

Garton told Daniels that even Carole had a code name from her IRA days. She had been known as "Sirene." He never explained where this code name came from, but he indicated that Josephine and Sirene had worked together.

Todd Garton wanted the main means of communication between Norman Daniels and Lynn Noyes to be by computer. This would keep things more private than communication being overheard as they talked on the phones. It also allowed one more thing—Todd could set up an account on a computer and make it look as if the messages were coming from someone else in The Company. Norm and Lynn obviously knew his voice, but an e-mail message coming "from The Company" could have been sent by anyone that Todd said it came from.

Todd was particulary inventive in this, and he had an unwitting ally in Dale Gordon, who was living in the Garton residence. Todd could send messages over Dale's computer. If anything ever went wrong, the messages and text would be traced back to Dale's computer, not Todd's.

Dale recalled, "I had a Pentium 166 computer at Todd's house. Todd and I set up an AOL account with a free disc. I was the one on the phone who set it up. He did some browsing. He talked with people in a chat room. There was some pornography he used it for. Todd's password was PATR3."

It seems that Dale logged on using Todd's screen name at some point. To stop this, Todd came up with a new screen name, PATR553, and a password. The 553 was part of Todd's social security number. He did not divulge the password to Dale. Todd also came up with an involved reason why he changed his screen name. Dale recalled, "Todd told me he was trying to access the CIA. Their computer system. He had a code memorized in his head, but he was one digit off. When he tried to access it, they sent a spike and it messed up the AOL account. You couldn't go into it anymore. It was like a virus they sent."

Todd told Norman Daniels to use the screen name Devlin when communicating with him, Lynn Noyes or The Company. Daniels already had screen names of Normbo for chat rooms and Valkymere for playing Internet computer games. Valkymere was named after the hero in his computer game mode and for use in the Internet game Vampire Tavern. But when Daniels tried to use the screen name Devlin, he discovered that it was already taken. So he tried Devlin 999. This was also taken. Turning the numbers over, he chose Devlin 666, and this was open for him to use. He adopted it. It was an interesting combination. In some circles 666 stands for the "mark of the Beast" and also refers to Satan.

In early May 1998 Daniels received a message via computer from The Company; it was called "a doorway message." It was an introduction and welcome to The Company. When Daniels opened this message, it read: *We would like to start by welcoming you to the family and hope you become an asset to our company of friends and family.* The next part of the message was very strange. It was an attachment that depicted a scantily clad woman with Todd Garton's pager number written backward. The pager number was superimposed over the woman's midsection.

Daniels saved this doorway message by printing it out as a hard copy. Just like the wax seal from the package, Daniels decided to save this doorway message just in case something went wrong. He would have some "proof" later that The Company existed.

On May 6, 1998, Todd Garton and Norm Daniels sent a reply to the doorway message. Daniels recalled, "Todd authored a message. I was sitting in the front room of his house when he was typing it. He was sending it to The Company to let them know that the doorway worked. The message said, 'New doorway opened.' This was to 'Company T' at USA.Net from PATR553 at AOL.com. Then there was a message to 'Confirm with Devlin and Josephine.'"

Daniels got an e-mail message from Company T (The Company's code name) that referred to the movie *A Prayer for the Dying*. He wasn't sure what it meant, except it had to do with the Irish Republican

Army. Daniels sent out a request for some help in killing Carole Garton. He wanted a more experienced assassin to help him. And he also wanted more time. The request was denied. He received an e-mail message: *Window impossible to meet due to weather, work and personal involvement.*

As Daniels said later, "I needed time to think. I just knew that it was going to be extremely hard to do."

Another message came from Company T to Daniels; it said, *Your best asset, Patriot.* That meant Todd Garton.

Todd had convinced Daniels that the shadowy Colonel Sean was directing him from The Company. Daniels was able to send messages to Colonel Sean at Company T. But, of course, there was no real Colonel Sean. There was only Todd Garton posing as Colonel Sean. Todd e-mailed the return messages to Daniels as if he were Colonel Sean. And Daniels bought it.

At one point Daniels wanted to put Colonel Sean on his computer's buddy list so they could send instant messages. Sean88 was given to Daniels as Colonel Sean's screen name. Even though he added this to his buddy list, he never did instant message Colonel Sean while Todd was in the same room as Daniels. Of course, he couldn't. Todd would have had to be at another computer to do so.

During this period there was no one Norman Daniels wanted to communicate with more than Lynn Noyes. She was his profiler. She was the one to keep him straight on his mission. And Daniels was definitely having trouble in following through on the hit of Carole Garton.

In the beginning Daniels just wanted to check in with Lynn via e-mails and discuss the mission. He was lucky in this regard, since Lynn had just obtained her own personal computer in April 1998. It might have been tough for her if she had to communicate with him using her husband's computer. Lynn asked Todd if it was okay to communicate with Norm via computer. Todd encouraged it. He told her, "He [Daniels] is really into computers. He's a techno geek."

Besides chatting in e-mails to Lynn Noyes about the upcoming operation, Daniels tried getting her interested in an Internet computer game called Vampire Tavern. It was a role-playing game that happened in real time. As Daniels explained, "We went to what was called the Vampire Tavern on the AOL chat room in a public area."

Lynn Noyes went into even more detail about this. "It was playing a game on a computer that had sexual overtones. There were numbers of people in cyberspace in this area and you went and kind of selected a person, and the object of the game was seduction. The only person I really played with was Norman Daniels.

"I always followed Norm's lead on what to do. Because there was something I never really understood, that dice were thrown and it was kind of like a point system. The time I spent on it with Norm Daniels, I really didn't understand or knew how to play it. It was entertainment. There was some enjoyment in it."

Todd encouraged Lynn to play these games with Daniels. He even popped into the Vampire Tavern once and told them to *have fun*. But Lynn Noyes was more adept at other seductions than in Vampire Tavern. And as time went on, Norman Daniels was increasingly enamored with her. She led him out of the Vampire Tavern and into cybersex. Her screen name for these episodes was indicative of her wiles. She used the name Pandoora 69. The 69 was self-explanatory. Lynn Noyes was always a very sexual woman. Her tastes and turn-ons ran the gamut from Todd Garton to Natalya.

Daniels said of his cybersex encounters with Lynn, "Instead of talking, you type out descriptive actions. In our first communication we were talking about copulating, having sexual intercourse. You know. Fellatio. Cunnilingus." He signed himself on as Valkymere, hero of his fantasy in Vampire Tavern. She was Pandoora.

Lynn Noyes's recollection of cybersex with Daniels was even more detailed. She remembered telling him: *I can't even fathom why you're so attractive. And your mind is so brilliant. I would gladly give more than take. It's the story of my life.*

They role-played a seduction until Daniels typed, *Stepping up behind her, he bends close to her neck.* Then he wrote, *Valkymere gently places Pandoora on the couch.*

Lynn replied, *Pandoora mounts him and takes control. She starts a rhythm. She reaches for a dagger on the nightstand. Cuts herself so she won't climax immediately.*

Fully into the vampire motif, Valkymere drank her blood as he became aroused.

At this point Lynn wrote Daniels that she was so turned on she needed to masturbate.

Daniels replied, *Can't type and do it at the same time?*

She countered, *I only need one hand.*

Daniels sent her a smiley face icon to demonstrate that he enjoyed the thought of her masturbating. He told her he wanted more cybersex that same evening.

By early May, Norman Daniels was in the incredible position of falling for Lynn Noyes, the mistress of Todd Garton. The same woman who was prodding him to kill Todd's wife, Carole. Just how smitten he was can be gauged by the stories and poetry he began to send her.

In one poem he told her that her face was invisible yet clear. He could almost feel her body in his hands. Images of her flowed through his head and he could smell her alluring scent.

He played out his Hamlet role to the degree that he said he was filled with despair of wanting her. Having her was only for an instant. Wanting her lasted lifetimes.

He told Lynn he had written this poem on the fly and he called her "Milady." Perhaps it was an apt description. Interestingly, Milady in *The Three Musketeers* was a woman involved with intrigue and murder.

On another day Norman told Lynn that he had gone to an actual tavern and was dancing with a young woman. But he revealed, *Do not be jealous my Queen. I did not touch her.*

This yearning for Lynn Noyes on Daniels's part was incredible, especially in the light of how Lynn felt about Todd. Norman might have been less enamored of her if he'd known that Lynn was also sending Todd cybersex messages during this same period. In these encounters with Todd, Lynn asked rhetorically if she was an angel or a devil. The romantic side of her was drawn toward the angelic. The steamy side of her was drawn to the devilish. He replied that she was his angel. His angel, Maliki.

Besides e-mails and phone conversations, Todd also instructed Lynn and Norm to keep in touch with each other via their pagers for important messages. In fact, Todd sent his pager number to Lynn in an e-mail that he'd used in the doorway message to Norm—the one superimposed on the belly of the scantily clad woman. About using her pager with Todd, Lynn said, "Usually I'd page him until he called me. If it was urgent, I'd page 'Call immediately' or '911.' I'd leave my phone number to call on the message and to get in touch with Josephine."

Garton must have become spooked about all the e-mails going back and forth at some point between him and Lynn. He wouldn't exchange an e-mail with her unless it had the notation of his pager number—in reverse order—in the title.

He also had a new elaborate way of communicating with Norm Daniels. This was by means of using a codebook and book drop. The book drops were an elaborate scheme concocted by Todd to convince Daniels that The Company was taking extra precautions on this mission. Daniels said, "Todd explained to me that *The Eagle Has Landed* book would contain messages that this company would want to give me other than through e-mails or any other way. It would be encoded by poking under each letter of whatever the code sentence was. Starting in the second chapter. It would always start in the second chapter. As long as you would look for pinholes under each letter, that would be the message.

"It made sense that it would be a subvertive [*sic*] thing. When you normally looked at the book, you wouldn't notice pinholes. I would find the book at the west side of the Moose Lodge. There's a small hole. Todd had taken me there and pointed it out to me. It was a crawl space in the building."

In a scene right out of a Hardy Boys mystery novel, Daniels was supposed to crawl under the building and retrieve the codebook every so often. There was also an e-mail message for him stating that if Patriot became a liability, then his new book would be *A Prayer for the Dying*. Daniels was under the impression that someone besides Todd was placing the codebook under the Moose Lodge. He also understood the term "liability" to mean anyone who tried to leave The Company without their permission. Such a person would be hunted down and killed.

As if it weren't enough that he was pushing Norman Daniels to murder his wife, Todd came up with another criminal scheme in early May 1998. He decided to go up by himself to Gresham, Oregon, and burglarize Dean Noyes's house. He wanted to find valuable information on Dean. He also wanted to be away from his home on Adobe Road on May 7 through May 9—the days he pushed Daniels to kill Carole. If he was in Gresham, Oregon, with a valid motel receipt, Todd thought it would give him a good alibi to the murder.

Todd checked into his favorite motel, the Hampton Inn, and obtained room 214. This was only a few rooms down from where he had fired through the window screen with a silenced rifle at the street below. Norman Daniels knew about this trip and related, "It was a reccon mission. Pretty much he was going to stake out Dean Noyes. If the opportunity arose to kill him, he would take it."

But Todd had no intention of killing Dean. And he gave the real reason for his being there to Lynn Noyes. She said, "It was to help orchestrate a break-in at my house. It was actually an idea of mine. As opposed to having Dean killed. Dean was embezzling money from the company he was working for, and I thought if somebody had certain information pertaining to the funds that he was embezzling—how he was doing it and all—if they held that over his head, he might have to come clean to his employers. This would result in him ending up in trouble with the law and then he would be out of the picture for a while. He probably would have served some type of prison term."

Whether Dean Noyes actually was embezzling or not, Lynn at least thought he was. And the figure of $80,000 came up in regard to this embezzlement. Todd liked this idea, but he changed it around to his advantage and didn't tell Lynn of the changes. Instead of having Dean go to jail and be out of the picture, Todd wanted to blackmail him. If he couldn't get insurance money by having Dean killed, then maybe he could squeeze some money out of him. Todd went to the Noyes residence and Lynn let him in while Dean and the children were away. He took some computer disks, a copy machine, a printer, one of Dean's laptops and a large three-ring binder. Todd also took records of Dean's bank account.

He took all of this material to the Hampton Inn and contacted Norman Daniels with Dean's laptop computer. He was miffed that Daniels still hadn't killed Carole, but he was also excited by having all this material belonging to Dean. Daniels, with his computer skills, could help him. Daniels recalled, "Dean Noyes's AOL screen name was Dean Noyes 1408. There were five sets of numbers that Todd wanted me to try as Dean's password." But Daniels tried this and they couldn't break into Dean's AOL account. They didn't figure out the right combination. But after looking through various documents, they discovered that Noyes's password wasn't numerical, rather it was a name—Chows, followed by Toulez.

Daniels recalled, "Todd asked me to search the Internet to see if we would be able to access Dean Noyes's bank account electronically. He wanted me to set up a fake Internet account and send a message to Noyes. He wanted to set up the account under the name Bladerunner. He wanted me to do it through USA.net. I wasn't able to do that. My understanding is that I did not have the proper software to access the USA.net's Web page to log on. I looked for another server so that I could set up the account. Eventually I got an account with Hotmail.com."

In a new twist on this blackmail scheme, Todd told Daniels he was going to flush Dean Noyes out with the embezzlement scheme so that Dean would come to talk to him in some secluded place. And then he would kill him. But Todd had no intention of really doing this. Basically he wanted to just blackmail Dean. In all these schemes Todd was constantly lying to Norman Daniels and Lynn Noyes.

With the Bladerunner screen name now on Hot

mail.com., Daniels set up a password of "a time to die." This was from the movie *Blade Runner.* Daniels thought this was an appropriate password concerning Dean Noyes. He still thought Dean was a wife-beating scumbag and deserved to die. Daniels also gave Todd another screen name for the Hotmail. com server. The name he gave him was John Carson.

Garton was so leery by now of having any connection to computers, he phoned Daniels from Oregon and had him type in a message to Dean Noyes. It was supposedly coming from an anonymous person named Bladerunner. The message was: *Someone has not been playing nice. Stealing money is a crime. Want to make a deal?* It was a none-too-subtle extortion attempt to shake loose money from Dean. In a short reply Dean e-mailed his unknown extortionist that he had no money and couldn't help him.

Once Garton was back in California, he gave Daniels pictures, business cards and floppy disks that he had stolen from Dean Noyes. Daniels was not sure what he was supposed to do with them. Todd Garton's reason for giving them to Daniels may have been if things went wrong, Daniels would have these items, not him.

With the embezzlement scheme bubbling along, Todd turned his focus back to the murder of Carole. Time was moving along and he was worried that Daniels might not ever act on his promise to kill her. The last thing Todd wanted was Daniels to flake out and not kill her before the baby was born. Once that happened, it was going to be a lot harder to kill mother and son. He encouraged Daniels to do it soon. He told him he didn't like going to bed at night knowing that his wife was going to be killed. It would be better for everyone concerned if he just got it over with.

About this time Grace Bell had an interesting conversation with Carole about Todd. Grace expressed her displeasure that Todd thought he could call Carole away from work at any time to have her help him with matters that concerned G and G Fencing. Carole explained to Grace that they were in serious financial trouble on this score and she needed to help him. The lawsuit by Rick Clark was a disaster for the fencing business.

To ratchet up Norman Daniels's anxiety about The Company, Todd pushed Lynn Noyes ever harder to prod Daniels toward the murder. Lynn said later that Daniels was contacting her daily now. In between cybersex episodes she reminded him about his mission. He replied that he was having a real problem following through. He liked Carole. He was worried about getting caught. He was so pent up with his Hamlet-like hesitations, he took a week off from the Kickin'Mule to try and build up his courage and focus on the operation.

Todd was making Norm once again watch training films to "help" him focus. They included another round of *The Jackal, Patriot Games* and *La Femme Nikita.* Learning of these movies from Daniels, Lynn told him that perhaps he should take a scene from out of these movies and adapt it to the murder of Carole Garton. Lynn told Norm he could kill Carole in her vehicle and make it look like a carjacking gone bad. Or kill her in her home and make it look like a robbery. The important thing, she said, was to do it quickly.

Daniels was so upset, he asked Lynn to send a message to The Company saying that he needed more time. He also wanted some money and a car. This was the last thing Todd wanted to hear, and he sent a message back to Daniels from Company T. In essence, it told Daniels to quit wasting time and accomplish his mission.

While all of this was going on, Todd put on a happy face around the house that he couldn't wait for the baby to arrive. Dale Gordon, who was living there, said, "Todd was treating Carole a little bit nicer. He assisted more around the house. I remember items showing up around the house for the baby. Todd and Carole worked a little bit together. Todd hired Sara [Gordon's girlfriend] to come down and help clean up. This was to help Carole during the pregnancy."

Todd knew that Lynn Noyes was his key to making Daniels follow through on the hit. And for some reason Todd deemed it was important that Lynn change her Internet profile to bring it more in line with an operator for The Company. Perhaps he thought Daniels might check up on this profile. Or maybe he just wanted to have Lynn get more in character. He decided to change it without her knowledge.

She originally had written her profile as having hobbies that included dancing and running. But she said, "He asked if I had seen my profile lately. That if possible I should look at it again. He had altered it so it would be more suitable, since I was involved in this company. Because I was part of the family."

Todd told Lynn that some of her profile information had been changed by The Company. It was in accordance with her doing a good job and their trust in her. She was now deemed to be a "closer" and a "mechanic." She was told that closer had something to do with the lyrics from the song by the Counting Crows—"A Murder of One."

Lynn recalled, "It was the situation he was in. If you look at the song lyrics, portions of the song are the fact that I was married to Dean, and it explains itself there." Lynn remembered that a part of the song said to look outside a window, and that the husband/boyfriend didn't need to know. Then the lyrics asked if the man kept her safe and warm. Lynn related, "Dean didn't do that for me. Todd always gave me what Dean didn't give."

Todd pointed out with these lyrics that a dead spouse, a murder of one, would allow him and Lynn to be closer together. The term "mechanic" seems to have come from the Charles Bronson movie by the same name. On top of all of this, he also called her a "cleaner." This came from the movie *Pulp Fiction*. It also made reference to a scene from *La Femme Nikita*. A "cleaner" cleaned up someone else's messes by eliminating individuals. Lynn said, "A cleaner was somebody who came in and cleaned up botched-up jobs."

To scare both Lynn Noyes and Norman Daniels, Todd began to rely more and more on the specter of the mysterious and dangerous Colonel Sean. That Colonel Sean was pure fiction, Lynn and Norm never had a clue. Todd told them that he recently had noticed a dangerous tagger following him around. This tagger was someone sent by The Company to check up on individuals and report back to Colonel Sean.

Todd also sent more e-mail messages to them from Colonel Sean. In one message to Lynn, Colonel Sean told her to keep tabs on Norman Daniels and report everything she witnessed to Todd. In another e-mail from Colonel Sean, he wrote, *Is there something going on that I am not aware of? My boy [Daniels] is getting weird on me. He seems to be in a very dark cloud. You must not push too hard. He will always break when bent. You must be in contact with me if his mood becomes more aggressive.*

But Norm Daniels was not aggressive enough for Todd Garton's liking. Daniels came up with one excuse after another why he couldn't kill Carole at the present time. He kept badgering Lynn to tell The Company he needed more time. In response Colonel Sean e-mailed Daniels in a series of threatening messages. One said, *We need you to deliver this package well and quick without any incident. I'm one inch away from pulling you down and personally handling this situation myself. We are in a crunch. Patriot only trusts you and sometimes Josephine and two others. Unfortunately, none of them [Lynn and the other two] are field operators.*

Daniels understood a field operator to be someone who actually went out and killed people.

Another message Daniels received from the fictional Colonel Sean insisted, *You have proven nothing to me and I sign the checks. But you may have something going on, because Josephine and Patriot are keeping you in good terms. You better live up to all the expectations I have been told of, or I will personally fly there overnight and see you.*

Daniels was very frightened by this message. Todd had told him Colonel Sean was a tough character. If he flew out to northern California, it would probably be to kill him.

As Norm explained, "Todd told me this Sean character didn't mess around. He would clean me up. I understood that to mean come out and kill me and everybody involved. He said if Sean was to get on an airplane, that he [Todd] would want to meet this Sean guy at the airport when he got off, but not up close. He [Todd] would want to shoot him before he got off the aircraft."

Colonel Sean also e-mailed Daniels: *Your request to meet me in person, denied. I do not meet newbies. They don't last long enough to bother. Perform to expectations or become a liability.*

To give the thumbscrews a last twist, Todd told Daniels he had received a final ultimatum from Colonel Sean about killing Carole Garton. Daniels recalled, "It was told to me by Todd, 'If you don't do what you're told, you or your son could end up either hurt or dead. Or your son could end up kidnapped and used against you to do anything they want.'"

That was the final incentive as far as Norman Daniels was concerned. He already partially believed he was a dead man no matter what he did. But the safety of his son concerned him greatly. It was this threat that finally made him decide to act.

Daniels said, "Todd suggested that Saturday would be a good day to do it because everybody would be away from the house and he'd be at a gun show." There was a gun show at the Anderson Fairgrounds and Todd had a good excuse for being out of the

KILL OR BE KILLED

house. It would also not seem strange that Norman was carrying a weapon around because of the gun show. Besides all of this, Dale Gordon and Sara Mann would also be gone. If everything went right, only Carole would be home.

Norman Daniels agreed to act then, on Saturday, May 16. He even spent the night over at the Garton house on Friday, watching videos with Todd, Carole, Dale and Sara. Once again they were videos that concerned hit men and assassins. Carole had no idea that some of the scenes were supposed to steel Daniels's nerve to murder her.

But even at this late hour, Daniels had one last round of Hamlet-like doubt. He said, "I thought this has got to be a setup. I just had a feeling. I was drinking heavily and thought about calling the police. But I didn't believe they would believe me. And if The Company found out I did that, I would wind up dead. The amount of information I was given by Todd, it forced the thoughts into submission. If I made a mistake, my son and my family—I worried about that."

On the night of May 15, 1998, Norman Daniels was afraid of killing Carole Garton. She was some-one he liked and also feared, because he had been told what a crack shot she was during her Irish Republican Army days. But as much as he feared her, he feared The Company even more. He screwed up his courage and decided that May 16, 1998, would be the day he would kill her—come hell or high water.

Chapter 7

Now or Never

May 16, 1998, dawned with scattered clouds and a prediction of sun and showers later in the afternoon. All the inhabitants at the Garton residence on Adobe Road awakened and made various plans for the day. Todd Garton, Norman Daniels and Sara Mann were going to the gun show in Anderson. Dale had a job at the Thunderbird Mill in Cottonwood and had to report there. Carole was going to visit the maternity ward at Redding's Mercy Medical Center with her friend Tracie Jones.

As Tracie said later, "We went to the Maternity Tea and Tour at Mercy Medical Center. We were both pregnant at the time, and she hadn't been up to visit the maternity ward, so we went together. We met, actually, at the gun show in Anderson and then drove together to the hospital. We went on the tour. The tour started at ten or ten-thirty. It took about an hour. We went to lunch around noon. We talked about going shopping, but given the time, and the time I told the baby-sitter I would be back, we decided just to pick my kids up. We went to the baby-sitter's house on the way back to the gun show, picked up the kids and went to the show.

"We went back there to trade cars. Traded cars with our husbands so that they could bring merchandise home that evening. I never saw her again."

It was sometime between 1:00 and 1:30 P.M. when Carole dropped by the Anderson gun show for the second time and talked to Todd and Norman for a while. Todd was displaying camouflage wear for Rancho Safari. Marshall Jones had a table right next to his with guns. Norman Daniels was nervous and fidgety. He knew that Todd expected him to do the "job" today. He also knew that the window of opportunity, mentioned in the package from The Company, was running out. His recollection of what happened next became a litany of anxiety, fear and ultimate determination.

Daniels said later, "I made an excuse to leave the gun show with Carole because we had been watching videos the night before and I wanted to get them back. Also, I wanted to finish one of the videos that we did not get to watch. It was called *Killing Time*. It was a real cheesy assassin movie. It had been suggested [by Todd] this would be a good time, so I made an excuse to leave with her. I had the forty-four Rossi with me."

Daniels had the Rossi in his holster. Apparently, Carole thought nothing of it because they were at a gun show and Norman, Todd and Dale were always carrying guns around. Since Carole was tired, she gave Daniels the key to the Jeep and he drove them both to the house on Adobe Road. No one was there except her and Norman.

Daniels continued his recollections. "We sat down and put the movie on in the front room. I was going to shoot her in the chair. I didn't know if I could do it or not. There were several times that I was ready but didn't do it. I had the pistol out one time and I was sitting as we were watching the movie. I had it under a blanket. Then something happened and I didn't.

"She went back into the bedroom area. She changed her shirt and came back out and told me that she was going to lay down. I went into the bathroom and I was going to come out and do it. But I got paranoid and didn't. Several times I had the opportunity and didn't.

"I finished watching the movie. I rewound it and informed her that I was going to take the movie back to the store. She was lying on the bed. I took the Jeep and drove to Valley Video in Cottonwood."

Frustrated by his timidity, Daniels drove to the Kickin' Mule and bought $5 worth of gasoline. He went back and forth whether he should do the hit now or later. He didn't want to do it at all. But the threats from Colonel Sean kept popping into his mind. He drove back to his house and decided he had to carry through on the hit. He changed clothing, somehow surmising that if he changed clothing, he would be less conspicuous when he went back to the Garton residence. He drove back on Fourth Street, crossed the Sacramento River at Ball's Ferry Road and then onto Adobe Road. He stopped about fifty yards from the Garton house.

Daniels said, "I had left the back door open so I

wouldn't make any noise coming in. I thought of going in the back door and surprising her. I'd go through the field across the street. I was going to jump the fence and go around the field and come in through the back door. I got back there. There's a fence that separates the BLM land and I was right at the gate corner.

"When I stopped at the fence, I could see the residence. I could see the back door and the back window. If she was there, I couldn't see into the area, but she could see out. But I didn't climb over the gate. I was nervous. I was afraid there was a weapon in the house. If she saw me coming over the fence, she would have a weapon. I'd been warned she would not hesitate. She would kill me if she knew her life was in danger. Todd Garton warned me. He warned me she was potentially dangerous."

Angry and desperate now, Norman Daniels parked the Jeep right in front of the house. He said, "Not until I entered the house did I actually come up with a plan of what I was going to do. Carole was lying on the bed. I made an excuse for why I was all wet, because at the time I was going through the field, it had rained. So I explained that I had got out of the car and had to pee. It started raining and that's what happened.

"I went back to the front room and shut the back door. I was nervous. I was pacing and running my hand through my hair, wondering if I could do it or not. I took the pistol out and cocked it so it would be ready to fire and I would not have to pull the trigger. Only squeeze it. There's a difference in your accuracy when you shoot with the hammer back and the hammer forward. I put it in my left pocket so it would be covered by my jacket. And she would be on my right side, so she wouldn't see the pistol.

"Finally it came to me, 'Well, I'll do it fast. I can get close to her.'

"I stood to the side of the bed as I was talking to Carole. The conversation was about Jack, which was her boss's dog that she was baby-sitting for the week. She was lying on her right side.

"I thought about my son. I thought about my life and my family. I said to myself, 'I've got to do this or I got to die. Now or never.'

"I turned around. I knew that I could get to the pistol without her knowledge. I had it in my hand and turned and fired at her."

Carole saw the pistol in Daniels's hand. For one split second she must have been startled and terrified. Norman Daniels was her friend. This couldn't be happening.

Daniels said, "She covered her face. Both of her hands she crossed over her face. I shot her in the head. I thought it was above the left eye. She was still moving. She shimmied off the bed. She was attempting to get under the bed. I didn't want her to suffer. So I continued to fire. I shot at her torso. I was aiming for the heart. I fired at her head again and then I shot at her torso. The last shot was at her head.

"After the last shot she was laying on the ground next to the bed on her left side. I immediately holstered the pistol and then left. All I remember is pulling the door shut before I left the house."

Chapter 8

"My Wife Has Been Shot"

At around 5:00 P.M. on Saturday, May 16, Sara Mann, who had been at the Anderson gun show most of the day, left the building. She arrived at the Garton residence a little after 5:30 P.M. and found the front door open but didn't think that was unusual. Even the fact that the television was on with a low volume didn't faze her. Sara knew that she, Dale, Carole, Todd and Norman were all supposed to go out to dinner soon, and she surmised that Carole had just stepped out for a while and left the television on. Sara sat down at Dale's computer and began playing the video game Centipede.

Dale Gordon arrived at the Garton home about fifteen minutes later, walked in and gave Sara a hug. He was mildly surprised that she had entered the house by herself with no one else there. He knew she didn't have a key. He even asked why the television was on if she was playing a video game. She told him she had found it that way.

Dale said, "I was worried at that point someone had robbed the house. I went from the kitchen area right by the master bedroom." Without knowing it, he had passed within a few feet of Carole's bloody body lying on the floor.

Dale continued his remembrance. "I went into my room. I saw my guns sitting around and I thought, 'Well, nobody came in and robbed them.' As soon as I saw my guns there, I was pretty much satisfied because they were out in the open. I remember my thoughts were to call Norman, but I didn't do that. We were all going to dinner that night. I kind of wondered where Carole was. She was supposed to be there because we were all going. She knew what time I was going to get off work."

Dale walked back toward the living room, but he stopped once again by the entrance to the master bedroom. Once again he was within feet of Carole Garton, but he did not see her lying on the darkened floor. Before Dale moved another inch, Todd arrived home and greeted him. Todd had a quizzical look on his face and asked, "Where's Carole?"

Dale answered, "I don't know."

Dale took a few steps toward the living room while Todd walked into the master bedroom. He gazed at a shape on the floor. It was a sight he had been waiting for—Carole lying in a pool of blood. But when he looked closer, he was shocked. He thought she was still breathing. It is highly unlikely that Carole was still alive after so many gunshots at close range. Todd knelt down and listened for a heartbeat. He would admit later that he was so rattled by the actual sight of her body on the floor, he didn't know if it was her heart beating or his. The

Young Carole Holman was good at many sports, especially soccer. *(Photo courtesy of Virginia Griffiths)*

Carole dressed up as an angel. *(Photo courtesy of James and Vicki Holman)*

Carole watched one of Mt. St Helens's eruptions from her backyard. *(Photo courtesy of James and Vicki Holman)*

Carole on her senior prom night.
(Photo courtesy of James and Vicki Holman)

Always a prankster, teenaged Todd Garton got his birthday cake all over his fingers and face.
(Photo courtesy of Collin Colebank)

Todd was the driving force behind Detente Touch, a popular band in Portland, Oregon, in the late 1980s.
(Photo courtesy of Collin Colebank)

Todd and fellow band member Ursula Desailles jamming on stage.
(Photo courtesy of Shannon Colebank)

Carole modeled a beautiful wedding dress before marrying Todd Garton in 1991.
(Photo courtesy of James and Vicki Holman)

Todd and Carole were married in Reno, Nevada.
(Photo courtesy of James and Vicki Holman)

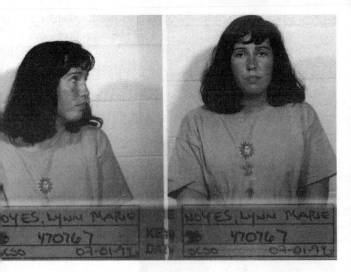

Lynn Noyes never gave up in her quest to have Todd
all to herself, even after she married another man.
(Photo courtesy of Shasta County Sheriff's Office)

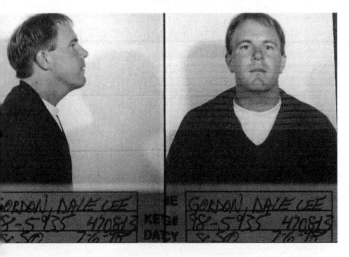

Todd Garton recruited gun enthusiast and wargame fan Dale
Gordon for his team of "assassins."
(Photo courtesy of Shasta County Sheriff's Office)

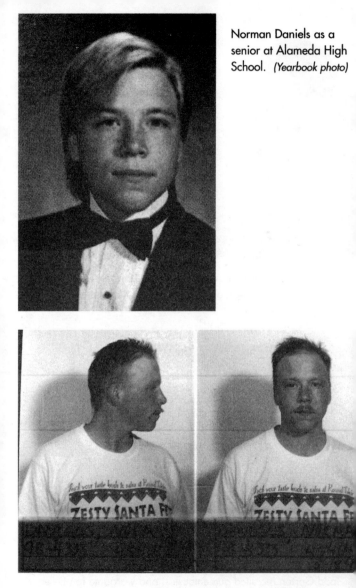

Norman Daniels as a senior at Alameda High School. *(Yearbook photo)*

Daniels was recruited by Garton for his team of assassins.
(Photo courtesy of Shasta County Sheriff's Office)

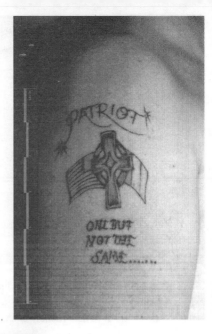

Todd showed his allegiance to Ireland and America by having a tattoo placed on his upper arm. *(Photo courtesy of Shasta County Justice Center)*

Lynn Noyes was so enthralled with Todd that she got a tattoo on her arm similarly stating "One." *(Photo courtesy of Shasta County Justice Center)*

Todd boasted of military medals that he had never earned, including a Purple Heart and Marine Lieutenant's Globe and Anchor pins. *(Photo courtesy of Shasta County Justice Center)*

Todd claimed that he wore this jacket while helping the Irish Republican Army in Belfast. *(Photo courtesy of Shasta County Justice Center)*

Planning to assassinate Lynn Noyes's husband, Garton and his associates amassed an arsenal of weapons.
(Photo courtesy of Shasta County Justice Center)

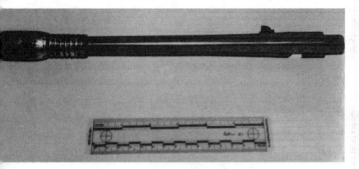

Todd Garton created a homemade silencer for his sniper rifle.
(Photo courtesy of Shasta County Justice Center)

Garton used a Lasersite on his rifle during target practice from a motel window in Portland, Oregon.
(Photo courtesy of Shasta County Justice Center)

Garton, Daniels, and Gordon planned to gun down Dean Noyes in this Portland parking garage where he usually parked before going to work. *(Photo courtesy of Shasta County Justice Center)*

When Noyes failed to show up at the parking garage, the trio of gunmen went to kill him at the home he shared with his wife, Lynn. *(Photo courtesy of Shasta County Justice Center)*

Todd pretended to be happy when Carole told him she was pregnant, but he did not want children with her. *(Photo courtesy of James and Vicki Holman)*

Carole Garton was seven months pregnant when she went to visit her mother in Oregon. *(Photo courtesy of Virginia Griffiths)*

On April 28, 1998, Garton went to Norman Daniels's mobile home and gave him a package that supposedly came from The Company. *(Photo courtesy of Shasta County Justice Center)*

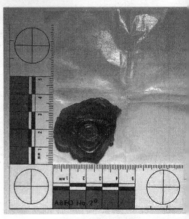

The package had a wax seal on its surface, which Daniels thought was in the shape of a ram's head. *(Photo courtesy of Shasta County Justice Center)*

The impression on the wax seal was actually made by Todd Garton's diving bubble pin. *(Photo courtesy of Shasta County Justice Center)*

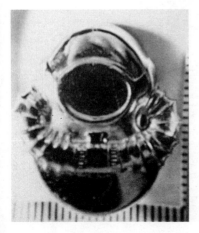

To get Daniels ready for his "mission" to kill Carole, Todd watched assassin videos with him. *(Photo courtesy of Shasta County Justice Center)*

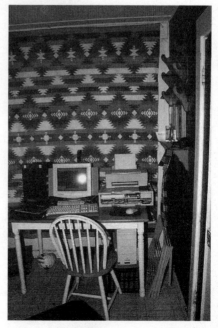

It appeared as though the elusive Colonel Sean, a high-powered operative in The Company, had sent e-mails to Daniels. In reality, Todd Garton sent the emails from this computer in his home. *(Photo courtesy of Shasta County Justice Center)*

Todd Garton's pistol had a Celtic Cross on the grip.
(Photo courtesy of Shasta County Justice Center)

Garton helped Norman Daniels buy this pistol. It was to be used to kill Carole. *(Photo courtesy of Shasta County Justice Center)*

Deputy DA Greg Gaul, with the help of Shasta County Sheriff's Detectives, put together a case against Todd Garton, Lynn Noyes, Norman Daniels and Dale Gordon in the plot to kill Dean Noyes and the murders of Carole Garton and her unborn son. *(Photo courtesy of Greg Gaul)*

A key piece of evidence against the conspirators was this label maker that Todd had used to print up instructions for Norman Daniels. *(Photo courtesy of Shasta County Justice Center)*

Miraculously, a Shasta County Sheriff's scuba diver was able to retrieve the label maker out of the Sacramento River where Todd had thrown it after Carole was killed. *(Author's photo)*

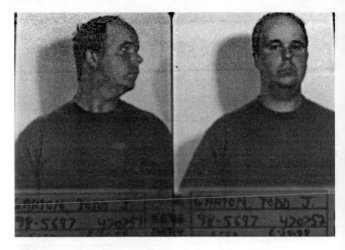

Todd Garton and his fellow conspirators were all either found guilty or pled guilty to various crimes. Garton was found guilty of first degree murder and sentenced to death.
(Photo courtesy of Shasta County Sheriff's Office)

Todd said that Carole and the unborn baby's ashes were deposited over beautiful Burney Falls, but their actual location remains a mystery. *(Author's photo)*

important thing at the time was that he assumed she was still alive and he was furious at Norman Daniels. He thought Daniels had botched the job and it put him in a precarious position.

Dale was just about to call Norman Daniels from a mobile phone when Todd walked up to him and in a calm but authoritative voice said, "Dial 911."

Dale recalled, "I didn't even ask why. I just grabbed the phone and dialed. There was some time, maybe five seconds or so, before I made contact with the operator for 911. I walked from the living room into Todd and Carole's bedroom. That's when I first saw Carole. I came real close. I saw a real bad bruise. I think it was around her left eye. Maybe toward the top, about her eyebrow. And I saw a lot of blood on her hair. Seemed like her hair was kind of up off the floor, and it was all red with blood. And there was some blood on the floor. My first impression was she fell off the bed and injured herself."

It was absolute chaos for a few minutes in the Garton residence. Dale was just beginning to talk to the 911 operator and Todd was kneeling down by Carole, pretending to help her. Inwardly he was enraged at Norman Daniels. Norman had been given a job to kill her and the baby and he thought she was still alive. Dale was staring down at the bloody scene as the dispatcher asked him what had happened. He answered, "I don't know. There's a lady passed out on the floor. She was just in bed and she's on the floor right now. I think she fell off and hit her head."

While Dale was trying to make sense of all this to the 911 operator, he watched as Todd pretended to give Carole CPR. Dale said, "Todd started to try and help revive her at that point. He was trying to get a flashlight to look into her eyes and check for dilation. Then I saw him doing, like, CPR. He blew in her mouth and then pressed on her chest. But he only did it a couple of times. It didn't appear like he knew what he was doing. We practiced CPR in boot camp in the marine corps. We did several methods. There's one when you blow in the mouth and push on the chest. Maybe fourteen pushes or something like that, and go back to the mouth. I remember him blowing in her mouth and pressing on her chest. But he only did it maybe fifteen seconds. Not very long. In the marine corps you do it until you get a response. You do it until you wear yourself out. You don't quit."

But Todd did quit and by now he was trying to get Sara to go down to the end of the block with a two-way radio and tell him when the ambulance was coming up the road. Apparently, she didn't go. Todd then dug around some boxes as if he were looking for something. Dale told the dispatcher that Todd was an EMT, even though nothing he did that day did anything to prove it. Dale also told the dispatcher that Todd was going to attempt to do a tracheotomy. But this wasn't coming off well because they were still searching around for a flashlight. Dale grabbed Todd's flashlight, but the batteries were dead. Then he went to get his own Maglite, but it didn't work. While he was in his room, Dale grabbed one of his knives in case Todd wanted to use it for the tracheotomy. Dale said, "I cleaned it. I sterilized it for Todd." Just how he did this, he didn't say.

While Dale went next door to get a flashlight, Todd got on the phone with the dispatcher as well. Whether this was another phone or not is not clear, but both of their voices could often be heard by the dispatcher. Garton yelled into the phone as if he were giving a soldier commands: "What is the ETA of my EMT? I need revival [equipment] and oxygen on stat!"

Then he said he had an airstrip cleared one hundred yards from the house for possible use of a helicopter. And somewhere along the line he added a crucial fact that Dale Gordon had not produced to the dispatcher. Garton told the dispatcher that Carole had been shot. He didn't know by whom or when it had happened, but he said that Carole was just barely alive.

Dale Gordon came rushing back in with a neighbor's flashlight and the voices of Todd and Dale mingled over the phone. By this point Todd clued Dale in about the gunshot wounds to Carole, and Dale told the dispatcher, "She has no pulse, is unconscious and has a gunshot wound on the head. But her body is still warm, so it hasn't been long."

Garton yelled in the background, "Streets need to be closed off! I think the gunman is still in the neighborhood!"

The dispatcher asked Dale if Carole had any enemies.

"We don't know," he answered. "Possibly."

Todd whispered to Dale, "Don't mention anything about the Oregon trip or Lynn." Dale promised that he wouldn't.

The dispatcher particularly had trouble getting

information from Todd. She even asked at one point, "Is there something you're not telling me?"

Todd didn't respond. Instead, he still prowled around Carole's body as if he were trying to help her. He even told Dale he was looking for some kind of hose to stick down her throat. Dale told the dispatcher that the driveway was cleared so that an ambulance could pull in there. He also said that Carole's white Jeep Wrangler was missing and no one knew why. He described it in detail and added something that Todd probably wished he hadn't. Dale told the dispatcher that there was a small Irish Republican Army sticker above one taillight.

Ten minutes had gone by without any real aid to Carole Garton lying on the floor. In fact, she had been lying there in a pool of blood for hours, and despite what Todd thought, she was probably already dead. When a medical examiner looked at her wounds later, he predicted she might have survived for twenty minutes at most from the time she was shot.

Sheriff's deputies were first on the scene, followed by paramedics. When the paramedics arrived, they took Carole into the living room for their examination because there was more room there. But their attempts at resuscitation were futile. She was pronounced dead at 7:22 P.M.

In a bit of acting, Todd Garton leaned up next to the tire of a police car and began to cry.

While all the pandemonium was occurring at the Garton residence on Adobe Road, Norman Daniels was long gone. He had driven Carole's Jeep to a park-and-ride lot near I-5 in south Cottonwood. This was just over the county line in Tehama County.

Daniels got out of the Jeep and threw the keys into the weeds by the side of the road. Then he walked back toward his mobile home by a long, circuitous route.

Daniels recalled, "I crossed the parking lot, walked on the opposite side of the road from the Texaco station and stayed on the right side. I walked north into town. I crossed over to the west side of the road. I continued north until I reached First Street. Crossed over First Street, heading west. I walked to just before the school and out north again, to Gas Point Road. And then walked west again until I reached my house.

"When I got back, I talked to my roommate, Jerry Enix. And I remember taking a shower. I paged Todd Garton and left a message, 'All done, going home.'

"Later I received a phone call from Todd. He said he was at his parents' house. He asked if the message was for him. I cleared my throat and told him, yes, it was. He sighed and said, 'Okay.' "

After Norman Daniels got home, he also contacted Lynn Noyes. He left a message on her answering machine. He said that he needed to talk to her because of what he had done. He didn't leave a message about exactly what he had done, but he was sure she would know what he was talking about.

Daniels also sent an e-mail message to Company T. It simply stated, *Package delivered.*

From this point on, Norman Daniels did very little to get rid of evidence. He took the Rossi .44 and cleaned it with gun oil to remove fingerprints. He didn't get rid of the weapon, though; he merely stuffed it under his pillows. And he only threw the casings from the expended bullets into his front yard. As to why he would leave such incriminating evidence around, Daniels said later, "I wasn't quite in my right mind. I didn't attempt to pick up any of my evidence. I didn't try to get rid of the pistol. I was distraught. I had just taken two lives.

"I was looking to get out of the house. Just go drinking. I was trying to alter my mood because of what I'd just done. I knew it was the last day or night I would be free."

Before Daniels went out drinking, he decided that he was hungry and stopped by a nearby store. He got some beer, a bottle of Jack Daniel's and a Take-n-Bake pizza. But as far as the liquor went, he said, "It didn't help. I was more relaxed, but it didn't stop the mental anguish I was feeling."

Before he left for the evening, he tried contacting Lynn Noyes again. He sent her an e-mail message via his buddy list and contacted her that way. He typed in that he had accomplished his mission and wanted to talk to her on the phone. He told her that his roommate was in the house and that he didn't want him looking over his shoulder as he typed. She agreed to take a call. Once she was on the line, Norm told her what he had done. She asked how he felt. He said he felt terrible. She asked if he had thrown away the evidence. Daniels said no.

"Well, I think you'd better get rid of it," Lynn said.

In almost a daze Daniels said, "I'll get rid of it later. I'm going to go out."

Lynn Noyes recalled this exchange: "I asked

him if he needed to talk. He was having a real hard time with it. He was freaking out. He was overwhelmed with what he had done and he didn't feel like he had a choice to what he was supposed to do now. He was so upset. He was crying. A lot of just rambling. He had paged Todd at that point but hadn't had a response. I said that I'd try. He asked if I could contact someone. Then he said he had to go, and I said all right."

Lynn Noyes did contact Company T on the Internet. She wrote: *Attention Sean. Sean, your boy has become a man.*

As to why she had written such a message, Lynn said later, "Todd had written a song long ago ("In My Mind"). There was some portion of the song that talked about a little boy. [He] grows up and would fight and end up dying. And just to make the e-mail sound professional, because I didn't really know what to say, I just played along with that. It was that Norman had killed Carole and that was it. In previous e-mails I referred to them as boys. Well, he had carried out this package, so he was a man."

After his conversation with Lynn Noyes, Norman Daniels did take a long day's journey into night. He walked across town to the house of a friend, Stephanie Bias. He had met her in a bar sometime in the past and they were only friends. In his own words concerning his time at Stephanie's that night, "I hung out there and got drunk. There were several people there. At some point I told her, 'I killed someone.' "

Stephanie did not believe him at the time. Daniels was clearly drunk and was prone to overexaggerating. She knew Norman was basically a good guy and she couldn't believe he would do such a thing.

It was a nightmarish evening for Norman Daniels as May 16 turned into the early-morning hours of Sunday May 17. Sometime after 3:00 A.M. he paged Todd Garton and Todd phoned him back. Garton was staying at his parents' home. His own house was now off limits. Yellow crime-scene tape surrounded the house. Todd said he had to be quiet. His own brother was sleeping on the floor of the room that he was in. Todd told him that he had already spoken with police and that they had mentioned the name Norman Daniels. They wanted to talk with him. This put Daniels into even more of a funk.

Todd asked Daniels if he knew that Carole was dead. He answered that he did. Todd also indicated that she hadn't been dead when he got home and that he was very angry about it. It nearly spoiled everything.

In a whisper Todd told Daniels that he had to go back to his house and get rid of the evidence, especially the gun. Daniels said later, "When he talked about the pistol, he got even quieter. I told him I was stuck. I had no ride to get back to remove the pistol."

Todd told him he was on his own. This news particulary distressed Daniels. He thought that Todd and The Company would help him. They would provide him with a safe house. They would secret him out of the area.

Daniels said, "I hung out all morning at Stephanie's house. And sometime around midmorning Lynn paged me. It was around ten A.M. I called her back. I knew I was in trouble and that if I went back to my house, I would get caught. I told her, 'I need to come in out of the rain,' which was a code word meaning to be picked up and taken somewhere safe. The Company would pick me up and take me to a safe area.

"She said she would find out if she could get ahold of these people in The Company or talk to Todd. In general, she told me that Todd said I needed to get back and get rid of the pistol. Finally I agreed to go back and try to get rid of it."

Lynn got in touch with Todd via an e-mail. She asked, *Do you want me to e-mail Sean?*

Todd answered, *Yes.*

Lynn sent a message to Company T that said, *Please instruct and advise me.* It also made mention of Patriot. Concerning the message, Lynn said, "Devlin [Norman Daniels] was in trouble. Todd said he couldn't speak because he was being questioned by the authorities at that time and he didn't feel safe talking. So if there was any message, to relay it through me so I could relay it to Norman. He [Todd] had read an initial article [in the *Redding Record Searchlight*] about someone killed in Cottonwood."

Having received very little help so far from Todd, Lynn and The Company, Norman Daniels became more and more depressed as the day went on. He said, "I finally found a ride [from Stephanie's] about noon or so. This guy gave me a ride back to my residence. He was a friend of Stephanie's. And as we were going by my place, I noticed there were two vehicles parked in the front of my residence. I knew they were the police. And so I told the guy to keep driving. I was in the backseat. I ducked down. The guy turned around and went back to where I worked. He needed to put some oil in his car. Then from there he went and dropped his girlfriend off. As we were going back, I started explaining about The Company, that I was in trouble and needed some help. I had to explain why I was acting so paranoid. I told him that I had committed a murder. I didn't give him details or anything.

"Then we went into Anderson. We went to his sister's apartment. I left and walked across the street to the Texaco gas station. I withdrew some money. I tried to get ahold of Lynn Noyes but only got her message machine. I ate something. I was there for a little while and then went up to the bowling alley just a hundred yards away. I attempted to page Lynn Noyes from there. I got the answering machine.

"I ate some fries at Bartels, waiting for a page that never came. I proceeded down Hilltop Drive to the Mount Shasta Mall and then I eventually ended up at the Hometown Buffet. At a phone booth right outside, I got ahold of Lynn Noyes. I wanted to let them [The Company] know there were police outside my place, that I couldn't get the pistol. And I needed to run. Lynn finally picked up and I explained to her that I needed help. And she said, 'Well, I'm on the other line with Todd Garton and I'm talking to him right now.'"

Lynn was on the other line with Todd because he had called and talked to Dean Noyes for a while before Lynn got to the phone. She had been out jogging. When she returned, Dean told her that

Todd mentioned something was wrong with Carole. Lynn remembered, "Dean first said it was some kind of accident. So I was trying to ask, 'Why did you say that?' without coming right out and saying it. It was a read-between-the-lines conversation on Todd's part, because he was extremely paranoid at this time that people were watching him. The police were there. He thought his phone was bugged. He did tell where Norman should hide the gun and ideas of where he could hide it. One suggestion was in his toilet. The other was, like, in a heating duct. If you pulled the grate off, you could put a gun in there and then put the grate back on the top."

Garton's ideas about where Daniels could dispose of his clothes were even more bizarre. He thought that he could try flushing them down the toilet. It never occurred to him that they would probably get stuck.

Garton also vented his anger to Lynn about coming home and finding Carole still alive. Lynn recalled, "Todd said that Norman had fucked up. Carole wasn't dead when he arrived and that he had to work on her and he was fairly irritated."

From the time Daniels got on the line with Lynn, it became a three-way conversation among Todd Garton, Norman Daniels and Lynn Noyes. She shuttled messages back and forth between the men. Daniels recalled, "She said something about me going to New York and something about Natalya. She wouldn't say what else except other than talking to Natalya about finding a place to stay."

Lynn talked to Todd for a while and then back

with Norm. Daniels recalled, "I was coerced into going back to remove the pistol and hide it somewhere. I kept saying I needed to run. And she kept switching over to the other line with Todd and then coming back and telling me that I needed to get back and hide the pistol at all costs. I asked her if there was anybody watching the place. And she came back after switch hooking and said yes. There was a detective watching my house. They were wanting to talk to me. Todd Garton had been notified by his brother they were getting a search warrant [for Daniels's house]. She said that Todd's brother knew this because he had been by Todd's residence on Adobe Road and run into the officers. He had overheard them talking about a search warrant." Todd may have lied about this last part, but the fact that the officers wanted search warrants was true. They not only wanted one for Norman Daniels's house, they wanted one for Todd Garton's as well.

Daniels continued his recounting. "She told me some details of what Todd told her he had to do to Carole. She said Todd had to do a tracheotomy and open-heart massage. That, in general, she was still alive when he found her. Todd was very upset about it."

Lynn pushed Norman to head for his house and told him before he hung up the phone, "Don't tell them about me. Just say we're friends on the Internet."

When Norm Daniels was off the line, Todd Garton kept talking to Lynn Noyes. She related, "Todd said Daniels was screwed either way, that there was a search warrant being proposed for his house. Daniels could run if he wanted to or not, but he was going to get caught regardless."

Norman Daniels finally felt this way as well. He decided he might as well go home, cops or no cops, and try to get rid of the gun. But basically he didn't much care one way or the other. He felt that no one was going to help him. He felt that the life he had known was just about over. He hardly cared anymore. He was racked with guilt and remorse. He said, "I got a taxi and decided to go home. I said to the taxi driver, 'Right here' as we were coming up to the house. He literally turned in across the street. I paid the taxi driver and tipped him. I didn't go to the front of my trailer. I was going through the neighbor's yard. I went up to the back gate. That's when I met Detective Grashoff and Detective Clemens."

Chapter 9

Dodging and Weaving

While Todd Garton, Lynn Noyes and Norman Daniels were dealing with the murder of Carole Garton in their own ways, law enforcement officers had been busy as well. As a matter of fact, they became involved the moment Dale Gordon picked up the telephone and dialed 911 on May 16. Detective Ron Clemens of the Shasta County Sheriff's Office began a narrative chronicling the events at 6:47 P.M. on May 16. He said, "SHASCOM received a 911 call requiring medical assistance on Adobe Road in Cottonwood. Additional 911 calls were made from the same location shortly thereafter. At approximately seven-oh-seven P.M. Deputy Bill Blair saw a white male, later identified as Dale Gordon, standing in the driveway talking on a cordless phone. Dale was placed in the rear seat of the marked patrol unit by Deputy Blair. Moments later additional deputies arrived on the scene. Deputy Blair then approached the threshold to the front door and saw a white male, later identified as Todd Garton, walk into the living room from another room. It was later learned that the other room was a master-bedroom area in the residence.

"Deputy Blair said he and Sergeant Ron Smith entered the residence. Deputy Blair advised that there were no lights on within the residence and it was dark. Deputy Blair entered the master bedroom and saw a white female lying on the floor. She was later identified as Carole Garton."

Deputy Blair noticed a large amount of blood around Carole Garton's head and body. He also saw bloody blankets next to her body. Blair checked Carole's pulse and couldn't find any. He observed what he took to be gunshot wounds to Carole.

Emergency medical personnel arrived on the scene at 7:09 P.M. They had already been told by the dispatcher that Todd Garton had been trying to perform CPR on the victim. The medical technicians removed Carole Garton from the bedroom and placed her on the floor in the living room. There was more room in there and better light. CPR was administered by one of the technicians, but he ceased trying at 7:22 P.M. It was evident that the victim was not responding. Carole Garton was pronounced to be dead at that time.

A curious thing happened around this time. Todd Garton's pager went off and a sheriff's deputy saw him throw it to the ground. He acted as if he'd just been snake bit.

At this point Todd Garton, Dale Gordon and Sara Mann were asked to come down to the Major Crimes Unit at the sheriff's office in Redding for an interview. They were not suspects at that moment, but they were definitely the first people who had witnessed a crime scene. In this particular instance, both Sara Mann and Dale Gordon knew nothing about the circumstances of Carole Garton's death.

But with Todd Garton it was a very different story, and he began dodging and weaving with his lies as he talked to Detective Steve Berg. Todd told him that Carole was eight months pregnant and that they both had been looking forward to the birth. He said she had gone with him to the Anderson gun show in the morning and then left with a friend to visit Mercy Medical Center. Her friend was pregnant as well and they were going to take a tour of the birthing room. Todd said that Carole had returned to the gun show about 1:00 P.M. She only stayed about twenty minutes because she was tired. She left with a friend named Norman Daniels, because Daniels needed a ride. Todd indicated that he didn't know Daniels very well, but that he was an acquaintance. He said that Daniels had been to his house before. He indicated that the only people staying over his house on the previous night were himself, Carole and Dale Gordon.

Asked what type of vehicle Carole was driving, he answered that it was a white Jeep Wrangler. Then he said that when he arrived home that evening, the Jeep was not there and no one had been given permission to use it. He told Detective Berg that he left the gun show at 6:00 P.M. He then drove to his parents' residence to drop off a photocopier. Todd said when he returned home, he was concerned that Carole wasn't there and neither was her Jeep. He immediately told Sara Mann to dial

911 because he was sure the Jeep had been stolen. Sara never did. (In fact, in the next room she said that she couldn't understand why Todd was so certain that the Jeep was stolen.)

Todd stated he knew that he and Carole and some others were supposed to go out to dinner that night. He didn't mention that Norman Daniels was one of the "others." All in all, he gave an impression that Norman Daniels was just someone that he barely knew. Todd said he started checking around the house and found Carole lying on the floor of the master bedroom at around 6:50 P.M. He yelled for Dale Gordon to call 911 as he tried to give her CPR.

The detectives wanted to talk with Norman Daniels because he was supposedly the last person who had seen Carole Garton alive, and at 8:58 P.M. the Jeep Wrangler was discovered by a Tehama County sheriff's deputy in the park-and-ride lot south of Cottonwood. A search for Norman Daniels at his home turned up nothing. Jerry Enix happened to be gone as well.

Very early on Sunday morning, May 17, 3:40 to be exact, Garton's neighbor Lenny Vanderburg was interviewed by the investigators. He recalled seeing the Jeep Wrangler at approximately 2:30 P.M. on May 16 parked in front of the Garton residence. Sometime around then he heard a male's voice, which wasn't Todd's, saying, "Get in your own yard." He assumed the male was speaking to a dog, since it had been barking. When he looked again at the Garton house, the Jeep was gone at 3:30 P.M. He had not heard any gunshots.

At 6:00 A.M. an investigator contacted the Kickin'

Mule and learned that Norman Daniels had not shown up for work—he hadn't called in, either. This was unusual for Daniels, according to the people who worked there. Normally, Daniels was very punctual and good about phoning if he couldn't make it to work.

Jerry Enix, Norman Daniels's roommate, was interviewed at 10:50 A.M. He told detectives that Norman had arrived at the mobile home at about 3:30 P.M. on May 16. He was driving the Gartons' white Jeep. Daniels took a shower, changed clothes and talked to him for a short time. Then he drove away in the Jeep and returned at about 4:30 P.M. Daniels had said that he was supposed to go to dinner that night, but it had been canceled. He said that he'd been dropped off at a bar by friends and had to walk home. He'd been caught in the rain while walking and that's why his clothes were all wet.

Enix said that he left the mobile home at around 9:30 P.M. and Norman Daniels was still there. When he arrived home again about 3:15 A.M. on May 17, Daniels was not there and hadn't returned home since then.

Detectives Ron Clemens and Steve Grashoff staked out the area on Gas Point Road near the Kickin' Mule on the afternoon of May 17. It was a long day of waiting and tedium. They were about to move, when around 4:20 P.M. a taxicab was headed up Gas Point Road in the direction of Norman Daniels's residence. They just happened to look at the passenger and the man bore a remarkable resemblance to the description of Norman Daniels. They decided to follow the taxi.

Detective Ron Clemens said, "A cab drove by Norman Daniels's residence and pulled into a neighbor's driveway. A male exited the vehicle and this individual was later identified as Norman Daniels. Norman walked to the rear of the residence and was contacted by sheriff's detectives [Clemens and Grashoff]. Detectives interviewed Norman outside of the mobile home at that address on Gas Point Road. Norman initially denied involvement in the case. Norman Daniels was transported to the Shasta County Sheriff's Office Major Crimes Unit and he was placed in the interview room. Norman was interviewed by Detectives Grashoff and Clemens."

Norman Daniels said of the interview, "I began to lie. Because this was a serious thing and I knew I was in deep trouble. Mainly, I was thinking of my son, but I was also thinking of [The] Company and Todd Garton and Lynn Noyes and who all was involved." In fact, at this point Norman Daniels was afraid of The Company as much as he was of the police. He didn't know whom he could trust. If he started talking and telling the truth, someone might sneak up and kill him. Or they might kidnap or kill his son. As far as he knew, there could be a tagger anywhere ready to pounce if he opened up about Todd and all the rest. The tagger could be posing as another inmate—or worse, he might even be in the sheriffs office, doing hits on the side.

Eventually, though, Daniels began revealing bits and pieces of the truth. He said later, "My conscience bothered me. Really seriously. I needed help. I was basically asking for help."

And he turned for help in the strangest of

places—to the detectives who were trying to determine if he was a killer. If they could help Norman avert being killed by someone in The Company, then he would help them implicate him for murder. He determined that it was better to be behind bars than it was to be dead. Norman said, "I was trying to protect Dale and Lynn, so I omitted the Oregon adventure." But he did start telling of his involvement in killing Carole. He mentioned Todd Garton's name a few times, but did not tie Todd directly to the setup of the crime. At least not yet. In fact, Norman took the blame upon himself and admitted that he had killed Carole Garton. For a motive he said, "I was jealous of the relationship Todd and Carole had. I was jealous of them."

With this admission of guilt, Norman Daniels attempted to build a wall between himself and the truth of what really had happened. At 11:57 P.M. on May 17, 1998, he was booked into the Shasta County Jail on an open count of murder.

A search warrant was obtained for his residence on Gas Point Road and executed soon thereafter. This initial warrant directed the officers to search for firearms, clothing and footwear. The murder weapon, the .44 Rossi, was easily found beneath Daniels's pillow, where he had stashed it.

A very small item appeared in the next morning's *Redding Record Searchlight* titled, WOMAN'S DEATH CALLED A HOMICIDE. It went on to say, *The shooting death of a 28-year-old Cottonwood woman is being investigated as a homicide, the Shasta County Sheriff's Department said Sunday. Carole Anne Garton was found dead Saturday in her Adobe Road home when Shasta County Sheriff's deputies arrived about 6:45 PM. The victim's*

*husband, Todd Garton, told Sheriff's deputies that his
wife's vehicle was missing from the residence. The white
1992 Jeep Wrangler was found thirty minutes later at the
Cottonwood Park and Ride.*

Early on Monday, May 18, Lynn Noyes knew that
she had reason to worry. Todd Garton had heard
of Norman Daniels's arrest and told her about it.
She recalled, "Todd told me to stick to the fabri-
cated truth that he had made up. If the police ever
contacted me, I never had met Norman Daniels in
person. I just knew him from the computer. And
not to mention the relationship he [Todd] and I
had. Also, to say that Norman was kind of a cyber
nerd. That Norman Daniels had an obsessive problem with Carole. Just that Norman was going to
cop a jealousy plea."

An autopsy on Carole Garton was performed on
May 18. In part it found that one shot had entered
her left cheek, and two shots had entered the upper
right side of her neck, with one bullet entering her
cerebellum. Stippling marks on her neck and face
showed that the gun had been fired from a very close
range. It was estimated that the gun had been four
to twelve inches away. A fourth gunshot wound had
entered the left side of her chest and exited on the
right side. The fifth gunshot wound had entered
Carole's left buttock and perforated her uterus before ripping through the head of the fetus and lodg-
ing in the baby's right shoulder.

Dr. Susan Comfort, a pathologist, concluded that
the baby would not have survived even if it hadn't
been struck by a bullet. She said, "The baby could
survive in the womb only for a very short period of
time. Once the mother's circulation stops and there's

no longer any blood flow, the baby would die because the baby would not be getting oxygen anymore. And so, probably the death of the fetus would occur in about two minutes at the most." As far as how long Carole survived after the gunshot wounds, it was estimated that she probably would have died within twenty to thirty minutes from the time she was shot due to shock and loss of blood. This contradicted Todd Garton's story that she was still alive when he returned home to find her on the floor.

Norman Daniels was cooperating with detectives up to a point by now. He took them to the park-and-ride lot and showed them where he had thrown the keys. They found the keys in the weeds. He also showed them where he had tossed the expended-shell cartridges from the gun he had used to kill Carole. The detectives recovered three shell casings from the grass.

Daniels also showed them one more important thing. It was the wax seal from the package he had received from The Company. The one that Todd Garton had handed him at midnight on April 28. The seal that looked like a ram's head to Daniels actually had the outline of Todd Garton's Navy SEAL diving-bubble pin. Daniels always thought it might be important and he had saved it.

Daniels was not yet fully implicating Todd Garton in the whole twisted plot, but he kept mentioning his name more and more often with ties to a strange plot. And the detectives wanted to know why. This was the same Todd Garton who indicated he barely knew Norman Daniels. That was not the story Daniels was telling.

* * *

Todd was less than pleased when an article appeared in the *Redding Record Searchlight* headlined, FAMILY FRIEND HELD IN SLAYING. Todd had to change his tune about how much he knew Daniels. Realizing that he had to shift gears in his story line, he pulled out all the stops concerning Daniels and Carole. The initial part of the article detailed the death of Carole and Daniels's arrest. Then it concentrated on Todd Garton's reaction to the murder of his wife. He started out by saying that he and Carole had done so much for Norman. They had him over to the house often and even let him borrow the Jeep on occasion. Todd said he gave Norman a job with his fencing company at one point. His tune had changed to the point of knowing Daniels so well that he admitted, "He [Norman] was a good close friend of the family. We would have given him anything he asked for."

Then to try and steer the detectives toward an unknown gunman, Todd said, "I want the person who did it, not the person who's convenient to get."

But Todd really saved his most expansive statements for a tribute to his wife. He told how they had tried for ten years to have a baby. Then a miracle had happened and she was going to give birth in June. They were both very excited about it. He said he knew that Carole would be an amazing mother.

Todd said that he always carried a small photo of Carole in his pocket watch. He said there wasn't an encyclopedia that could list all her good qualities. She was an accomplished archer, musician and animal lover. When she hit a horse on Adobe Road, she wished she had broken her own leg instead of the horse's leg. He said if she was that way toward animals, just think how she was with humans.

Summing it all up, he said, "I know people in retrospect, they always say good things. But she was perfect. No one could ever hold a candle to her."

So many things weren't adding up from statements Todd made and statements that Norman made, so the detectives cooked up a scheme of their own. Todd Garton would have been impressed by their machinations. The detectives talked Norman Daniels into placing a phone call to Todd from the Shasta County Jail. They wanted to see what Todd's reaction would be to the call. And they also had authorization to tape the conversation. The call took place on the evening of May 18 and Daniels said later, "I was posing as Dale Gordon when I made the call. If anybody picked up the phone other than Todd, they would think it was Dale." (This call was placed to Todd's parents' home, where he was staying at the time.)

Daniels began talking to Todd, and Garton berated him for telling the detectives he had killed Carole out of jealousy. Todd told him that he shouldn't have told the police anything at all. Then Garton calmed down and said, "I'm going to get on the phone to the big boys and see what we can work for you. We'll be there for you, man. We'll try to help you out as much as we can. Whatever money you had coming goes to your kid or family or something." (Daniels understood that he had $25,000 coming to him for the murder of Carole.)

All of this was very interesting to the detectives.

First of all, Todd Garton didn't seem to be angry at Norman Daniels for killing his wife. He only seemed to be angry that Daniels had confessed. Then there was all this talk of money and helping Daniels in his legal defense. Why would he want to help someone who admitted to shooting his wife? And who were "the big boys"?

Norman Daniels entered a plea of not guilty in his initial appearance at Shasta County Municipal Court on Tuesday, May 19. Among the people in the courtroom was Stephanie Bias. She told a reporter later that Norman had been at her house on Saturday, May 16, and mentioned that he had killed someone. She said she thought he was just drunk at the time and ignored the comment. Learning the truth about him had come as a complete shock to her. Norman didn't seem to be the cold-blooded killer type.

Daniels was held on a bond of $1.5 million and Stephen Kennedy of Redding was appointed as his attorney. Because of multiple deaths (both Carole and the eight-month-old fetus Jesse), lying in wait and possible murder for hire, the district attorney's office kept open the option of seeking the death penalty. District Attorney McGregor Scott told reporters, "I can't talk about the specifics. All I can say about that—we would not allege about that [the murder for hire], unless we had good faith we can prove it in court."

Because of Todd Garton's strange phone conversation with Norman Daniels on May 18, and continued statements Daniels made about Todd, a search warrant was issued to search Todd Garton's home on May 21. During the search detectives seized a Navy SEAL scuba-diving bubble pin. It had reddish wax adhering to the edges. They also seized insurance company records that revealed both Todd and Carole had received physical exams at their home on March 12, 1998. Policies in the amount of $125,000 were issued to Carole on March 25, 1998, and to Todd on April 1, 1998, with each being the sole beneficiary of the other's policy.

Things took a huge turn for the worse on Todd Garton's cover-up on that same day. Still afraid of The Company, but wanting to talk, and especially wanting police protection from The Company, Norman Daniels began telling Detective Grashoff and Sergeant Mark VonRader everything concerning the murder of Carole Garton. For the first time he brought up the name The Company and told of its deadly implications. He also told about Todd Garton's role within The Company, how he was a paid assassin and had been a go-between urging him to do what the organization said or suffer the consequences. The only part he was leaving out was about Lynn Noyes, Dale Gordon and the trip up to Oregon to assassinate Dean Noyes.

Detective Grashoff and Sergeant VonRader had heard a lot of things during their law enforcement careers, but nothing like this. It was something right out of a Tom Clancy novel. All of it was almost too fantastic to believe, but during the whole interview Norman Daniels was calm, coherent and decidedly focused. He kept telling the police more and more of the twisted plots. There were enough factors that rang true to give them credence and Daniels appeared to be someone now telling the truth, rather than just someone trying to save his own skin. After all, Todd Garton had hardly acted like a grieving husband, and there were those new life insurance policies that had gone into effect only a few weeks before Carole Garton had been murdered. Norman Daniels had been right to worry—the police know that in more than 80 percent of all domestic murders, a spouse or someone who knew the victim is involved. And it was looking more and more probable to the investigators that Todd Garton was somehow involved in this particular case.

Todd had scheduled a memorial service for Carole on May 23, 1998. He was about to get two more guests there that he never counted on—Detective Steve Grashoff and Sergeant Mark VonRader. They would monitor the scene and try and determine who was telling the truth—Norman Daniels or Todd Garton.

Chapter 10

Into the River

The news of Carole's death hit her mother, father, stepmother and stepfather like a thunderbolt. That it came in the middle of the night gave it an even greater aspect of a nightmare. Vicki Holman recalled, "The week after Carole died was the worst in all our lives. It started about four-thirty A.M. On May seventeenth we were awakened by the phone, and my husband answered it in a bit of a fog. He listened awhile and dropped the phone crying. I took the phone and asked who it was. He said he was detective somebody from the Shasta County Sheriff's Office. He was sorry to tell us that Carole and the baby were deceased. She had been shot in the home. He explained that they didn't know who had done it and that they had questioned Todd for several hours and released him. He said that Todd had asked him to call us.

"When I got control of myself, the first words out of my mouth were, 'Has Todd been arrested?

Oh, I'm sorry. You said he had been released.' To this day I don't know why I said it. Intuition, I guess. The rest of the day and the next, we tried in vain to get ahold of Todd. We learned from his mother Sunday night that one of Todd's friends had been arrested, but they didn't know the details. She said that Todd was too upset to talk to anyone."

Virginia Griffiths had also been hammered by the tragic news of the murder of her daughter and the baby. She had to spread the terrible news to all of Carole's brothers. The fact that one of Todd's friends had killed Carole was just as incomprehensible to Virginia as it had been to Vicki. She never thought that Carole had any enemies, much less someone who would want to murder her.

When Todd finally did contact Carole's relatives, he had very strict guidelines about the upcoming memorial service in Anderson. Vicki remembered, "He wanted all of us to arrive in Anderson together and check in at the AmeriHost hotel. He said the owner was a friend of his and he had gotten us a deal on the rooms. He said do not talk to anyone, do not read the paper or watch TV. He wanted all of us to meet in one room, and he would be there at eight P.M. on May nineteenth and he would explain everything. We followed his instructions to the T."

Both the Holmans and the Griffiths arrived in the Anderson area on Tuesday, May 19, the same day Carole's body was released by the coroner's office. Just as planned, Todd showed up at the AmeriHost hotel at 8:00 P.M., and Vicki recalled, "There were Jim and I, Carole's mother and her husband,

Gary, and Carole's brothers, Scott, Mike, Donny and Donny's girlfriend, Irina. Todd showed up right on time. He brought two people with him that none of us knew. They were Dale Gordon and Sara Mann. Todd explained that they were at his home when he came home and found Carole. Todd stood leaning against a wall and, in a very calm and unemotional way, gave us details of coming home, getting angry about the dogs being in the house, looking for Carole and finding her under covers on the floor of the bedroom. He spoke of doing CPR and doing a tracheotomy. He said there was a cash box under the bed with five thousand dollars in it that was stolen. When asked about that, he said it was money they had saved for the baby. The more he talked, the more I felt something was not right about the story. I kept quiet. He didn't like when anyone asked questions.

"He told us that he had received a call from Norman Daniels after he was arrested and that he had said he did it because he was jealous of Carole and Todd's relationship. I wondered why he didn't kill Todd if that was the reason. Later in the conversation, Todd said he thought the DA was just looking to hang someone, so he arrested Daniels. That didn't make sense because he already told us that Daniels had told him he did it."

In fact, Norman Daniels may have foiled Todd's plans of lying about a cash box, stolen money and an elusive, unknown burglar who had killed Carole. The "jealousy story" threw a monkey wrench into this scheme, even though Todd was still trying to make it fly and make it seem like Daniels had only confessed out of confusion and fear.

Vicki said, "Todd was with us about an hour, and then he said he had to go. He did bring a newspaper article, which ran after Todd said that he went to the newspaper reporter and told her she had it all wrong." (The article he brought was an early version of the murder.) "As we were saying our good-byes, he looked at me and said, 'You're not all right, are you?' I thought it was the strangest question anyone had ever asked me."

Todd had a lunch for everyone at the Old Town Eatery the next day. His parents were there, as was Dale Gordon, Sara Mann and all of Carole's relatives. Vicki recalled, "Sara was very upset and cried most of the time we were there. During the meal Todd left. Later, I think I knew why."

Todd left for a very special reason. He was meeting Lynn Noyes at the local airport. As Lynn flew down from Oregon, she chatted with the male passenger who sat next to her. He was a man from the Redding area, and when Todd picked her up, he said he knew the man. Lynn recalled, "Todd asked how the flight was. He said the gentleman on the flight next to me was from Cottonwood. He asked if I knew the person that was sitting next to me on the plane was an undercover police officer. (This has never been confirmed.) When we were back in his vehicle, he patted me down to see if I had some kind of wire on me."

Satisfied that Lynn was not wearing a wire, he took her to meet his parents and Carole's relatives. There was already friction developing between the various relatives. By now Vicki was very suspicious of Todd. Virginia and Gary wanted to give him the benefit of the doubt. It was unthinkable that he was somehow involved in Carole's murder. But as Vicki said later, "It must have shown in my face, because I hadn't said anything to anyone. But I just knew that Todd was not telling us the truth. Jim wanted to give him the benefit of the doubt, but I just knew that something wasn't right."

It must have shown so much in Vicki's face that Gary Griffiths took her aside and told her to lighten up with Todd. His thinking was that Todd was now a widower and had suffered enough without undo suspicion thrown upon him.

After lunch Virginia asked to see the house where Todd and Carole had lived. They all caravanned out to the residence on Adobe Road. Virginia said, "Todd offered to show us the inside of the house, even though there was still yellow tape around. None of us wanted to go inside, of course."

Vicki remembered, "Todd seemed to be having a good time showing us around. We went over to the park and stood around him while he recalled Carole walking the dog and other stories. Not once did he shed a tear or get choked up. After a while he took us to the Moose Lodge, where the memorial service was going to be. That is when he showed us a handout he made up with the help of Carole's mom. I asked about the poetry on it and he glared at me and refused to answer."

This handout was just as extraordinary as Todd's comments in the *Record Searchlight* about his murdered wife. It began by stating, *In Loving Memory of Carole Anne Garton 1969 to 1998*. It contained a photo of Carole holding a puppy in the upper left-hand corner. Below it were lines of poetry that Carole had written. They were ironic in the extreme.

They seemed to be accusatory of Todd. The lines read:

> *This glass heart has been broken 100 times*
> *and put back together . . . with glue of my tears.*
> *When you said goodby and dropped it again*
> *something happened because this time it won't mend.*
>
> *You said it hurts too much to stay with me*
> *and watching up close is like watching me bleed*
> *You said I need to heal what's broke inside me*
> *can't you see what's healing you is killing me.*
>
> *All my tears are grinding into sand*
> *all my dreams have washed out to sea.*
> *But this time I swear you won't win*
> *when you come back, I won't come back again.*
>
> *Why love hurts and anger feels so good*
> *I'll not understand as long as I live*
> *You can't ignore what you want to be true*
> *whatever happens, I'll be in love with you.*
>
> *Now this glass heart has been shattered again*
> *and the pieces cut through my kin*
> *But like that heart, I see right through*
> *you don't deserve a love that's true.*

On the rest of the page Todd said that most people knew Carole as a friend, a writer, a mother-to-be. But that they didn't know the artist in her. He said, "Those graced enough to have heard her perform were blessed with a gift that will never be matched."

Todd also spoke of Carole as a painter and that her talent there was natural and beautiful. He said he would cherish every painting she ever made. At the end of the piece he recounted her life and mentioned all the friends and family she left behind who would miss her.

The poem by Carole particulary struck home with Vicki Holman. It was like an accusation against Todd from the grave. She said, "In retrospect I could see how true the words were."

Whether Todd gave one of these handouts to Lynn Noyes isn't recorded. But she was now very much of the group awaiting the memorial service. Lynn said, "The first night I stayed at Todd's parents' house. On one of the sofas. He slept on the opposite one. We had an intimate moment. Some foreplay. A kiss. A hug. There was a little bit of self-gratification by Todd. He did it in my presence."

As far as how to act around the others, Todd told her to act normally. Lynn remembered, "He said just be normal, friendly and roll with whatever conversation is going on. Because he told a number of people that Carole and I were very close."

By the morning of May 21, Vicki Holman was so upset by Todd's strange behavior, she had a talk with her husband and they agreed to go speak with someone at the district attorney's office about their concerns. She said, "Early the next morning, Jim and I talked with Donny and he also felt something wasn't right. We decided we needed to talk with the DA. Don called them and they said they were anxious to talk to us. Virginia and Gary refused to go. Scott, Carole's oldest brother, declined to go, too. So Jim and I, Don, Irina and Mike went to meet with McGregor Scott and a female assistant DA and several detectives. McGregor Scott told us that Norman Daniels had confessed about shooting Carole, but that he said that Todd had planned the whole thing. They said some of it sounded pretty far-fetched, but they would be investigating Norman's story. They told us they had a tape of a phone conversation between Daniels and Todd that was suspicious. They split us up and each one went with a detective. I don't know about the others, but I was asked how long Carole and Todd had been married, what I knew about their relationship, when we had seen them last, when I had talked to Carole last and how long they had been trying to have a baby. I found out later that Todd had told them that they had been trying to get pregnant for ten years. That was a lie.

"The detective asked me how we learned of Carole's death. He asked if Todd called us or tried to communicate with us before we got to Anderson. He wanted to know everything that happened after we got there, and exactly what Todd had told us.

"After the interviews we met back at the conference room and they told us that Todd had been downstairs being questioned. When he learned that we were there, he demanded to be let upstairs to see us. But they wouldn't let him. They asked that we not talk to anyone about what they had told us, including Todd. They would be in touch, and if we had anything more to add, please contact them."

Todd was indeed downstairs at the DA's office, and he had taken Carole's friend Krista along with him. It's not apparent if she was with him while he was being grilled, but he certainly filled her in on what happened soon thereafter. Grace Bell had a telephone conversation with Krista soon after this meeting, and Krista was very upset. According to Grace, "Krista said she was with Todd and had gone with him to the interview with the police. She said he came out of it saying, 'They think I did it.' She said her reaction was that she wanted to get away from there. She felt afraid and unsafe. Her husband arrived about that time and said she needed to stay for Carole's memorial service. She said she did not want to but did it anyway. She said Lynn [came by] and she was relieved to have someone for Todd to interact with and not her."

Vicki was also upset by what she had just heard at the DA's office. She recalled, "No one knew what to think at this point. It was really frightening. We all went back to our motel and I don't remember anything more about that day."

Around this time Vicki seemed to recall that Todd offered to give Carole and the baby's ashes to them for transportation back to Oregon. But both Vicki and Carole's dad thought the proper place for Carole was with Todd. They would regret not taking him up on the offer at the time. The issue of Carole's and the baby's ashes would become a nightmare for them later.

May 22, 1998, was the day of the actual memorial service at the Moose Lodge in Anderson, and everyone who was there would come away with slightly different reactions about what they had witnessed. One thing they all agreed upon was that Todd was in control of the proceedings. In fact, he ran the whole affair like a master of ceremonies. Vicki remembered, "We had asked about a minister, but he said there would be no minister. He wasn't going to have someone who didn't know her speak about her. I know that both Jim and I were in a daze throughout the memorial service. I remember at one point Todd's brother came over and introduced himself and told us how much everyone loved Carole. Everyone said the same thing. I don't know how we got through the day."

Collin Colebank and his wife, Marty, were also there and Collin remembered the scene vividly. He said, "The whole service was emotionally charged. No one gave a eulogy except Todd. He wanted to direct it all. He told what a powerful woman Carole was. Krista was very emotional. She was a train wreck. She seemed both tearful and angry at the same time. People were crying all around."

Grace Bell was not there at the time, but she got secondhand reports and commented, "The memorial service was bizarre. Todd was controlling and hamming it up. I didn't hear about any grief on his part. It was all about him. Later I went to the dictionary and looked up narcissistic disorder. Lynn Noyes sat across from the family. I wondered to myself, 'Who is this woman?' Apparently, Todd was making eyes at her the whole time."

Later on, Krista would tell Grace Bell how Carole had felt about Lynn Noyes. According to Grace, "Krista said that it took a lot of balls for Todd to have her there. Krista said Carole had mentioned Lynn as the 'other woman.' She was not comfortable with Todd continuing to be in touch with Lynn."

The memorial service was an eye-opener for Lynn Noyes as well. But for very different reasons. She said, "Todd was acting numb. Nonemotional. Just kind of cold; well, not cold but in between. He was nothing like he usually was around me. I learned that Carole wasn't the mean, nasty person that Todd had told me that she was. That in a nutshell she did care for him as much as I did."

Collin and Marty Colebank were astounded that Lynn Noyes was at the memorial service. They knew that Carole had never liked Lynn and certainly didn't like her hanging around Todd. Collin said later, "My direct response to seeing Lynn there was, 'What the hell is she doing here?' I didn't regard her as anyone who belonged at a memorial service for Carole. And she was going out of her way to be nice to people at a funeral. For one thing, she walked up to Marty and was very bubbly and happy to make her reacquaintance. I think she said, 'Hi, Marty, do you remember me?' And Marty didn't care for her in any way, shape or form. So she simply said, 'Yes. I know exactly who you are!'"

Tracie Jones also noted Lynn Noyes's presence at the memorial service. She said later, "Todd introduced her as a friend. He had told me that he had dated Lynn before Carole. At the service she sat up front near Todd. He gave the eulogy, but afterward they sat together. She was staying close by him. Sitting next to him in a comforting manner."

Vicki Holman recalled, "As soon as the memorial service was over, the Moose ladies served a lunch and Todd seemed to be having a wonderful time. He talked about how he and Carole had spent so much time at the Moose Lodge. Then Todd brought

Lynn to the table and she sat across from us. He introduced her as Carole's friend from Portland and said that she had been teaching Carole Lamaze exercises. He said Carole and Lynn spent hours on the phone talking about babies."

Jim and Vicki were so weirded out by Todd's excessive behavior that they wanted to leave right away, but they stuck it out for form's sake. But what happened when they actually got back to the motel room was one more in a series of altercations between Vicki and Todd. He knew on some level that she didn't trust him. He mainly blamed her for the trip to the DA's office. Todd talked to Carole's mother, Virginia, and told her how unsupportive Jim and Vicki were. Virginia, still believing that Todd was innocent, was not pleased about this latest disturbance. After all, he was the widower of a wife who had supposedly been murdered by his friend. It was not a happy scene that afternoon at the AmeriHost.

According to Vicki, "Todd had already talked to Virginia and asked her to get our key so that some of his friends [Collin and Marty] could use our room that night, since it was already paid for. We were thinking of leaving anyway. I hesitated for a moment, and Gary took the key out of my hand. I just wanted to get out of there at that point. So I let it go. We left about three P.M. and drove straight home."

Even with this latest scheme of turning one set of relatives against another, Todd was not yet through with his antics for the day. He, Lynn, Collin and Marty, Sara Mann, Dale Gordon, Krista and her husband, Ryan, and Gary Griffiths all used the swimming pool and hot tub at the motel. Todd was constantly talking and apparently having a good time, hardly the embodiment of a grieving husband.

Collin remembered, "Lynn was all over Todd. She was not there to grieve for Carole. She was there to move in on Todd because, obviously, he was available now. There was a time when Todd was in the pool, actually sitting on the side, and she was between his legs. They were together like a couple. I would say he was a willing participant. He definitely wasn't resisting. It wasn't the body language of a grieving husband."

Gary Griffiths was so offended by Todd's stories and behavior with Lynn that he left and went back to his room. He told Virginia, "He's [Todd's] full of shit." And he mentioned what he had seen and heard. Todd may have fooled Virginia and Gary for a while, but now they, too, had doubts about his innocence in the murder of Carole.

Todd and Lynn raised even more eyebrows when they stayed in the same hotel room that night. There were two separate beds, but Lynn did not stay in hers for long. She admitted later that she climbed into Todd's bed and they had sex.

Even with all this strange behavior, Todd was not through taking people by his house on Adobe Road, despite the fact that yellow police tape still adorned its exterior. At some point he took Collin and Marty there, and Collin could not remember exactly when this was, because of the hectic schedule. But he seemed to recall that it happened after the memorial service. Collin said, "It had been a couple of years since we had seen each other. We were catching up a lot in a very condensed period of time. It looked like Todd had a couple of businesses going. Had friends around town. Had a comfortable house on the edge of the country. I was happy for him—except for somebody having just killed his wife. But basically Todd was happy about where he was in life. He said that it was nice and peaceful and quiet on the edge of the BLM land. Lots of free, open space. It was a peaceful homestead.

"We went into an outbuilding on the property. It was like a garage with some couches in it. Like an artist's space or party room. We just went in there and kicked back on the couch and had some drinks and relaxed. He told the story of how somebody broke into his house. The police were holding his best friend in jail for the murder. He didn't believe his friend did it."

Collin and Marty knew that everyone reacted differently after a tragedy, but the impression they got from Todd was that he didn't miss his wife very much. He basically seemed happy and relaxed and enjoying himself.

Collin and Marty left on May 23, as did all of the rest of Carole's relatives. But there was one person still very much in evidence with Todd: Lynn Noyes. She finally had him all to herself. He took her to the house on Adobe Road and they met his neighbor and talked to him for a while and walked around the property. Afterward they went shopping in Redding at a couple of malls, and Todd bought some clothes. Lynn shopped as well, and got a very unusual item. It was a nipple ring. They went to a tattoo parlor and Lynn had the nipple on her left breast pierced. It was Todd's idea. She wanted to do it for him. She knew that it would not please Dean. She didn't care—Todd was the one she wanted. It would be one more reminder of him, like the tattoo ONE and the self-inflicted scar on her thigh of a heart and a very faint letter *T*.

With such contempt for Dean, it was curious what both of them decided to do next. Lynn and Todd cooked up a scheme where Dean would be induced into moving down to the Redding area. They would dangle the bait in front of him that he could come and work for Todd at G and G Fencing. Whether this was to get him in the area to be assassinated, or just so Lynn could be closer to Todd, neither one elaborated on later. Though Lynn did mention that Dean "might have an accident while he was on the job," this scheme never really got off the ground.

Another scheme of Todd's actually did begin to take place. Lynn wanted to move to the Redding area near Todd, and he went to a real estate office that dealt with house rentals in the area. He obtained some forms just in case Lynn did make the move.

Lynn said, "It was to kind of lay the foundation if I was to move to California. The Redding area. To get a fresh start and be closer to Todd. There was some kind of rental deposit."

Todd desperately wanted to take care of one last thing while Lynn was in the area. It was to destroy the label maker that was still in his home on Adobe Road. It didn't matter that there was yellow police tape all around the house barring everyone from going inside. The label maker and tapes that went in it were the few physical items that could tie him to Norman Daniels. This was the label maker he had used to construct the message on the package Daniels had received from The Company at 12:01 A.M., April 28.

Lynn recalled, "He had forgotten something very important. He said it was something that was incriminating and he had to get rid of it because it was one of the few things that could tie him physically to this case. We went to his house. I followed him through a window into the living room, the kitchen and, maybe two or three steps, into a bedroom area. He got a package of tapes, a stack of magnets and it looked like a little portable computer. [It was the label maker.] They were cassette-type tapes that were interchangeable with his little computer thing he had.

"We went back to the vehicle. We were just driving down a paved road. On the side there was some dried grass, wheat, I don't know. A couple of sporadic houses on one side of the road and on the other side there were trees. He said he needed to get rid of the little computer machine that had the tapes. There was one tape inside the machine, and when we were driving, I took the tape out and I was looking at it. He said, 'You don't need to read the tape.' He took the tape and he was driving with his arm and trying to pull part of the tape out.

"At some portion [of the road] we stopped. There was kind of a gravel embankment that dipped down. He had taken the tape out because there was writing on the tape. Then he was kind of unraveling it. When we got out of the vehicle, we went down by the river. We went down and there were some Mexican males down there. I don't know what they were doing.

"We went off to the side. To the Sacramento River. There was kind of an overpass bridge and we walked right down underneath the bridge to the water's edge. He broke a piece of black [tape] off and put it in the water. Then we went back to the vehicle. He was in the back of his truck and he had a little kind of, like, hunter's pack that had materials that you could light things on fire. And he burned a portion of tape that had writing on it. After he burned that portion of the tape, the ashes from it and the computer [label maker], we went back to the river and threw all of these in the river.

"The other two tapes weren't ever used. They were still in the vehicle, and after we left the river, we stopped at a Toys 'R' Us because we were going over to the senior Jones house for a birthday party. There was a bunch of garbage in the vehicle and I put the two remaining cassette tapes with miscellaneous stuff, and threw them in the trash."

After this expedition Todd and Lynn went to the birthday party and celebrated with the others, as if they had not been on an evidence-destroying mission in an off-limits crime scene. Tracie Jones recalled, "He and Lynn had gone shopping. He said that they had gone to a Toys 'R' Us because it was one of Carole's favorite places. They bought toys for the kids. At the birthday party they were sitting next to each other. Enjoying the boys opening the presents.

"Then he told me that she was thinking about moving down here. That her husband was in trouble with embezzlement in Oregon and that she and the children were thinking of moving to Redding." Just how much Todd told Tracie about the embezzlement is not clear. One thing he did not tell her was that he had tried to blackmail Dean in conjunction with this embezzlement scenario.

For the most part Lynn was happy that Carole was dead and Norman Daniels had taken the fall. She seemed closer than ever in having Todd all to herself. The police were still asking questions, but as far as she knew, everything would soon die down and Norman Daniels would take the blame for everything.

Chapter 11

House of Cards

It didn't take long for Todd Garton to try and make a claim on his wife's life insurance policy. He was very much looking forward to claiming the $125,000. Ironically, the claim had to go through the Bell Agency in Anderson. The same agency Carole had worked for with her friends Kenneth and Grace Bell, and where a playroom had been constructed for her and the baby. Kenneth Bell told Todd by telephone he would get the ball rolling when he got home from the East Coast.

On May 26, 1998, Grace Bell spoke with claims specialist Tony Aranda. At some point Todd joined in on a three-way call. Todd spoke with Aranda and gave Carole's date of birth and other information. He even told Aranda that Carole had been killed by a jealous friend.

Pat Garton, Todd's mother, went by the Bell Agency that same day and gave Kenneth the original death certificate for Carole. Grace, in turn, gave

Pat all of Carole's plants and personal items that were around the office. Pat said that Todd hadn't broken down yet, but she expected him to do so at any time. She also told Grace that she was going to clear out the house on Adobe Road for Todd. He had told her to put everything Carole owned out in the yard and let people take whatever they wanted. He said he couldn't stand looking at it. But Pat said that she knew that was just his "pain" talking. She intended to box up everything of Carole's and put it in storage until he could deal with it at a later time.

That same day the detectives were busy as well. They searched Norman Daniels's mobile home again and discovered a box of .44-caliber shells, pictures of Lynn Noyes and burned material in his barbecue pit. The material was not completely burned and it matched the description of the envelope Daniels had received from Colonel Sean. The investigators recovered the wax seal that Daniels had saved. The seal with Garton's diving-bubble imprint in it. They also seized Daniels's computer. This item was invaluable. They turned it over to a Redding police computer technician named Jim Arnold, who was an expert in this field.

The next day the investigators executed a search warrant on Todd Garton's residence and discovered the two life insurance policies—one for Todd and one for Carole. Each of the policies was worth $125,000. The real eye-opener as far as the detectives were concerned was that the policies had been purchased in late March 1998, not even two months previously.

Because of stories Daniels had been telling of

black labeling tape with instructions on the envelope, the detectives also searched for a label maker in Todd Garton's home. Detective Grashoff seemed to remember such an item on a shelf in the Gartons' master bedroom. But when they searched now, there was no label maker to be found. There was, however, an empty space about the right size on one of the shelves, as if such an item had been removed recently. Detective Grashoff took a photograph of the empty space as a reminder that the item should be tracked down if possible.

Detective Grashoff said later, "The label maker was being searched for due to information received by Norman Daniels."

The investigators also looked for a photo album that held photos of Carole Garton. They discovered the album and it was of special interest. Daniels had told them that one photo he received in the package from The Company had been of Carole near a creek and small waterfall. There was a similar photo in the album they seized in the Garton residence.

Also seized during the search was the video *Patriot Games,* which Norman Daniels said Todd had used as a training video for him before the murder. The video not only contained a key character named Sean, but Patriot was supposedly Todd's code name with The Company. Todd had business cards with the word "Patriot" on them as well.

Evidence kept mounting against Todd's involvement as Detective Grashoff and Sergeant VonRader interviewed Grace and Kenneth Bell about a life insurance policy Todd recently had taken out on Carole. When they learned that Todd was in the process of trying to collect a $125,000 claim, it magnified their growing suspicions about him. This seemed just too coincidental that he should have instituted the policy in March and Carole was dead by May.

On May 29, 1998, Norman Daniels contacted the investigators by means of an inmate request. When he sat down with Grashoff and VonRader, he had a whole new set of stories to tell, and they were almost more fantastic than what he'd already been telling them. He said that Todd Garton got his orders from an assassination organization called The Company. He also said that Lynn Noyes had been his "profiler" for The Company. She was a go-between and kept him on track as far as the murder was concerned. He told of his trip up to Oregon with Todd and Dale to attempt an assassination on Dean Noyes. This was the first the detectives had heard about the Oregon mission. Norman had dates, places and names all lined up for them. He was still afraid of The Company and wanted police protection. As far as he knew, another operative could be posing as an inmate, just ready to kill him.

Even with all the evidence starting to point in their direction, Todd and Lynn were still not through with their clandestine operations. As she said of this time period, "Things were very up in the air. It was scary. Todd said he was questioned by police. He wasn't available to talk freely on the phone or computer. I sent him an e-mail message. It said, 'My loyalty (to you).'"

In fact, she wanted to show her loyalty with one more gesture—a new tattoo that would bind her even closer to him. She said, "I was trying to figure

out the spelling of something in Gaelic. The word
'angel.' That was one of the names he called me
off and on. In the tattoo the word 'angel' would be
written in Gaelic. It had to do with Todd and
Ireland. He said he could speak broken Gaelic and
it would be something only he would know when
he saw it."

As far as Todd's concerns about bugged phones
and tapped e-mail messages, Lynn said, "He
wouldn't talk over the telephone or computer about
Carole's death. He would be very guarded in what
he said. Because of the police involvement. He believed my phone was tapped."

Lynn, however, still wanted to express her
thoughts to him about Carole's death. She decided
she would describe how she felt by using some
song lyrics. She said, "I would do this by song lyrics
or occasionally a poem." But Todd was incensed
when Lynn got too close to the truth with one
poem. She started to recite it over the phone and
he hung up on her in anger. Lynn recalled, "It was
a poem I had run across and it made me think of
Carole. It was a sad poem and I just wanted to read
it to him. He hung up. I paged him numerous times.
There was a 911 in one of them. One message said,
'Call Lynn ASAP,' regarding the poem I had just
read. It was double edged. It had another meaning. I thought he misinterpreted it. I mean, I was
going through a lot of different emotional cycles. I
was in shock. I was sad. Sad at the whole situation.
That [poem] was meant for Carole. It was obvious,
going down for the memorial service, that she had
loved him."

Todd did not want to hear anything about Carole

from Lynn Noyes. Especially on an open phone line or e-mail message. In fact, he ordered Lynn to pick a new screen name for herself, something not already associated with The Company. She thought about it and came up with Cowboy. As she explained, "There was a song that had the word 'cowboy' in it. If I remember, it was by the group Devo. In the song called 'Big Mess.' " Lynn related that it spoke of a cowboy on a mission with a gun. He had a picture in his pocket of someone he was supposed to kill. She added, "So that is one of the reasons I chose the word 'Cowboy.' That and the fact that his area [around Cottonwood] is kind of cowboyish."

As far as Todd's connection to the song, "Big Mess," Lynn said, "He just mentioned that it kind of went along with the military. Things associated with The Company."

Incredibly, with all the police questions swirling around them and Todd's paranoia, Lynn Noyes was still not through cooking up schemes to have her husband, Dean, murdered. She began the process by taking out a $500,000 life insurance policy on Dean. She even mentioned to Todd that there were now five hundred thousand new reasons to get rid of Dean. She said, "I came up with an idea and I presented it to Todd. One of my friends—her birthday was coming up. And it was Dean's and my anniversary. We were all going out to celebrate at the Newport Bay Restaurant on the riverfront in downtown Portland. It would take place preferably after dinner when Dean and I were going back to our vehicle.

"Since Todd always portrayed that he's a great

marksman, from a distance he could shoot Dean and then myself. Just so it wouldn't look too obvious. Just a flesh wound on me. But kill Dean."

Lynn might have thought twice about this plan if she had known Todd was not quite the marksman that he claimed to be. His consistently missing the paper cup while he fired out of the Hampton Inn window was proof of that. And his missing the target with an arrow at the bow shoot, and hitting a pickup truck instead, was an even more flagrant example of how off the mark he could be.

It was all a moot point anyway. The last thing Todd wanted by now was something to stir up more suspicion. He told her, "Be patient. Wait until all this calms down."

But it wasn't calming down. In fact, everything was heating up to the degree that stories were starting to surface about Todd and hitting the front page of the *Redding Record Searchlight*. One article was titled CHARGE IN KILLING PUZZLES VICTIM'S FAMILY. The article went on to say that certain family members related to Carole Garton wanted to know who benefited financially from Carole's death. Although it didn't say so directly, Todd understood this to be coming from Jim and Vicki Holman. In response Todd told a reporter that when the detectives asked him if he had killed his wife, he replied, "It broke me mentally and physically. It's barbaric. What gain could you get from the death of your wife and child?" He went on to say he only had a $10,000 insurance policy on his wife. He said this amount barely covered her cremation and memorial service.

Grace Bell knew this was a lie. Todd was trying to collect on the $125,000 life insurance policy. This statement that he was only going to collect $10,000 added to her already deep-seated suspicions about his involvement with Carole's murder. In effect, it turned her into a sleuth along the lines of Jessica Fletcher in *Murder, She Wrote.* From this point on, Grace Bell started her own private investigation of Todd. She did it by contacting people he knew and those who lived around him. She was even quoted in the newspaper: "We definitely want justice on her behalf. "We need answers because none of this makes any sense."

The sheriff's detectives were also looking for answers that went beyond Norman Daniels as the "lone gunman." They were sure Daniels pulled the trigger, but it was becoming more evident all the time that he might have been coerced into pulling the trigger. With clues leading off into a myriad of directions, they contacted the Gresham Police Department and filled them in on the new angle of Lynn Noyes being involved, especially with a possible intended hit against her husband, Dean. Gresham police officers showed up at Lynn Noyes's door on June 3, 1998. And just like Norman Daniels before her, she went to an interview room and began concocting an initial mixture of truth and lies.

Lynn said of this first interview, "My intention was to stick with what Todd told me to say. I told them I really didn't know that much. I didn't know Norman Daniels except on the computer. That Norman Daniels had used Todd's identification on his computer. Sometimes he used Todd's computer."

She also told the Gresham police that Todd had a lot of animosity toward Daniels because he had killed his wife. Perhaps Daniels was just trying to get back at Todd. As to a question about a box of items she might have sent Todd containing photos of Dean, as well as keys, she said she never sent any photos because Todd already knew what Dean looked like. And she certainly never sent any keys. She told them she was not involved in any way in some plot to kill Dean or Carole Garton.

But at some point Lynn messed up during the interview, either out of nervousness or just plain carelessness. She admitted she knew about a small computerlike object, a label maker. She indicated that she and Todd had thrown it away in the Sacramento River. She did not say what kind of writing might have been on the labels.

The police let Lynn Noyes return home and she knew by now she was very much under suspicion, as was Todd Garton. In fact, the next day Jim Holman, who no longer believed in Todd's innocence, phoned Grace Bell and asked what was going on. Grace filled him in about the discrepancies in Todd's statements and the true nature of the life insurance policy taken out on Carole.

In her sleuthing role Grace had a conversation with Todd's next-door neighbor Chris Lamm, a teenager. Chris told her about Todd, Dale and Norman with guns in the fields. He had been frightened by them. They had been acting "secretive and weird." Chris also had overheard Todd on a cell phone talking to Lynn Noyes. He stated that these two had a lot of conversations over the past year, and something wasn't right.

On June 9, 1998, Todd called Carole's mother, Virginia, to try and stanch all the rumors. But it was as useless as trying to hold back the waters of a dam that's ready to burst. A woman named Susan Stone told Grace Bell about Todd, Dale and Norman's obsession with everything military. She also said that Todd had abused Carole's dog, KD, and that she worried what he would be like with a new baby in the house.

Grace began writing down a list of her suspicions about Todd. She then had a conversation with Julianna Metcalf, Chris Lamm's mother, on June 12. Metcalf added stories about how odd Todd had been behaving just before Carole was murdered. So did people at the Kickin' Mule. They told Grace that Norman Daniels had been acting funny a couple of weeks before Carole's death. They said that Todd and Norman had lunch together every day before Carole's murder, something they had not done before. This was a bit of an exaggeration, but not by much.

After her questions at the Kickin' Mule, Grace had another conversation with Chris Lamm who said that he knew about Lynn and Todd for almost a year. He said that during the summer of 1997 he worked for Todd and was often in his house. He overheard phone conversations that Todd had with Lynn. He also picked up the phone, with Lynn on the other end of the line, asking for Todd. At one point Todd told Lamm, "My life will be very changed next year." Chris didn't know at the time how correct this prediction would be.

Grace talked with Julianna Metcalf again as well and Julianna told her that Todd had a terrible temper. Chris would sometimes come home crying because of the way Todd treated him. He yelled at and verbally abused the boy. It got so bad that

Chris was afraid of Todd and didn't know what he might do. He often saw Todd and his friends target practicing out in the woods. Chris told his mother that Todd had some illegal guns stashed in the back of his house. Then on the day of the murder Chris was in Todd's house and the guns were suddenly gone.

Jim and Vicki Holman were so concerned by now, that Jim phoned Pat Garton that they were going down to witness Norman Daniels's plea in court, which was coming up soon. Jim said he wanted to speak to Todd. She told him he wasn't there. Jim then said that he and his wife would like to have Carole and the baby's remains. Pat became upset and hung up the phone. But within a minute Todd was on the line talking to Jim. Vicki recalled, "Todd called Jim every name in the book. He said how dare Jim think that he was involved. He would never hear from him again. And we certainly weren't going to get the remains. We wondered how he knew we were suspicious of him. From that point on, I was afraid. Paranoid would probably describe it better. Even cars with California license plates scared me."

Vicki's fears were not without foundation. On previous occasions Todd had badgered Dale Gordon into trying to kill people who had irritated him, such as Rick Clark, the man who sued him over the bungled fencing job, and the man who had bought Dale Gordon's alignment business.

The Shasta County investigators were also following phone number leads that verified what Norman Daniels was saying. They discovered that there were phone calls from Todd Garton's parents' house to Norman Daniels's pager in the hours after the murder. There were also phone calls from Daniels going out to both Lynn Noyes and Todd Garton. A twelve-minute phone call originated from Stephanie Bias's house to Lynn Noyes at 11:01 A.M., May 17. A one-minute call from a phone booth at a Texaco station occurred at 1:35 P.M. Another call was placed from the same phone booth at 1:44 P.M. to Lynn Noyes. There was a one-minute call from the phone booth at the Hometown Buffet at 3:46 P.M., followed by a fourteen-minute call at 4:15 P.M. All of these phone calls were from Norman Daniels to a woman who indicated that she barely knew him.

Up in Oregon, Detective Kerry Taylor of the Portland Police Department went to the Hampton Inn and recovered the window screen from room 218. He discovered that it had several small bullet holes in it, just as Norman Daniels said. Taylor passed this information on to the Shasta County investigators and Gresham Police Department.

Lynn Noyes had a couple visitors on June 16, and they weren't just Gresham policemen. They were Detective Grashoff and Sergeant VonRader of the Shasta County Sheriff's Office, and they had a lot more ammunition in their arsenal as far as allegations against Lynn and Todd went. Norman Daniels had been telling more and more about Lynn's involvement, and there was physical evidence to back up his claims. Lynn had done fairly well holding up in her interview with the Gresham cops, but the sight of the Shasta County investigators really threw her. She recalled, "I was in my kitchen looking down the staircase. And the doorbell rang. They looked official. I grabbed Dean's cell phone and I went into my bedroom and called Todd. I was nervous and scared. He said, 'Well, do you know the police are questioning just about everybody I know? Just remember the "truth." ' We discussed that I stick to that."

Lynn went voluntarily with Detective Grashoff and Sergeant VonRader to the Gresham Police Department and they all sat down in an interview room. The interview lasted for hours. Lynn initially told the detectives she only knew Norman Daniels via the Internet. She said she had never met him in person. She also told them she believed Daniels had some kind of obsession with Carole Garton.

Lynn lied when they asked her if she had ever heard of something called The Company. She said no. Lynn said later, "Todd had said if I revealed anything about it, that my family would be killed and possibly myself. The whole situation—I was scared. It was very overwhelming."

The two investigators were not letting Lynn off the hook easily. They came armed with a manila envelope full of information. She said, "They had some type of manila folder. And it had to do with phone records that Todd and I talked quite a bit on the phone. I thought, 'Oh wow, the phone records will reflect that there was definitely some type of relationship going on. They probably know more than what they're letting on.'

"I was really, really scared. I just started babbling bits and pieces of the truth. There were portions of it that were contrary to what I had already said. I was very selective and guarded. But I was petrified, too."

At some point one of the detectives pointed at her Celtic cross necklace. She said, "It was identified to me they had seen the same type on Todd. The necklace was of such emotional significance to me. I knew that Todd had a matching one. I mentioned that at one time we were boyfriend and girlfriend. And I admitted that Todd is my best friend in the whole entire world."

The interview was a marathon that day. It lasted more than six hours. At that point Lynn Noyes's world was collapsing like a house of cards. Even though the interview had been grueling, she went back for another one the next day with Detective Grashoff and Sergeant VonRader. They wanted to know about her computer involvement with Norman Daniels. They already knew about some of the things he talked about concerning his computer affairs with Lynn. They asked about the game Vampire Tavern and Lynn said, "We started playing this game. We played for . . . I don't know how many times. I mean, it was a really addictive game."

But after a while she began to change her statements about the game and her interest in it. She said she didn't know how to play it very well and she and Norman started to drift off from it into another direction. She told the investigators, "It ended up he and I just got to a chat room, doing what I now know is called cybersex. It was easy for me to do and get the sex into the vampire thing."

During this tale of cybersex, Lynn mentioned Norman Daniels's various screen names, Valkymere and Normbo. She also mentioned her own, Pandoora 69.

The discussion turned toward Easter, 1998. She lied and said that she had neither seen Todd nor Carole that week, when, in fact, she had sex with

Todd in her Bronco. She told Sergeant VonRader that she had thirty kids over her house that day for an Easter egg hunt. Then she said, "They were in town for Easter, and I didn't see him. Jeez, they may have been in town several times and I didn't see them. I know Carole and Todd and Krista and Ryan—they were all really tight and they may have been by there and not seen me."

Sergeant VonRader said, "Yeah, I got the idea that your feelings were hurt."

Lynn admitted, "Well, yeah. I never got to see her pregnant. I would have loved to see her pregnant."

Lynn was still trying to play a game of cat and mouse with the investigators, giving up some of the truth and hiding the rest, while still trying to place all of the blame on a jealous and troubled Norman Daniels. Most of all, she tried to keep hidden her relationship with Todd. She said later, "I very guardedly revealed just portions of our relationship. I remember sitting there and some hotel brochures were shown to me. The hotel brochures were places that I had been with Todd. And I thought, 'I've said very little about the relationship with Todd and I. Well, if they have these records—' I just panicked."

Lynn began to blurt out more details about herself and Todd, and this was not wise. Once again the interview was long. It lasted at least four hours. She either gave new information that corroborated what Norman Daniels had already said, or she gave a different version than she had told before. In both cases it made her and Todd look more and more guilty.

When Lynn returned home, she was so concerned about her future that she boxed up her Celtic cross necklace and nipple ring and sent them to Natalya in New York for safekeeping.

It was a wise decision. Detectives soon conducted a search and seizure at her home. Some of the items seized included an address book with Todd Garton's and Norman Daniels's names in it. They also seized Lynn Noyes's computer. Perhaps most damning of all, they seized *The Anarchist Cookbook,* which held many photos and articles related to snipers and Northern Ireland. This was a direct link to Todd Garton and all the stories that Norman Daniels had been telling about him.

Detective Grashoff and Sergeant VonRader spoke to Dean Noyes about all the alleged attempts on his life. They advised him it might not be safe under his own roof. This news struck Dean Noyes like an earthquake. He grabbed his children and went into hiding. He later would tell a *Redding Record Searchlight* reporter, "It's an eye-opening experience. If you don't have an appreciation for life, you do after this. My opinions have changed drastically as to what anybody is capable of."

Officer Rich Boyd was a computer forensics investigator for the Gresham Police Department. He was a self-admitted computer nerd. Within the department his office was hardly any larger than a walk-in closet. It was crammed with seized laptops and CPUs that had ties to crimes. His job was to see what information the criminals or alleged criminals might have left behind within the computers. So far, he had helped tie information to crimes as varied as counterfeiting, credit card fraud and a child pornography case. But this alleged tale of conspiracy and murder was the biggest thing ever dropped on his desk. If he could find e-mail messages between Lynn Noyes and Todd Garton relating to the conspiracy, it would go a long way toward their arrests.

Of course he knew they probably hadn't left damning messages out in plain sight. Many e-mails might have been deleted, but even deleted e-mail messages are not truly gone. As Boyd said, "Finding evidence from a computer is like finding a needle in a haystack the size of Oregon. Passwords may be obscure and it is an art as much as a science to figure out what the passwords might be. Also, e-mail messages may be deleted, but the pointer, or name of a file, is not. It's about knowing where to look."

As Rich Boyd wound his way through Lynn Noyes's computer, he came across screen names for her, such as Pandoora 69, Josephine and Cowboy. He discovered screen names coming from Norman Daniels such as Normbo and Valkymere. Nothing was spelled out in black and white with a message such as *Kill Carole Garton,* or *Kill Dean Noyes.* But there were references to a Company T and some individual named Colonel Sean. Also a window of opportunity that ended on May 20.

Jim Arnold of the Redding Police Department was also looking at computers, especially the one seized from Norman Daniels's residence. By 1998 he had been a policeman for twenty years and an investigator for six years. In this capacity he had investigated the use of computers involved in a crime. As he explained, "A forensic examination is taking a computer, a floppy disk or any computer item and examining it for evidence. Information is stored in several different ways. The most common way is to go to a Windows environment. When you delete a file on a computer, it's not normally permanently deleted. Usually what happens in what's called a file application table—it just gets rid of the first letter or number or character of that file. The file can be overwritten, but normally this takes time, and the document is still out there.

"Once you empty the recycle bin on a computer, it takes some forensic tools to find a file. But the file is still on the hard drive until the computer operating system decides to write over the space. To find deleted files we use a program that's called EnCase. Initially what EnCase does is make a mirror image of the source hard drive. And it takes it sector by sector, copies it into a file on a destination hard drive, taking every bit of information without changing anything. That's called 'acquiring the source drive.'

"From there we add it to evidence. It is opened up into a Windows environment of EnCase. What it does is give us a screen almost like the Windows Explorer screen. We can sometimes bring up full Web pages that were written to the original hard drive when they were looked at or written to. Sometimes you only get part of a Web page. When a person goes to the Internet, each Web page that you view is spooled onto a swap file. And most of the time these Web pages are on the hard drive unless they've been written over."

With the computers concerning Norman Daniels,

Lynn Noyes and Todd Garton, Arnold discovered material that passed back and forth through AOL, USA.net and Hotmail.com. AOL did not save e-mails to the hard drive. But USA.net and Hotmail.com did because of the way they spooled information. With these two, and by using EnCase, Arnold typed in key words he thought might link these three people together. Through a very long and winding path, he discovered messages and bits of messages concerning the likes of PATR553, Devlin 666, Josephine and Company T. All of these led into a strange and tangled conspiracy.

Lynn Noyes was so worried about her future that she took a flight to Redding on June 19 to talk once more with Detective Grashoff and Sergeant VonRader. And this time she was all but giving Todd Garton up to try and save her own skin. During the interview she confided, "Todd said such things as, 'Let's get rid of Carole and Dean.'" According to written reports, she told VonRader, that Todd had always been tied to The Company and they assassinated people for money. She said that she had never wanted either Dean or Carole killed. She also said that Todd had broken into her house and burglarized some files related to Dean.

Sergeant VonRader wasn't buying her innocent routine. He said to her, "Isn't it true you gave Todd the key to your house? And not for some burglarized file crap, but for the purpose of him going and killing Dean."

Lynn answered, "No."

As a last gasp she said if Todd knew what she was telling them, "He would take me out and kill me in a second."

Even more than what she told them, it was what she showed them that had disastrous effects not only for Todd, but her as well. Lynn went with the investigators to the Sacramento River and showed them where Todd had thrown the label maker into its waters. Normally, the river through there can be very swift with a large flow of water, especially during May when there are releases from Shasta Dam upstream. On some occasions, an item as large as an automobile can be swept downstream for hundreds of yards or more. On one occasion an entire pickup truck was washed downstream and never recovered. The chances of finding the label maker after a month in the river seemed slim at best.

Detective Grashoff was part of the Shasta County scuba dive team. He said later, "We went there to dive for the label maker machine to see if we could locate it in the river. This was in an area toward the Deschutes Road where it crosses the Sacramento River. We found it [the label maker] approximately ten to fifteen feet from the shoreline. The west shoreline of the Sacramento River."

This was an amazing bit of good luck. The label maker was one of the few pieces of physical evidence that led straight back to Norman Daniels's "package" from The Company. It also led the detectives to receipts seized in Todd Garton's residence. The receipts proved that he had purchased the label maker and other items at a Redding Office-Max on April 17, 1998, by check # 1605 of G and G Fencing, a business that Todd just happened to own.

In the long run, Lynn Noyes's last gamble to

save herself didn't work. Things had progressed
beyond her control. Norman Daniels and physical
evidence both lined up to put her and Todd Garton
squarely in the crosshairs of the Shasta County investigators and the Shasta County District Attorney's
Office. And by now these agencies had a lot. It
doesn't take foolproof evidence to arrest someone—it only takes probable cause. And by the end
of June 1998, the probable cause against Todd
Garton and Lynn Noyes was winding its way from
mere rumor to actual documents—signed, sealed
and delivered.

Chapter 12

Mug Shots

The ax fell upon both Todd Garton and Lynn Noyes on June 29, 1998. Todd was arrested in Anderson at 4:00 P.M. The sheriff's investigators who arrested him had a declaration of arrest warrant, approved by the municipal court. Charges included an 187 (first-degree murder) and an 182 (conspiracy to commit murder). The amount $1,000,000 was issued for bail.

At the time of Todd's arrest his Celtic cross necklace was taken into custody—the Celtic cross that Lynn Noyes had given him so many years ago. The officers also obtained an active pager from his belt. On the same day his house was searched again and several violent videotapes were seized. Of particular interest to the investigators were the tapes, *Sniper, Pro Sniper* and *Ultimate Sniper.* They also seized a calendar with the date May 20 x-ed out. This was the date that Norman Daniels had told them was the end of his window of opportunity to kill Carole Garton.

The official charges brought against Todd were:

Count 1—Murder 187. Todd Jesse Garton, on or about the 16th day of May, 1998, did willfully, unlawfully, and with malice aforethought murder Carole Anne Garton, a human being.

Count 2—Murder of a Human Fetus. Todd Jesse Garton, on or about the 16th day of May, 1998, did willfully, unlawfully, and with malice aforethought, murder the human fetus of Carole Anne Garton.

Count 3—Conspiracy. (Note: this was a long count with several alleged Overt Acts.)

Act 1—A conspirator obtained a hand gun.

Act 2—A conspirator provided an envelope containing photographs of Carole Garton and written materials to a co-conspirator.

Act 3—One or more conspirators communicated via computer e-mails.

Act 4—A conspirator shot and killed Carole Anne Garton.

Act 5—A conspirator shot and killed a fetus belonging to Carole Anne Garton.

There were also counts in the conspiracy to murder Dean Noyes, which included the possession of a key to his house and a photograph of him. There was also the count of constructing a home-made silencer.

Special circumstances at the bottom of the list brought the possibility of a death penalty. These were:

PC—Special Circumstance Murder for Financial Gain.

PC—Special Circumstance Multiple Murders.

Many miles away in Portland, Oregon, Lynn Noyes was arrested on the same day by Gresham policemen at her parents' home. She was held in the Justice Center Jail on similar charges to Todd's. And just like Todd, her bail was set at $1,000,000.

The *Redding Record Searchlight* recorded these startling developments. On July 1 it reported the headline HUSBAND ARRESTED IN SLAYING. In the article Sergeant VonRader explained that a person could be involved in a murder even if they weren't at the crime scene at the time it occurred: *"You can still be a principal, although you are not involved in the act."*

The reporter also contacted Carole's father, Jim Holman. He told her that he already had suspicions about Todd's involvement. Jim said, "I didn't see any remorse from him at the funeral [memorial service]. He was calm and putting on a show. He has to be a monster to do something like this."

The next day's addition of the newspaper expanded its focus. Under the headline KILLING WAS LOVERS' PLOT, OFFICIALS SAY, the newspaper depicted photos of Carole Garton, Todd Garton, Lynn Noyes and Norman Daniels. A little farther down the page was a subheading that said, *The husband of a slain pregnant woman and his girlfriend could face the death penalty for allegedly plotting to kill their spouses for insurance money.*

The article delved further into the whole twisted affair, revealing what investigators knew at this point. Shasta County sheriff Jim Pope said, "In my thirty-three years in law enforcement, I don't know of a case similar to this."

Pope also had a dire warning for anyone else connected to the crimes, "More arrests could follow."

Of course there was still one more conspirator on the loose, Dale Gordon. But by now he was in another county.

With all the allegations, fact-finding and circumstantial evidence turning up, Dale Gordon had plenty to worry about. By early July, Todd, Lynn and Norman were all in jail and the investigators had tracked Dale down to neighboring Trinity County and were asking him questions. Gordon was now a firefighter working in Trinity National Forest at a place called Big Bar. The "bar" referred to an area along a river where gold was in abundance during Gold Rush days. It was rough work in the forest and rugged mountains of the area, but Gordon did his job well and his supervisors and coworkers there liked him. His main duties were that of a fire-suppression hand crewman. This involved using a shovel, chain saw or Pulaski on a fire line. The Pulaski was a combination pick and shovel especially designed for fighting wild land fires.

Dale Gordon realized that the investigators already knew a lot, so just like Lynn Noyes and Norman Daniels before him, he began giving a concoction of truth and lies. He hoped the truth would match what they knew. He also hoped the lies would lead them astray from what they didn't know. But Dale was not a fabricator of stories like Todd Garton was. He admitted later, "I was under a lot of pressure. They were showing me pictures. Telling me things. I knew I was guilty and not a good liar. I began telling them the truth."

On July 7, 1998, Dale Gordon was arrested, completing the net of all the conspirators. He was the last one to step in front of a police camera and have his mug shot taken—front and profile. Dale's charges dealt with the attempted murder of Dean Noyes. Since he had not been involved with the murder of Carole Garton, there were no charges on that score.

Gordon's arrest shocked his fellow forestry service workers. They knew and liked Dale. One of his bosses told a *Record Searchlight* reporter that Dale was a good worker and got along well with the others. The whole thing came as a shock. The article began by saying: *Dale Gordon looks like your typical all-American boy.*

Even at his arraignment at Trinity County's historic old courthouse in the Gold Rush town of Weaverville, Dale Gordon lived up to this image. He politely answered all the judge's questions with "yes, sir" and "no, sir." He seemed truly abashed for being caught up in the whole sordid affair. His grief-stricken parents watched from the gallery. They never had a clue that their son was involved in such terrible crimes.

Soon thereafter, Dale said, "I was very upset. I felt betrayed and angry. Betrayed by my friends, Norman Daniels and Todd Garton. They knew every little detail. He [Daniels] told everything. He told all about what happened in Oregon, which was enough to send me to prison."

Dale Gordon pleaded innocent to the charges against him.

On the same day that Gordon pleaded innocent, Lynn Noyes sent the judge in her case a handwritten letter from jail. It contained an unusual request. Lynn wrote *I'm writing to plead with you not to allow cameras in the courtroom with the regard to my case.* She said it caused her extreme difficulty in her pod (a secure area within a jail or prison.) She said she wanted to protect her family in Oregon and claimed that the adverse publicity would affect them. She concluded the letter by saying, *I'm asking, if not for my own safety and mental health, then for my children, husband and family.*

Her plea fell on deaf ears. The judge allowed newspaper reporters and television film crews into the courtroom during proceedings. And the husband she referred to was soon to be her ex-husband. Dean Noyes started divorce proceedings against her with inclusion that he would have sole custody of the children.

Two interesting developments occurred around this time concerning Todd Garton. He was under a lot of stress and perhaps lost some of his customary caution. In a recorded phone conversation with his mother, Pat, she told him that she couldn't find a "little, tiny sticker" with I LOVE YOU, BABE on it. The sticker in question had been made by the label maker that Todd and Lynn had thrown into the Sacramento River. The same label maker that Garton had used to create the package he gave to Norman Daniels from The Company. If this sticker was discovered, it could lead right back to the label maker, one that Todd was trying to say he never owned. Garton wanted her to get rid of the sticker at all costs, and told her so. All of this was recorded by the investigators.

The second adverse occurrence, as far as Todd

Garton was concerned, happened when Marshall Jones realized he had something in his possession from Todd that was "hot." If he didn't inform the authorities about it, he could be in hot water himself. Jones contacted the investigators and said they might want to check out some "stuff" of Garton's that he had in storage for safekeeping. When the investigators checked these items, they discovered the "stuff" was a large silver-colored case. It was hot indeed. It contained a large sniper rifle, plastic gloves, cleaning equipment, communication devices and subsonic ammunition. All of these were items that had been used in the February attempt to kill Dean Noyes. And they all were the property of Garton.

As the summer wore on, the amount of evidence against Todd Garton kept multiplying. And two key players were about to arrive on the scene. These two would decide his fate.

Chapter 13

Warnings to the Angel Malichi

By mid-July 1998 all four co-conspirators had their respective attorneys, and the Shasta County District Attorney's Office was putting together their team. But of all these individuals, two men would have more impact on the fate of Todd Garton than any of the others. They were Greg Gaul, senior deputy district attorney, and Russell Swartz, Garton's defense lawyer.

On first glance these two hardly could have seemed more different. Greg Gaul was a lean man, almost patrician-looking, in his pressed suits and air of calm. Russell Swartz, on the other hand, was a large man, with balding head and expansive gestures. He conjured up the images of a powerful mountain man, television's Detective Cannon and Friar Tuck all rolled into one. In the courtroom Swartz often eschewed a suit coat and rolled up the sleeves of his shirt, as if to demonstrate he was a man at work. Both men, with such different looks and styles, were equally shrewd, learned in law and knew their way around a courtroom. They both had devoted their lives to the instrumentation of law and were worthy adversaries. Neither one of them was afraid of a difficult case, which the present one with Todd Garton and his co-conspirators was sure to be.

Greg Gaul had a solid foundation in both law enforcement and the judicial branch. He began his career as a crime-prevention specialist for the Redondo Beach Police Department in 1979. In this capacity he presented weekly crime-prevention meetings for neighborhood watch groups and conducted commercial security inspections. From 1980 to 1984 he was an administrative crime analyst, providing daily crime analysis for seven southern California police departments. These duties included identifying suspects for undercover surveillance and a crime-suppression team. One of his analyses led to the arrest of two bank robbers who had pulled off seven bank jobs. Moving up the ladder, he headed the Career Criminal Apprehension Unit from 1984 to 1987. This unit targeted serial criminals who engaged in robberies, burglaries, rapes and homicides in Los Angeles and Orange Counties.

A big change came for Greg when he moved to Redding from southern California in 1987. This area was for the most part rural with one medium-size city, Redding. Its residents were mainly white, as opposed to the mixture of races in the urban sprawl of cities near Los Angeles. But that didn't mean the county was a bucolic landscape without crime. In fact, there was an element of lawlessness that went clear back to the Gold Rush. In some respects, the new gold rush in the area were meth labs, which produced and distributed methamphetamine throughout the West.

In 1987 Gaul joined the judicial branch of law enforcement as a deputy district attorney I. He prosecuted all misdemeanor cases in Anderson, Central Valley and Burney Justice Courts. By 1988 he had moved up to deputy district attorney II. His caseload now included numerous major narcotics felonies following a lengthy undercover drug investigation by the Shasta County Sheriff's Office. From 1988 through 1990 he was working at the level of deputy district attorney III, where he delved into adult and child sexual assault cases, as well as complex white-collar crime.

In 1991 Greg became senior deputy district attorney for Shasta County. Along with trying major assault and homicide cases, he instituted a sexual assault response team to help in rape cases. By the time the Garton case landed on his desk, he was a veteran of about everything that law enforcement and the judiciary could come up with.

His legal opponent across the aisle in Todd Garton's defense was no stranger to a courtroom as well. Russell Swartz was born to be a defense lawyer. He had the savvy, the knowledge and the drive to present his client's case in the best manner possible. By 1998 he had handled some of the most notorious homicide cases in Shasta County history. One of his earliest had been one of its most volatile. It concerned a serial killer named Darrell Rich, of Redding. In 1978 Darrell had gone on an absolute rampage of rape and murder in the area. Among his murder victims were Linda

Slavik, twenty-eight, Annette Edwards, nineteen, and Pam Moore, seventeen. But it was his fourth victim that particulary angered residents of the county. Rich raped and murdered an eleven-year-old neighbor, Annette Selix. After raping her, he had taken her to a 105-foot-high bridge in the mountains and had thrown her off. She did not die immediately.

This was a very tough case for Swartz, but he did his best. And unlike many another criminal, Darrell Rich truly did seem remorseful after his rampage. It was as if he'd been mad during the months of terror he had inflicted upon the region. It didn't matter in the end, the jury found him guilty and he eventually died by lethal injection. But in March 2000, as he was strapped in, awaiting the needles that would stop his heart, his last word was "Peace."

Perhaps the most interesting direct link between Russell Swartz and Greg Gaul began in the summer of 1998, even as the Garton case began to take shape. At 6:00 P.M. on August 22, 1998, pretty sixteen-year-old Tera Smith went jogging near the Old Oregon Trail, north of Redding, and simply disappeared. Tera was not the runaway type, and soon Redding police and Shasta County sheriff's deputies were looking for her, but to no avail. It was known that Tera sometimes liked to run near the mountains up by the Shasta Dam. The investigators began to focus on a twenty-nine-year-old instructor of martial arts, Troy Zink. He told them he had given Tera a ride to the corner of Old Alturas Road and the Old Oregon Trail at about six o'clock on August 22. She had jogged away and he hadn't seen her since. Then he said he went to pray at one of his favorite spots, up near the Shasta Dam. Zink was of particular interest to the police since he had pled guilty to a charge of rape in 1992. When the police searched his residence, they discovered four rifles and three shotguns. They booked him into jail, since he was an ex-felon and should not have had firearms in the house.

In response to this arrest, Zink posted bail and was released. He also hired Russell Swartz to be his attorney. Swartz immediately went on the offensive. He told local reporters that the police were harassing his client simply because they didn't have any clues about the disappearance of Tera Smith. He said that the firearms in the Zink residence belonged to Zink's father and grandfather and were used for hunting. Swartz also said, "Zink and his family feel harassed by the police. He disassociated himself with the karate business because of the attention to the case. The authorities are just trying to make it look bad [in connection with Tera Smith]. How many times are you supposed to talk if you tell a person [the police] all you know?"

Interestingly enough, Greg Gaul was heading up the prosecution against Zink. He told a *Record Searchlight* reporter, "Zink is someone we're certainly interested in because his actions have caused us to focus a lot of attention on him. He just gave us very minimal information about that last contact with Tera Smith. He knows more information. But he has not provided it."

The "harassment" against Troy Zink only increased as time wound on. The Smith family, who owned a business called Oasis Fun Center, north of Redding, put up a billboard on their property that read, WHERE'S TERA? ZINK KNOWS. $40,000 REWARD.

When Troy Zink went to trial on the firearm possession, the courtroom was packed with Smith family supporters wearing yellow ribbons. In the end, Judge Bradley Boeckman, the same judge who was going to preside over the Todd Garton case, gave Zink the medium possible sentencing for his crime, which was four years in prison. Russell Swartz said of the decision, "Because of the fact I don't think he's guilty of the crime, I don't think the sentence is fair." And Swartz called the wearing of yellow ribbons, "game playing."

Swartz may have lost the battle with his client, but he won the war as far as Troy Zink's connection to Tera Smith. No charges were ever brought against him for her disappearance. Zink would have suffered a lot more than just four years in prison if he had somehow been connected to kidnapping and possibly murder. If Swartz could do as well with Todd Garton, and get him some lesser charge, it would certainly beat a death penalty conviction.

Even with the notoriety of these other cases, Russell Swartz and Greg Gaul had never seen anything like the Todd Garton murder and conspiracy case. Portions of it were so fantastic and outlandish that it seemed more like a work of fiction than reality. Something indeed out of a Jack Higgins spy novel.

There was so much evidence to compile—so many e-mails and documents to go through that concerned the various co-conspirators—that the paperwork grew into pyramids within the offices of Gaul and Swartz. And, of course, there were other ongoing cases with which they had to contend. By the autumn of 1998 there were thousands of pages of documents and more discovery happening all the time. The cases of Lynn Noyes, Norman Daniels and Dale Gordon were so interlocked with that of Todd Garton that Russell Swartz had to worry about what these other people were saying as well as discovery about his own client. Any deals the others might make were sure to spell trouble for Todd. And as the autumn of 1998 wore on, Greg Gaul was dangling deals before all the others. Only Norman Daniels did not bite. He had adopted a melancholy and fatalistic view on everything developing, almost as if he were doomed to wear the mantle of Hamlet. He told Gaul that he would make no deal, but he would cooperate in the prosecution of Todd Garton nonetheless. It was almost in expiation for his sins. It left him very vulnerable if a jury failed to find Garton guilty of murder. After all, Daniels was the one who actually pulled the trigger on Carole. Without a deal, it was he who could be looking at the death penalty, not Todd, if Todd Garton was found to be innocent. Even with this information Daniels would not budge. He carried the responsibility on his shoulders and moved forward to bring Todd Garton down. There was always somewhat of a noble, yet flawed aspect about Norman Daniels.

It took all summer just to hammer out the charges against Daniels, Gordon and Noyes. In October 1998 Lynn Noyes's charges were finalized and looked like a carbon copy of Todd Garton's. Counts 1, 2 and 3 were in connection with the murder of Carole Garton and the unborn baby. And Overt Acts 1–4 concerned the conspiracy to commit murder against

Dean Noyes's. Norman Daniels's charges were very similar to Garton's and Noyes's. And on October 28, 1998, Greg Gaul and the district attorney's office showed how far they were willing to go in this case. He wrote an official letter that stated in part, *The District Attorneys' Special Circumstances Committee met yesterday regarding Mr. Garton's case. After a full discussion of the facts and appropriate mitigating/aggravating circumstances, the committee has tentatively decided to seek the death penalty against Mr. Garton.*

Even if Daniels was stonewalling about making a deal, the same could not be said of Lynn Noyes and her attorney, and Greg Gaul focused his attention on her. Receiving permission to photograph Todd Garton's tattoos, he compared them to those on Lynn Noyes. Especially the writing ONE BUT NOT THE SAME on Todd, and ONE on Lynn. He gathered new evidence concerning the silencer found in Gresham and some notes by Lynn.

She certainly did not want to go down in flames with her lover, Todd Garton. Frank O'Connor, her attorney, sought to get a severance and change of venue to Oregon. O'Connor wrote a notice and motion to dismiss for improper venue. The thrust of it was that all of the connections to Lynn Noyes and the conspiracy took place in Oregon. According to O'Connor, Lynn should not be facing trial in Shasta County, California—especially where feelings ran high about the case. He cited the United States Constitution, Article III, Section 2: *The trial of all crimes shall be held in the state where the said crimes shall have been committed.* And the Sixth Amendment: *In all criminal procedures, the accused shall enjoy the right to a speedy and public trial, by an impartial jury of the state and district where the crime shall have been committed.*

In his rebuttal to this argument, Greg Gaul pointed out that Lynn Noyes was helping Todd Garton, who hatched the plan in Shasta County, California. Garton was the chief conspirator in the plan to kill Noyes's husband, Dean. Greg argued, "The defendant [Lynn Noyes] was a willing participant in the conspiracy and provided a portion of the means and information necessary to carry out the intended murder of Dean Noyes. There was no direct testimony elicited at the preliminary hearing regarding when or where the defendant gave Garton the key to her residence, the photographs of her husband or intelligence information concerning his activities. However, there was sufficient circumstantial evidence presented to substantiate both that the defendant had discussed with Garton to plan to murder Dean Noyes and that the defendant provided Garton with above-referenced items *prior* to execution of the plan to kill Dean Noyes."

Greg Gaul cited evidence of what he already knew about the conspiracy:

1. The defendant (Lynn Noyes) revealed to the detectives that for many years prior to the attempted murder, she and Garton had a romantic/sexual relationship.
2. During discussions with the defendant concerning her request that her husband be killed, Garton told the defendant that he would need a group of people or a team to carry out the murder. The defendant left the specifics to Garton.

Gaul went on to cite five more instances that the plan was hatched in California, not Oregon, and that Lynn Noyes should be tried in Shasta County along with the others. He said, "The above testimony demonstrates that the intent to enter an agreement to kill Dean Noyes was formed by at least three of the conspirators while in the state of California and that the defendant had formed the same intent and was aware of the existence of the conspirators who were participating in the plan."

The presiding judge reviewed the arguments and came down on the side of the prosecution. Lynn Noyes would stay in Shasta County, California, and she would remain linked with Garton, Daniels and Gordon.

Lynn Noyes realized she had to do something or be dragged down with Todd Garton. On June 21, 1999, after almost a year of mulling over her situation, she signed a plea bargain with the district attorney's office. The document she signed said in part: *I plead guilty to Counts 1 (187 a PC) and 5 (182 a) and admit to the Overt Acts alleged in Count 5, all remaining counts and special allegations to be dismissed with a Harvey-waiver for all purposes. The stipulated sentence will be concurrent terms of 25 years to life in a state prison with the possibility of parole. I waive all my appellate rights. The six page typewritten agreement that I have entered into with the District Attorney is incorporated by reference in this plea agreement. I understand the maximum possible imprisonment is 25 years to life in state prison, the maximum fine is $10,000. I will be required to pay restitution to the full amount necessary to compensate any victims for economic loss.*

There was one more important clause that she

acknowledged: *The state of California has jurisdiction over the conspiracy to kill Dean Noyes.*

She also signed off on the acknowledgment: *On and between the 1st day of October 1997 and the 30th day of May, 1998, I did willfully and unlawfully conspire together with another person and persons to commit the crime of murder of Dean Noyes.* She admitted to providing a photograph of Dean Noyes and the house they lived in, as well as a key to the house.

Lynn Noyes finally signed an agreement stating: *Other than what is written in the Plea Agreement part of this form, no other promises have been made to me by anyone to convince me to enter this plea. No one has made any threats to me or anyone close to me. I am entering this plea voluntarily and of my own free will. These convictions are strikes under California's three strikes law. My conviction of any felony in the future could result in a sentence of up to 25 years to life.* This would be on top of the twenty-five years to life she was already serving.

One more stipulation was that she would have to give testimony against Todd Garton when it was time for his trial. Greg Gaul in a later court appearance told her exactly what would happen if she began to lie during testimony:

> Gaul—In addition to agreeing to plead guilty on these charges, the purpose of the agreement is to ensure the tryer of fact, in this case the jury, as well as prosecutions against Dale Gordon and Norman Daniels, that the jury would be able to hear your truthful testimony. Correct?
>
> Noyes—Correct.

Gaul—And that the only consideration you were given in exchange for the agreement is that you will answer truthfully all questions asked of you either by the court, the prosecution or the defense, correct?

Noyes—Correct.

Gaul—Also you shall not assert any Fifth Amendment privileges, resort to silence or feign any lapse of memory in an attempt to avoid answering questions. Correct?

Noyes—Correct.

Gaul—You also understand that if you commit perjury or subornation in these procedures against Todd Garton, Dale Gordon or Norman Daniels, that doing that, you could be punished by death or life imprisonment without the possibility of parole. Do you understand that?

Noyes—Yes.

It remained to be seen exactly what Lynn Noyes did understand about her plea agreement. Certainly it was explained to her, both by her own counsel and by the prosecution. But perhaps Lynn Noyes was overwhelmed by the whole experience and frightened of the death penalty which had been on the table against her. She didn't read the document fully until it was nearly time for Todd Garton's trial to begin.

Meanwhile, on the same day that Lynn Noyes signed her plea bargain agreement, Dale Gordon signed a similar one. With his plea agreement he was sentenced to ten years in prison, not the twenty-five to life that Noyes would serve. He agreed to a count of attempted murder against Dean Noyes.

He had never been part of the plan to murder Carole Garton, and Greg Gaul took that into account. As part of the agreement, he would have to testify against Todd Garton at his trial. This was something that Gordon relished. He hated Garton by now.

Things got even worse for Todd Garton at the end of June 1999. Tracie Jones had been storing items for him that had come from his house on Adobe Road after the murder of Carole. Many of the items were Carole's clothing and things that had been purchased for the baby. There were baby clothes, a crib, a rocker and cradle stored in the Jones garage. Tracie had not looked at the items for a long period of time. She said, "After Todd was arrested, it was an emotional time. I didn't go through the stuff, even the baby items, because it was just too hard."

But by the end of June 1999, she and her husband were ready to take a look at what was stored in boxes and bags. Tracie said, "There were things of Carole's. A box of shoes. Her wedding dress. My husband had been in the garage looking for something and came across a bag. And he said, 'Hey, there are some photo albums in there.' And so I went to see if I could find a picture of Carole. "

Tracie Jones found more than just a photo of Carole in the bag. It contained many of Todd's pay stubs, work receipts for G and G Fencing and a spiral notebook. In the notebook were cutout newspaper clippings related to the Irish Republican Army. One of the clipping's headlines read, IRA ATTACK KILLS TWO POLICE OFFICERS. Another had a photo with the caption: *At right a British soldier lies on the ground after having been stoned by rioters.* It was just the kind of material that had been in Norman Daniels's package from The Company, the package that Todd Garton had handed to him at midnight on April 28, 1998.

There was also handwritten dialogue in the notebook supposedly between someone called Sean and Carole. But to Tracie's eye, the handwriting looked like it came from Todd Garton.

Tracie took many of the items to a local copy store and photocopied the contents. She said, "I wasn't ready yet to let go of a friendship that I'd had for ten years. And I knew I would never see those things again. I wanted to make sense of Carole's death, and I was hoping that something in there would help me make sense of it."

Knowing that the items she looked through were important, Tracie Jones took them to the district attorney's office on July 1, 1999, and handed them over to Detective Steve Grashoff.

By the late summer of 2000, the early stages of setting up the parameters of Todd Garton's trial began. Everyone knew that it would be a massive undertaking, with dozens of witnesses and mountains of documents. The trial would be in the Honorable Bradley L. Boeckman's courtroom. Judge Boeckman laid down a schedule of procedure on August 14, 2000, and the planning looked like the order of battle for a major army campaign. These included:

Unresolved Motions—Counsel are to be prepared to discuss and argue the following—
People's Motions

1. *To photograph scars and marks on defendant.*
2. *For Pre-trial discovery order.*
          Defendant's Motions
1. *To Prohibit Jury Commissioner from excusing any prospective jurors.*
2. *To exclude Opinion Testimony of Guilt.*
3. *To dismiss for lack of jurisdiction.*
4. *To exclude hearsay.*
5. *To exclude photographic evidence.*

Other matters to be discussed were:

1. *Information of wording to be read to jury.*
2. *Jury instructions—date for submission.*
3. *Witness lists—date for submission.*

Even such minor topics such as special needs for a long table, filing cabinets and one clear row in the gallery, as well as the defendant's attire in court, were to come under discussion.

Judge Boeckman knew that jurors in a capital punishment case were under extreme pressures outside the normal routines of their lives. For many of them the whole experience was not only disruptive but very stressful as well. He did everything he could to explain the process and lay down the ground rules in the most understandable terms possible. He addressed the prospective jurors with sympathy for those concerns in a conversational tone. He knew that to explain things clearly would go a long way toward ensuring a fair trial in a case that was certain to be a marathon affair.

In his capital-trial initial orientation Judge Boeckman said, "Good morning, ladies and gentlemen.

You have been summoned as prospective jurors for the case of the *People of the State of California* versus *Todd Jesse Garton.* The district attorney has accused Mr. Garton of first-degree murder with special circumstances, and is seeking the death penalty. The defendant has pleaded not guilty, and is presumed by law to be innocent unless and until the prosecution proves his guilt beyond a reasonable doubt.

"I want you to have some idea of the nature of the proceedings in which you will be participating should you be selected as a juror. Defendant Garton is accused of a capital crime, which means a crime for which capital punishment, or the death penalty, is sought by the prosecution. Because of the fact that a capital crime is charged in this case, there may be separate phases to the trial proceedings. If the jury were to find the defendant guilty beyond a reasonable doubt of first-degree murder in the first phase and find a special circumstance which is charged to be true, there would follow a second phase or trial regarding appropriate penalty to be imposed. In this type of case the jury makes that decision. Choices, under the circumstances I have outlined, would be between the imposition of the penalty of death or a sentence of life imprisonment without the possibility of parole.

"Mr. Garton has entered a plea of not guilty to all charges against him, and he has denied the truth of all special allegations and circumstances alleged in the information. Mr. Garton is presumed innocent until the contrary is proved beyond a reasonable doubt. The trial of this action will require a considerable amount of time. Jury selection will take several weeks. The trial will begin with evidence on approximately Wednesday, October 4, 2000. We will generally be in session Tuesday, Wednesday, Thursday and Friday from nine A.M. to noon and from one-thirty to four-thirty in the afternoon.

"During the time you serve on this jury, there may appear in the newspaper, or on radio or television, reports concerning this case. I do not know if such coverage will occur, but because of this possibility, you are prohibited by order of this court from reading any newspaper articles and from watching or listening to any news program on television or radio concerning this case until you are excused from service on this trial."

Judge Boeckman may have looked forward to smooth sailing from that point on, but Lynn Noyes was about to disrupt all these well-laid-out plans by her actions in September. On September 18, 2000, she suddenly requested to speak with Greg Gaul, Detective Steve Grashoff and Sergeant Mark Von-Rader. Once they were together, she told them, "I haven't been truthful about some things. I had been in denial about a lot of what happened and I wanted to be a little more forthcoming. It was tragic. Very overwhelming just dealing with it. On a personal level I had a hard time going back through it all."

This threw a monkey wrench into the time schedule laid out for trial. But it was nothing compared to her next move. She attempted to withdraw her plea agreement with the district attorney's office. Lynn obtained the services of another attorney named Sharpe and sought to change portions of the plea agreement. Incredibly, for over a year she had not taken the time to read the agreement fully.

When she finally did, she was astounded that she had agreed to a charge of first-degree murder against Carole Garton. Lynn said, "One of the counts in my deal was a stipulation that I had to plead guilty to murder one. And I wasn't guilty of murder one. I thought I was only guilty of conspiracy. The paperwork is so long. I reread it and thought, 'Wow, I'm not guilty of murder one!'"

Because of this sudden change of heart, the news of her change of plea passed on to Todd Garton's attorney, Russell Swartz, and through him to Todd Garton. It precipitated a very unusual letter to Lynn while she was in jail. A letter that was supposedly written by a person named "Gabriel Michaels," but the letter had all the earmarks and style of having been written by Todd Garton. The return address was to Russell Swartz's office, even though he had nothing to do with the writing of the letter. The worst part of this, as far as Lynn was concerned, was that the letter seemed to be threatening not only her, but her family as well. In a panic she turned the letter over to Greg Gaul.

The letter began: *Dear Lynn, Malichi, My Angel. Straight to the point. Your love is not lost. No, your love is renewed. Do not hold fascination as to their ship of fools but look to those who have always held the faith.*

It went on to say that bad things had been said about her and that stones had been cast against her because she was playing in a den of snakes (the prosecutors and her own attorney, Frank O'Connor). He mentioned how the Bible said to take up the snakes, Mark 16:18: *They will pick up snakes in their hands, and if they drink any deadly thing, it will not hurt them; they will lay their hands on the sick, and they will recover.*

But the letter warned that this was only a parable. It warned her that a snake would bite her. She would not recover. She would suffer a life in prison: *Look what Frank O* [her former attorney, Frank O'Connor] *has done for you. Look at promises made by your friend Gregie* [Gaul], *Steven* [Grashoff] *and Marky* [VonRader]. *Now towards the end as you face the abyss, and see your life ending, the truth slaps you in the face like a cold wet storm. You are alone. None of the people know or feel your pain. You cry out for help and help knocks at that door.*

The letter went on to say that Frank O'Connor, her former attorney, and Deputy DA Greg Gaul were trying to block the door. He compared them both to serpents who only wanted to bite her. The letter said that on the other side of that door were real friends. Friends who wanted to help her. It promised her love and support if she would take it. She was the only one with the key.

The letter went on to explain that Russell Swartz had written Frank O'Connor a letter that he wished to talk to her, but O'Connor said no. The letter contended that O'Connor was not trying to help her because he was trying to keep her in the dark and "screw her." It stated that Gaul and O'Connor were friends and that all O'Connor wanted was the plea agreement to stay in place because he was afraid of Gaul.

But now, the letter contended, she had a new lawyer who should reach out to Russell Swartz. It said, *Tell Sharpe, you want to give a statement of fact to Swartz. This is your key.* It then asked why her old lawyer, a serpent, proclaimed to want to help her when he wouldn't even reach out his hand to Swartz. It even alleged she had sat down with Greg Gaul without her lawyer present. Was that watching out for her interests? it asked.

The letter stated she had friends, friends who believed that women and children came first. It stated she had a choice: jump into the abyss with Greg Gaul's connivance, or cross toward the light and help Todd. *Do not let the snakes coil and pull you over the side,* it implored.

The letter told her to watch the mail. That love came in many forms. It promised her a concordance of the Bible and other things that were on the way. It also promised that the friends of Todd Garton would help her get back to her children. At the end it said, *If you do not respond in a week to Swartz by letter, then this is farewell, Malichi, and be lost with the others, banished to eternal darkness.*

The letter told her to read Revelation 12:9 and Jude 1:6 in the Bible.

Revelation 12:9 states, *The great dragon was thrown down, that ancient serpent who is called the Devil and Satan, the deceiver of the whole world—he was thrown down to the earth and his angels were thrown down with him.*

Jude 1:6 states, *And the angels who did not keep their own position, but left their proper dwelling, He has kept in eternal chains in deepest darkness for the judgment of the great day.*

Both of these quotes were a warning to his angel Malichi, Lynn Noyes, if she abandoned her proper place in regard to Todd Garton.

Lynn immediately suspected that Todd was the

author of the letter. She said, "Who else would it be? There was nobody else that I could help and save myself by helping him. The term 'Malichi' and 'my angel' were ones he used for me. The reference to friends and help and wanting the truth to come out. Friends meant to me, people who supported Todd. He had mentioned friends and family in connection with The Company. It was alarming because it mentioned my family."

Afraid that The Company might really exist, and what they might do to her children, Lynn Noyes showed this letter to Greg Gaul. She also sent a short note to Russell Swartz, only a couple of lines. She recalled, "I said that I'd become aware through another party that I should speak with him. I didn't say I would talk to him. I said I would meet with him. And I think that was pretty much it. Because I believed, from the letter I received—it caused me great concern that people that knew my family, and my children especially, would harm them. I wasn't in a position where I could do anything for them except pray for them. I took all of this as a threat."

Russell Swartz had nothing to do with his client perpetrating this new threat toward Lynn Noyes. But that the letter must have come from Todd was highlighted by another letter that apparently came from him soon thereafter. It had a return address of 124 Judith Lane. As Lynn explained, this was a code for Jude 1:24 in the Bible.

Jude 1:24 said. *Now to Him who is able to keep you from falling, and to make you stand without blemish in the presence of His glory with rejoicing*. Whether Todd Garton viewed himself as the "glorious one" is not clear.

Todd wasn't the only one sending letters to Lynn Noyes during her incarceration. Letters that were just as bizarre arrived to her from Dale Gordon. Dale was slowly breaking down mentally from the stress of imprisonment. He wrote to Lynn about getting revenge against Todd Garton, the man he blamed for ruining his life. He wrote, *If he hadn't done what he did to Carole, I wouldn't be sitting here.*

Dale said, "Me and Lynn became good friends in jail. She's a Christian. A good Christian. We wrote Bible verses together. I talked about how much I hated Todd. She told me I needed to forgive him."

But then Dale admitted, "I am a terrible Christian."

Dale was having such severe bouts of depression and anxiety that he had to go on medication while in jail. He even said, "For a while I was insane. I was going through a lot of terrible things. I was seeing visions. Hearing voices. I was in the safety cell on two different occasions. A week at a time. I was out of my mind. I was being attacked by the Devil. And God came into the picture. Somebody else in the pod cast spells on me. Sorcery. It's in the Bible." Dale Gordon believed the man behind the sorcery was Todd Garton. He compared him to pure evil.

Sitting behind bars himself, Norman Daniels couldn't have agreed more. Todd Garton had helped him destroy his own life. He wasn't as psychotic as Dale Gordon, but he struggled through profound bouts of depression. He knew his life of freedom was essentially over. The one last weapon he had was to bring Todd Garton down with him. Todd hid behind the defense that all the others had somehow managed to cook up these schemes without his knowledge or approval. If Daniels had his way, he would tell at Garton's trial just how implicated he was in the entire scheme.

With Lynn Noyes's turnaround, followed by its quick reversal, the trial date was off track now. And Russell Swartz asked for an extension of time. On November 14, 2000, he explained to Judge Boeckman that 40 percent of all the discovery he had received had arrived within the last month. This totaled over three thousand pages. Eight hundred pages alone had arrived during the jury-selection process. Swartz said, "The defendant would advise the court that we have been making a diligent effort to process and absorb this additional discovery, but as of this date have not been effectively able to do so. Much of the new discovery is in the form of handwritten letters and the documents are very hard to read and interpret. Since much of this comes from one of the principal witnesses against the defendant and provides important insights into his thinking, it is important that it be carefully analyzed."

Swartz noted that all this new discovery had changed his defense strategy significantly. He had an investigator working extended hours following up on issues created by the new discovery.

Chapter 14

The Main Event

On December 5, 2000, opening arguments finally resonated in Judge Bradley Boeckman's courtroom in the trial of Todd Garton. The courthouse sat on a rise in the city of Redding, facing towering snow-covered Mount Shasta in the distance. If Norman Daniels and Todd Garton had a pair of binoculars, they easily could have seen where their fateful meeting had begun at Shasta Community College.

Senior Deputy DA Greg Gaul portrayed Todd as an evil mastermind who manipulated his friends in the murder of Carole Garton and the attempted murder of Dean Noyes. Gaul then played the phone call in which Norman Daniels called Todd Garton from jail and the investigators listened in. Greg pointed out that Garton didn't seem shocked or angry that Daniels said that he'd just killed his wife. Instead, he seemed angry that Daniels had confessed. Garton exclaimed to Daniels, "So, you said you did it? I just went to the wall for you with the *Record Searchlight*. I can't believe you did that, man!"

At that point Garton offered to help Daniels in his defense and promised help from "the big boys." Gaul told the jury that "Todd Garton convinced Norman Daniels he was part of the organization which he called The Company."

Gaul then went into all the manipulations Todd had perpetrated with Daniels, Gordon and Lynn Noyes in the implementation of his schemes. He explained that even though Norman Daniels pulled the trigger on the gun that killed Carole Garton, it was Todd Garton who directed where to aim those shots.

Russell Swartz, on the other hand, had a very different take on what occurred during the months prior to May 16, 1998. He portrayed Todd Garton as the unwitting victim of all the others' conspiracy plans. Russell depicted Dale Gordon as someone clearly not in touch with reality, who loved guns, role-playing games and violence. He portrayed Lynn Noyes as a woman scorned by Todd, who would do anything to get him back. And he depicted Norman Daniels as a man used as a pawn by Lynn Noyes to get rid of Carole Garton. Daniels's e-mails to Lynn proved that he was in thrall of Lynn Noyes. He would do anything Lynn told him to do. Swartz portrayed him as a lovesick flunky.

Opening arguments are one thing, and memorable to the jurors, but the nuts and bolts of a trial are often conducted outside the hearing of jurors. And the Todd Garton case was no exception. A trial is like a battle in some respects, and the prosecutor and defense attorney are like generals. But the judge can be seen as a quartermaster who allows the opposing generals to have various weapons on the field of battle. The "weapons" are evidence, and if the judge does not let them have certain evidence on the field, it can hamper the "general" in his plan of attack. These behind-the-scenes legal battles were in some respects just as interesting and volatile as anything the jurors ever heard or saw.

One of these contests came very early in the proceedings. It concerned the two investigators, Detective Steve Grashoff and Sergeant Mark Von-Rader. Russell Swartz noticed that these two were able to pass right by the security check point at the entrance of the court, while he and all the jurors waited in line to empty their pockets. Swartz met with Judge Boeckman, along with James Pearce, his co-counsel, and Greg Gaul as well.

Swartz—I do have a very legitimate objection. When we go through that line and those jurors queued up, I think it is inappropriate for them to see the people on defense table having to unload our pockets, go through the searches, while the two officers simply flash their badges and walk on through. It shows some level of trust on that side of the courtroom that is not being accorded to us. I think those gentlemen, Mr. VonRader and Mr. Grashoff—they should go through the same procedure that we go through.

Gaul—Well, I just want to say that I have to go through the same process. I have to empty my pockets. I understand what Mr. Swartz is saying. But this side of the table hasn't got carte blanche just to walk through.

Pearce—It does present an inappropriate appearance of credibility to the officers being allowed to pass through without a proper search.

Boeckman—Interesting argument, Counsel. First time it's come up. I'm going to take it under advisement.

The next day Judge Boeckman told Swartz and Pearce, "Here's my sense of it. The purpose of weapon screening is primarily to screen for weapons. When peace officers who are on duty come into the courtroom, the weapons-screening staff assume that they have weapons and they are permitted by law to have them. So there is no point in having them go through the weapon-screening process. I don't see any prejudice. I don't think it is likely that any jurors take any kind of improper inference from that."

Detectives Grashoff and VonRader took the stand and laid out everything that they had found linking Todd Garton to the crime. "Computer cop" Jim Arnold did as well, going into detail about the messages on Todd's computer that were aligned with Company T and the conspiracy. Garton seemed to be deeply implicated in this because of his numerous messages not only to Norman Daniels but to Lynn Noyes, too.

Jurors were shown graphic autopsy photos projected onto a six-foot screen while Dr. Susan Comfort, Shasta County pathologist, explained the various wounds. In one photo red flecks, gunpowder burns, surrounded a bullet hole in Carole Garton's cheek, evidence she was shot at close range. A photo of one black eye portrayed the fact that a bullet fired at the back of her head had penetrated through her head and came to rest behind the eye socket. She was also shot once more in the head, in the chest and in the buttocks.

On viewing these photos, Todd Garton acted as if he were sick and leaned over to vomit into a trash can. Some of those who saw it were sure he was acting. They said it looked more like someone trying to dry heave than actual vomiting. But defense lawyer Russell Swartz said later, "I'm having to talk to him and divert him all the time. His hands are always shaking."

Greg Gaul's first main witness from the trio of co-conspirators was Norman Daniels. On December 8, 2000, he sat down for a long and grueling round of testimony. At least in Daniels, Gaul had an eager and articulate witness. Dressed in a blue jail-issued jumpsuit and ankle shackles, Daniels began his testimony with no deal in place from the DA's office. In fact, he was still looking at the death penalty for his own actions in the murder of Carole Garton. Only Norman Daniels knew for sure why he was doing this high-wire act without a net.

Gaul—Why are you in custody?
Daniels—I'm being accused of first-degree murder, of lying in wait. Monetary gain. Double murder. Use of a firearm in the commission of a homicide.
Gaul—Since you are in custody, I assume that you have an attorney?

Daniels—Yes, sir.

Gaul—And who is that attorney?

Daniels—Richard Maxion.

Gaul—At this time have you pled guilty to any charges against you?

Daniels—No, sir. I have entered a plea of not guilty.

Gaul—All right. And are you prepared to proceed to testify without your attorney being present here in court?

Daniels—Yes, sir.

Gaul—Do you understand that what you say in this courtroom, and in this trial, could be used against you in some future prosecution?

Daniels—Yes, I do.

In a clear voice Norman Daniels answered all of Greg Gaul's questions that dealt with first meeting Todd Garton at Shasta College in 1993 and Garton's claims of being in the IRA, a marine and a DEA sniper, plus being an assassin for The Company. He also told of receiving the package from Todd Garton's hands with instructions to kill Carole Garton. Daniels told how he had saved the wax seal from the package, a seal that bore the imprint of Todd Garton's Navy SEAL pin. Daniels then uttered the phrase "I'm a trusting person. For example, if you told me you had a million dollars in the bank, I wouldn't ask for your bank statement. It's a fault, I guess."

Gaul asked Norman Daniels how he felt when he realized that the person in the photo with her head circled was Carole Garton. Daniels replied, "Terrible."

Gaul then asked, "But you were still going through with this?"

Daniels answered, "I felt I was in a corner. Because of the documents stating that if I didn't complete my mission, that I could end up dead."

He told of being constantly in fear for his life and the threats hanging over his son. He constantly asked The Company for help and they gave him none. Rather, each new request was answered by a response to accomplish his mission or become a "liability."

During a break from the courtroom proceedings, both Greg Gaul and Russell Swartz were quoted by a reporter for the *Record Searchlight* outside the court, and it caused discomfort for both of them the next day. To stave off any implications of impropriety, they both had a meeting with Judge Boeckman.

Gaul—There was an article in the newspaper this morning that both Mr. Swartz and I are quoted, so I'll hit on it. The article quotes me as saying in reference to Norman Daniels—it says that I said, "I think he wants to tell the truth." Says that I said that outside the courtroom. And I probably did say that. I don't have any reason to disbelieve the reporter, although she wasn't taking notes. But she was hounding me all the way down the stairs, asking me all kinds of questions about whether Norman Daniels had some kind of deal to testify. What's he getting out of this? Has he pled? And I kept saying, "No, no, I can't talk to you." And finally I just, out of frustration, said to her, "I think he just wants to tell the truth." Something like that. And again told her I really couldn't talk to her. So she again called me at my office later; she was asking questions about the testimony and I said I'm not going to talk to you about the testimony. And generally my policy is when I'm in trial on any case, I will talk about procedural matters, but I will not talk about testimony or witnesses. And Mr. Swartz has to take a hit, too. I'm a little concerned about his quotes in the paper. He stated, regarding Mr. Daniels, "He's a sleazy, little, lying murderer. We noted the friendship ended when he unloaded five rounds into his friend's wife." The Holman family and Griffiths family have not talked to the press. Even though I'm sure the press has been trying to get statements from them.

Boeckman—Do we have any reason to believe that Mr. Garton's family is conducting themselves any differently than the victim's family in terms of avoiding talking to the press?

Gaul—Yes. Mrs. Garton, Patricia Garton—well, there was a news reporter filming her. And Mrs. Garton was stating that I made several errors in my opening statement. I think she made a comment about her son's innocence and a comment about what a great daughter-in-law Carole Garton was.

Swartz—I was misquoted [in the newspaper]. I did not use the word "sleazy." "Sniveling," I think, was the appropriate word. Sounded like she [the reporter] weaves some statements in with her own observations.

Boeckman—Well, Mr. Gaul is not asking for a

gag order, or any other kind of order. He's asking, I think, for the exercise of discretion on what's said to reporters on the off chance some juror may inadvertently see something in the paper. And I think that's appropriate.

With all of that out of the way, Norman Daniels continued testimony, which was very emotional and potent. He spoke of how he felt more and more ensnared by The Company, and that if he didn't act, either he or his son would be killed. It did become a matter of kill or be killed in his mind. He told of how Todd Garton bought the murder weapon at Jones Fort and of Garton's continued insistence that Daniels kill Carole or he would bring the wrath of Colonel Sean down on all of them.

When Daniels told of the actual murder, he was shaking and crying on the stand.

Gaul—Did you make a decision that you were going to shoot her?

Daniels—Yes, I did.

Gaul—Tell me what happened.

Daniels—I said, "Now or never" in my mind. As I was talking to her about Jack the dog, I was contemplating on what I was about to do. And I thought about my son. I thought about my life and family, and I said, "You know. I've got to do this or I've got to die." Because I really seriously thought I was a dead man. So I did it.

Gaul—What's the first thing you did?

Daniels—I turned around and at that point I knew that I could get to the pistol without her knowledge. It was in my hand. I turned and I fired at her.

Gaul—Okay. Where did you shoot first?

Daniels—I shot her in the head.

Gaul—Do you remember what part of the head?

Daniels—I thought I hit her above the left eye.

Gaul—Was she looking at you?

Daniels—Yes, sir.

Gaul—When you fired the first shot, what did she do?

Daniels—She covered her face.

Gaul—With what?

Daniels—Both of her hands. She crossed her hands over her face.

Gaul—Then what did you do? Just tell me what happened next.

Daniels—She was still moving. I didn't want her to suffer. So I continued to fire. I shot at her torso. I was aiming for the heart. As she was on the ground, I fired at her head again and then I shot at her torso. And then the fifth shot at her head. I even cocked the pistol again and re-aimed to make sure she was dead.

Gaul—So you pulled the trigger a sixth time?

Daniels—Yes, sir.

Gaul—What was going through your mind when you were doing that?

Daniels—I wasn't thinking. I can't explain.

By the time Norman Daniels was through with this portion of testimony, he was shaking and sobbing. So were Carole Garton's friends and family members in the courtroom.

In another section of the testimony, concerning the attempt on the life of Dean Noyes, Greg Gaul and Norman Daniels got tangled up in semantics and confused. In trying to extract themselves from this, Greg Gaul became amused and laughed. He then said, "I'm sorry, I don't mean to be laughing."

As soon as Gaul said this, Todd Garton yelled from the defense table, "He's just a murderer! Why don't you go ahead and laugh!"

There was a moment of stunned silence in the courtroom before Judge Boeckman brought his gavel down and signaled, "Order in the courtroom."

He then said, "Mr. Garton, this is not the time for you to speak. Don't speak again."

After this outburst, while the jury was out of hearing, Judge Boeckman addressed the counselors and Todd Garton. "Mr. Garton, it's not going to work for you to speak out in these circumstances again. When you get to speak, sir, if you choose to and only then, is when you take the witness stand and are subject to cross-examination. And I don't want to have to make any comments to you to cause you not to behave like that in front of the jury. So that's why I'm addressing you in this way now. I want you to exercise self-control. Understood?"

Russell Swartz spoke for Todd. He said, "Mr. Garton asked me before the break to apologize."

Judge Boeckman replied, "That's fine. Frankly, one of the reasons I'm saying what I am, Mr. Garton, is making it clear on the record that you've been warned."

After Todd's outburst, it was time for the defense's turn to cross-examine Norman Daniels.

And they did so by trying to portray him to the jury as a liar who was under the spell of Lynn Noyes. That was the reason he attempted to kill Dean Noyes. And it was the reason he actually killed Carole Garton. Lynn wanted her murdered, and Norman Daniels was like a lovesick puppy dog, ready to do anything she demanded, including murder.

James Pearce did the actual questioning of Norman Daniels's and he hit on Daniels's initial lying to police during the interviews.

Pearce—Do you recall how many interviews you had with the police?

Daniels—Several.

Pearce—The police would come in and talk to you several times about the evidence in the case, over a period of two years?

Daniels—Yes, sir.

Pearce—So after May of 1998, you never lied about anything to the police?

Daniels—No, sir.

Pearce—Now to your conversations of May 1998, did you tell them about Todd's involvement in these matters?

Daniels—Yes, sir.

Pearce—But you lied in those initial conversations. Was that in relationship to Lynn Noyes?

Daniels—Yes, sir.

Pearce—So, they would ask you a question whether or not Ms. Noyes was involved and you said, "No."

Daniels—Yes, sir.

Pearce tried to make it appear that Norman Daniels was trying to protect the real mastermind behind all the plots—Lynn Noyes. In furtherance of Noyes's schemes, Pearce questioned Daniels about using Todd Garton's computer.

Pearce—So, at some point in time you had written down Todd Garton's Internet password?

Daniels—Yes, sir.

Pearce—If I understand the Internet correctly, you could take one of Mr. Garton's screen names, take his password and get on-line from your home?

Daniels—Yes, sir.

Pearce—In fact, you could get on-line from anywhere you had a computer?

Daniels—No, not necessarily.

Pearce—Okay. Why not necessarily?

Daniels—Because unless you have the AOL software, you could not access AOL.

Pearce—Assuming you had AOL software, you could access Mr. Garton's computer with his secret name and password wherever you were at?

Daniels—Yes, sir.

Judge Boeckman later asked Pearce where he was going with all this. Pearce answered, "This individual [Daniels] can and, in fact, does have enough expertise in the operation of computers that he can go in and create accounts, use other people's passwords to get on the Internet and re-forward messages back and forth without too much difficulty. A majority of all information, outside of what this witness claims, is direct conversations with Mr. Garton via the Internet. And a person's ability to use the Internet is going to be highly critical in this case.

"I would indicate to the court, at least in jailhouse interviews, Mr. Daniels believed himself to be somewhat of a computer expert. I also believe that eventually in testimony, it was Mr. Daniels who established the AOL Internet accounts at Mr. Garton's house profusely during the course of events. E-mail messages that are attributed to Mr. Garton. We already know that he has Mr. Garton's password at his house. This individual's expertise, along with a co-conspirator's, has a tremendous amount to do with the amount of guilt or innocence in this case."

Soon after this discussion with the judge, Pearce asked Daniels about why he saved the gun. It was an act so flagrant that Pearce wondered if Daniels had done it to try and build an insanity plea if he ever got caught. It would seem that no sane person would keep the gun around his house in plain sight.

Pearce—Why did you save the gun?
Daniels—After I committed the murder, I really just didn't feel like trying to pick up anything. I had done something terrible, despicable, and I was not happy with myself. Otherwise, I would have done differently.
Pearce—But if my memory is correct, you went home and cleaned the gun after the murder?
Daniels—Yes, sir.
Pearce—And the purpose of cleaning the gun was what?

Daniels—I don't know, Mr. Pearce. I was not in my right mind.

Pearce—The fact that you were not in your right mind, did that occur to you after you had read the documents on temporary insanity, duress and coercion?

Daniels—No, sir.

Pearce—So, you weren't thinking about preserving evidence when you were cleaning your gun?

Daniels—I wasn't thinking of anything.

Pearce—Then why . . ."

Daniels—Other than to get drunk, get out of my house.

Pearce—Outside of the fact that you had just put five shots into Mrs. Garton, were you thinking about anything else besides going out, eating and getting drunk, when you were cleaning the gun?

Daniels—The action of putting five bullets in Mrs. Garton was going over and over in my head continually. I did not have any conscious effort of trying to pick up my mess.

The next high-profile witness in the trial was Lynn Noyes. Dressed in a dowdy jail jumpsuit, she hardly looked like a temptress who could incite men to murder. Greg Gaul took Noyes through all the different details of her connection with the plot to kill Dean Noyes. And once again the jury was able to hear only what was placed upon the field of testimony. Other factors were debated outside of their hearing and decided in what direction the trial would go. The rules of law were the conduit of the "truth," but unlike concrete walls, these conduits were always fluid and open to interpretation.

Much of Todd Garton's trial depended on the admission of e-mails as corroborating proof to witnesses' statements. And Greg Gaul argued that the pager Todd Garton had given Lynn Noyes was just as important. Some of the messages related to The Company. Others related to her code names, such as Josephine. Greg Gaul told Judge Boeckman, "What I'm trying to show is more than just a friendship between these two. It's a much greater relationship."

Judge Boeckman answered, "Okay. Is it your belief when she looks at the message, her memory will be refreshed and she will be able to say that this document reflects messages that she sent to the defendant?"

Russell Swartz jumped in and said, "Your Honor, this is a charade. I think everybody knows it. What she's doing—she's been shown the message outside of court. She's going to be shown the message again. She's simply going to say, 'Yeah, that's right.' This is two years ago she saw the messages. We don't know if they were recorded by Mr. Garton or not. I submit it's not appropriate."

Boeckman—Do the documents reflect any messages sent by her?
Swartz—No.
Gaul—No, because they are just messages transmitted to his pager. He either calls her back or doesn't.
Boeckman—But this document wouldn't show whether he called her back or not, would it?

Gaul—No. But I don't believe that's relevant. It's also in these documents where Norman Daniels indicated, "All done. Going home." There is a reference to the flight to come to Redding for the memorial ceremony. And where they were talking in circles because the defendant was concerned that his phone was tapped. All I can do is show her the records, and have her explain why did you send that message. What was the meaning behind it. And some of the messages have enough specific relevance, either to the conspiracy or the relationship with Todd Garton—that's all I'm trying to show.

Boeckman—Okay. It seems to me, the ones that are sent by this witness, that they are admissible as far as hearsay exception under 1223.

Swartz—She did not put this in the machine. The procedure was that she would call a telephone number, say something that someone else would put in the computer.

Gaul—The company that has the records can't do that. Their purpose is to receive these calls and transmit them to the person that's being requested.

Boeckman—Then I think you can have her testify to statements she made in furtherance of the conspiracy, which she transmitted or tried to transmit by way of calling the pager number. That's her direct testimony . . . In other words, she can't be shown a document and say, "See this? Is that the message you sent?" Because then she's just reading the document that's coming into evidence without any other foundation than from the custodian of the records.

Swartz—Your Honor, I'm sorry. It's a scam. They have shown her documents outside of the court. She is going to be given the documents. She is going to state she can't remember them. Then they will show her the document and she reads it off.

Boeckman—Well, I understand that's your position, Counsel. I don't agree. I think the law permits Mr. Gaul to do what he says he's going to do. With the understanding, Mr. Gaul, you need to exhaust present recollection before you even show this document. And then only show a redacted portion.

After this exchange Judge Boeckman made an interesting remark about this case in general. He said, "The extent I seem critical of you attorneys, I don't mean to be. These are pretty unique evidentiary issues. It's not the kind of thing you guys see everyday. It's certainly not the kind of thing I see every day."

One such point of unique evidence was when Lynn Noyes had her screen name's profile changed by Todd Garton. Greg Gaul wanted it into evidence, and Russell Swartz argued there was no relevance. But Gaul argued, "It shows that he doesn't have any problem accessing profiles, moving around in the computer, manipulating things that other people have done. And manipulating people. It's all a control thing to him. I mean, that's Todd Garton."

These arguments over evidence even came down to photographs and tattoos. Greg Gaul said about one of Lynn Noyes's tattoos, "I believe she would testify that she wanted to add the words 'But not the same,' [to her tattoo that declared 'One']. It would go along with the song 'One' by U2. And it would also go along with the defendant's tattoo which says, 'One but not the same.' Just another way to show this connection. This strong connection between the defendant and Miss Noyes."

Swartz argued back: "Your Honor, what this witness in her mind intended to do at some future date is not part of a conspiracy. It has no relevance to anything that is before the court in this trial."

And then the topic came up about the life insurance policy she had taken out on Dean Noyes, just before she was arrested. Greg Gaul wanted this admitted into evidence to show that Lynn Noyes had plans to use it and be with Todd Garton after Dean was dead. He said it was a very strong indicator about how far she was willing to go to be with him.

Gaul—The relevance is that if Dean was killed, she would share that money, or commingle it, with Todd Garton if they got together at some point after the murder.

Swartz—Her intention in this case is irrelevant.

Gaul—I think her intent is relevant, because she's one of the co-conspirators. She's going to testify at some point that the defendant was attempting to help her move to Shasta County after Carole was murdered.

Boeckman—Well, it would be relevant if you

were prosecuting Ms. Noyes. Whether it is relevant to Mr. Garton, I think would relate
whether or not he was aware of what her intentions were.

Gaul—I believe he was. I believe her testimony
will be he wanted some money for killing Dean
Noyes. Like maybe a husband and wife who
would share the money. I suppose I could go
the opposite way and ask her what knowledge,
if any, the defendant had of that money. Maybe
that would be a better way to approach it.

Greg Gaul questioned Lynn Noyes extensively
about *The Anarchist Cookbook*, which she had kept
for Todd Garton. And in his questioning he
proved more and more how romantically tied to
Todd Garton, Lynn Noyes was. But in some ways it
was a double-edged sword. He showed how she
might have become tied to the conspiracy, but it
also gave the defense ammunition to show how
obsessed and unbalanced Lynn was when it came
to Todd and how she could have cooked up schemes
and murderous plots without his knowledge. Everything that Greg Gaul presented as evidence, and
everything Lynn Noyes said, could be approached
from a different angle on redirect.

Everything in a trial of this magnitude is a potential
train wreck waiting to happen, and even the most trivial incident, if construed the wrong way, can lead to a
mistrial. Such an incident occurred on January 3,
2001. While Greg Gaul was in a courthouse rest
room, a juror spoke to him. This was strictly off limits.

Gaul reported it to Judge Boeckman and said,

"When I went down to the rest room during the break, one of the jurors came in and said to me, 'Did you have a nice Christmas?' And I said, 'I can't talk to you, sorry.' I would request you advise all the jurors that counsel cannot talk to them. We can't even acknowledge them. I don't want you to focus on any particular juror or embarrass him."

Judge Boeckman asked Swartz, "Any comment from the defense?"

Swartz replied, "What can I say?"

Judge Boeckman said, "I don't think there's any need to identify the juror. I think it's harmless."

Nonetheless, Judge Boeckman did speak with the jurors when they came back. He did it in a way not to embarrass any specific juror by telling all of them they couldn't speak with any counsel, no matter how trivial the subject. He said, "There was a harmless incident that happened moments ago in the rest room, where one of the jurors came in contact with one of the attorneys and basically said, 'Did you have a nice Christmas?' That's harmless, but it reminds me to remind you folks that that kind of conversation has to be avoided because if somebody else were to see such a conversation and not be able to hear it, they might jump to the wrong conclusion that it's an inappropriate communication. And so, out of an abundance of caution, let me remind you jurors that you cannot talk, even so much as to pass pleasantries of the day or anything of that nature, with these attorneys or parties or witnesses. And I know that's uncomfortable when you're in a close proximity to one of these persons I've named. It's not the natural thing for you to say nothing and to ignore one another. Nonetheless, that's what you must do."

But incidents kept arising in the case and had to be addressed with an "overabundance of caution," as Judge Boeckman pointed out. Greg Gaul brought to his attention that Ellie Smith, a reporter for KRCR-TV, had told him that Todd Garton wanted to be interviewed by her. Not knowing what was legal, she went to Gaul with Garton's request.

Gaul told Judge Boeckman, "Obviously, I have concerns about that, if he starts talking about the case. She didn't know what to do. She didn't want to do anything that might cause problems for the case. So I told her I would bring it to your attention. I'm concerned about anybody in the case in any way talking about the facts, or their feelings about the case. I have no idea what Mr. Garton wanted to do. I can only surmise it."

Boeckman—Mr. Pearce. Mr. Swartz. Any response?
Swartz—I'm thinking about something over steak and wine. No response, Your Honor.
Boeckman—Well, I think I need to do something other than just silence from the defense. Do you have any knowledge one way or the other, Mr. Swartz, about whether this occurred?
Swartz—Personal knowledge? No. But there wouldn't be any violation of any rules.
Boeckman—Not that I'm aware of.
Swartz—My client has contemplated talking to various people in the media. This wouldn't cause any problems because jurors aren't going to read or watch it anyway.

Gaul—Regardless of whether the jurors are going to read it, or intend to read it, or listen to it, accidents happen. And I'm doing my best not to do anything that would prejudice anybody in this case.

Boeckman—Well, as you know, Mr. Gaul, I just give wings to my imagination here in terms of what I can and cannot do in terms of restraining parties from doing various things. I need some authority to suggest that I have the ability to prevent the defendant from doing that, or prevent the media from publishing the latter.

Gaul—Okay. Well, unfortunately, I don't have time to do that. I'm just bringing it to the court's attention. If Mr. Garton wants to talk to the press, I guess that's his business.

Boeckman—Right. And I'm not an expert in the law of prior restraints, First Amendment rights, and probably not going to become one in the next hour or two. So, I think members of the media have to use their good judgment. I'm generally not in favor of gag orders of any type.

With that said, Judge Boeckman once again instructed the jurors not to read newspapers, listen to the radio or watch television when there might be any accounts of the ongoing trial. And the trial did go forward with questions to Lynn Noyes about her relationship with Todd Garton over the years, her discontent with Dean Noyes and the elaborate plans to have Dean killed. Greg Gaul even asked how her children and parents were supposed to be protected when Lynn Noyes went to the hospital with Dean while Todd, Norman and Dale were all up in Gresham with guns. Her answer that he would know she and Dean were gone, because the Bronco was gone, was flimsy at best.

Gaul also asked her about all of her communications with Todd Garton and Norman Daniels via e-mails, pagers and telephone. Her responses were pretty much in line with what Norman Daniels had said. Greg Gaul was happy with her testimony for the most part.

But there was always something that could throw the trial off track. And it happened in another trivial way, which could have been devastating if it had gone on too long, undetected. Judge Boeckman happened to look over toward the jurors and noticed that one of them, Juror #5, had her eyes closed. It appeared to him that she was sleeping. Just how long she had been sleeping was anyone's guess. Judge Boeckman called a recess. If this had been a pattern with Juror #5, there would be big problems.

With all of the other jurors out of the courtroom, Judge Boeckman asked Juror #5 to stay in the courtroom along with Gaul, Swartz and Pearce. Then he said, "I'm not trying to dehumanize you by not using your name. Hopefully, you will recall the reason we're doing that so the court reporters don't have to work overtime to delete jurors' names from the record. The reason I asked you to remain is because I noted at least on one of the questions and answers asked of this witness in the afternoon session, not too many minutes ago, you appeared to me to be asleep. And I'm not saying that to criticize you.

But I need to find out if you missed much of the testimony and if you have difficulty in staying awake."

Juror #5 responded, "There is, like, about two sentences that I missed. I wasn't actually asleep. My eyes were closed. I wasn't really listening to two of the sentences that were asked. But I remember hearing the response."

Judge Boeckman said, "Okay. You know it's difficult for me, and probably others, to tell the difference when someone simply has their eyes closed and when someone is asleep. It's probably important that you not only be awake, but that you manifest that." Then he told her, "I'm going to ask you to step outside for a moment so I can discuss this with counsel."

When she was gone, Judge Boeckman asked everyone for their opinion.

Russell Swartz said, "I think the court probably handled it as well as it could be handled. And I don't know that there is anything we can do about it at this point."

The others agreed.

With another procedural bullet dodged, Greg Gaul went on with his questioning of Lynn Noyes. And he reached a critical point about the label maker, one of the few physical items that tied Todd Garton to the conspiracy.

Gaul—Have you seen that object before?
Noyes—Yes, I have.
Gaul—What is that object?
Noyes—It's that little computer thing that Todd had retrieved out of his residence and threw in the river.

Gaul—Is there anything different in the photograph than when you saw Todd Garton throw it in the river?

Noyes—Yeah.

Gaul—What's the difference?

Noyes—It's waterlogged. It has dirt and sediment in it. A portion of it is missing. The tape isn't in it and it's all banged up.

Then she told of Todd saying to her at the time that if the "little computer thing" was ever found, he would go to prison for a long time.

On cross-examination Russell Swartz pounded away on Lynn Noyes's credibility. And he got to a point where he wanted to get his own evidence in just as much as Greg Gaul had sought to have his introduced. Much of this evidence had to do with Lynn Noyes's sex life, and one of the areas of contention boiled down to her tattoo. Greg Gaul had tried linking it to Todd Garton, but Swartz had a whole new angle. It concerned the tattoo and how Lynn Noyes controlled people, including her lesbian lover, Natalya .

Swartz—Your Honor, it's our contention that this lady [Lynn Noyes] is controlling people. She's controlling Todd; she's controlling Norm Daniels; she's controlling her husband by using sex. It's a common element from the time she starts the relationship with Todd Garton to everybody she's had contact with and that she strings them along. She gets them to do what she wants them to do by the use of sexual favors, sexual contact, innuendos—and the same thing happens with Natalya. She's [Lynn's] admitted she's engaged in a homosexual relationship with Natalya and the evidence is going to show that this is an ongoing relationship and it's going to relate to the tattoo. It's going to relate as well to Natalya's name in a number of communications. She is using her association with this lady and we have a right to explore it.

Gaul—I don't see the relevance. All we have is an assertion of this. I'm not sure that there's any evidence to support it.

Swartz—Support what?

Gaul—Support your claim that she's manipulating people with sex. There is relevance of her relationship with Norman Daniels and others in this case. But not with those parties.

Boeckman—First of all, Natalya has been put in issue and the use of her name. Apparently, Mr. Swartz has a theory. I think the witness's relationship with co-conspirators, her husband, are clearly at issue, including the sexual nature of their relationship. I also hear Mr. Gaul when he says so far that's just your assertion, Counsel. And before I conclude that somebody's alleged homosexual relationship is admissible, I'd want more than just an assertion. In other words, not that she had the relationship, but that she's manipulative and uses sex to manipulate people and that the relationship with Natalya is proof of that.

Swartz—That's why we're bringing it up. They put the issue of her tattoo in. They put in the issue of Natalya. We're going to show the relationship between Natalya and that tattoo and what the tattoo really means—that it's linked to a homosexual relationship."

Gaul—Quite honestly, what I think is they're hoping to assassinate this witness's character because they know that this Natalya isn't willing to come to California and testify. And that we're not going to be able to bring Natalya here and help establish what the true nature of their relationship is and that she would not consider Lynn Noyes to be manipulative. And that's my good-faith belief.

Boeckman—I don't think your offer of proof is complete, Mr. Swartz. Mr. Gaul has his theory about the tattoo. You have yours. But I haven't heard what it is.

Swartz—The yin and yang association of male/female refers to her sexual nature. The tattoo was actually paid for by Natalya. She has previously stated to police officers that she does have this relationship. She had previously stated to police officers that Dean was okay with it. We have the right to argue the implications of that. It shows a whole lot of different meanings to that tattoo than what she's tried to give in direct testimony.

Boeckman—(turning to Greg Gaul) I think what I have to do, Counsel, is your case relies very significantly on circumstantial evidence. And there are inferences you want the jury to take on certain evidence. And I've allowed you to put that evidence in because I think it's probative. The defense is entitled to try and develop theirs. And although I think the court has a duty to avoid inappropriately assassinating the character of any witness, I'm mindful of the fact this witness is not the victim. It's not a case where the defense is trying to taint the victim herself in such a way that jurors think the crime less significant or something of that nature. We have a co-conspirator, a person who's admitted her involvement in a murder. The fact she was engaged in a homosexual relationship, if that's brought out, I don't think is greatly prejudicial to your case. It may be uncomfortable for the witness, but in terms of her credibility, I don't feel the same way that you do about it. What I do feel is that I'm going to permit the evidence.

This contention that Lynn Noyes used sex to manipulate everyone around her became the focal point of Russell Swartz's defense of Todd Garton. He portrayed Lynn Noyes as the mastermind of all the plots of murder. And sex was her weapon. Swartz said, "We're trying to show that this lady is into sex, uses sex to achieve her goals and, specifically in this particular murder, was doing just that, controlling parties. We contend that she may be running the show and she uses her sexual favors because it's part of her basic character. She is very blatant about it in the use of the number sixty-nine. She knows what it means."

This whole sexual side of Lynn Noyes really heated up the debate about admitting evidence between Russell Swartz and Greg Gaul when the topic of her episode of the hot tub came up. Swartz argued, "The testimony of Bill Johnson indicated that he and Todd, Lynn and an unknown female, were together for a sexual rendezvous in a hot tub. And that there was a contemplation of switching partners. More, what we're trying to do is show, and this is only one element of it, that this girl, when she was sixteen years old, fixated on Mr. Todd Garton. We intend to show that she was a groupie. She has maintained this illogical, pathological fixation on Mr. Garton from the age of sixteen, through several relationships, up to and including the murder. That this was the motivation for her involvement in the attempted murder of her husband and murder of Carole Garton. She was the one with motivation for it."

Swartz also brought up the fact that Norman Daniels had become her tool for murder, by his own obsession with her and her manipulating of him by sexual means. He said, "She assumed the name Pandoora sixty-nine. And that is exactly what she is doing with Mr. Daniels in the chat room. It explains the type of relationship she had with Mr. Daniels, which is relevant to why Mr. Daniels did things that he did."

Judge Boeckman finally ruled on all of this by saying, "Counsel, I previously ruled on the source ideas based on the people's theory of this case. From books, movies, et cetera. And I feel comfortable letting the defense do the same thing with Miss Noyes. Keep it within reason, though, Mr. Swartz."

Russell Swartz answered, "I'll try. I'm not getting the same level of active cooperation from this witness as the district attorney did. But I didn't expect that. It will get worse tomorrow."

Worse it did get, when Lynn Noyes said she often couldn't remember certain conversations or evidence. She claimed she had nothing to do with the murder of Carole Garton, but she could only run so far from her involvement in the plot to kill Dean Noyes.

Swartz—Did you want Dean killed?

Noyes—Sometimes yes, sometimes no.

Swartz—On the occasion that you say that an attempt was made to kill Dean, did you help in it?

Gaul—Objection, overbroad and vague.

Boeckman—Sustained.

Swartz—Do you consider yourself a murderer?

Gaul—Objection, it's argumentative.

Boeckman—Sustained.

Swartz—You're a liar, aren't you?

Gaul—Well, I'm going to object. It's argumentative.

Boeckman—Sustained.

Swartz—Since the police first contacted you back in June of 1998, have you lied to them?

Noyes—Yes.

Swartz—Did you lie to Dean?

Noyes—Yes.

Swartz—Did you lie to Todd?

Noyes—Yes.

Swartz—Did you lie to the deputy district attorney Greg Gaul?

Now Lynn Noyes was in tricky territory. If she agreed she had been lying to the DA's office, her plea bargain could be out the window and she could be facing death penalty charges or life in prison.

Noyes—It really kind of narrows down to the date.

Swartz—I'm not asking about time, I mean a reference about a document you signed. At that time had you decided that you were actually going to tell the truth?

Noyes—I can't pinpoint if that was the specific time.

Swartz—Did you lie at all to this jury?

Noyes—No, sir.

Swartz—So, at some time you decided to tell the truth. When was that?

Noyes—Sometime between 1998 to the current time.

In another interesting exchange during her testimony, Lynn Noyes told how she still felt about Todd Garton, even though he was very involved in her present predicament.

Q.—Did you love him?

A.—Yes.

Q.—Do you care for him still?

A.—Yes.

Q.—Why do you still love him?

A.—The Bible says we have to love everyone.

Q.—Do you feel that you are in custody right now and facing prison because of the defendant?

A.—Yes.

Q.—But that doesn't change your feelings about him?

A.—On some levels, yes, it does.

Q.—But not on all levels?

A.—Not on a basic human level.

Q.—Is it hard to testify against him in this case?

A.—It's not easy.

Lynn Noyes was a difficult witness for both sides, but nothing compared to the person up next on the witness stand—Dale Gordon. Gordon was completely agitated like some windup toy out of control. He was initially all right until he looked down from the stand and saw Todd Garton. When asked if he saw the defendant in the courtroom, he grimaced and answered, "I don't really even want to look at him."

Pearce objected by saying, "Nonresponsive."

Gordon growled, "Yes, he's there."

According to the *Record Searchlight* reporter, "When deputy marshals brought Gordon into the courtroom, his hair was rumpled and he had a vacant look. He answered the initial questions calmly. When Deputy District Attorney Greg Gaul asked the witness to identify Garton, Gordon's demeanor immediately changed. His face twitched with anger."

Gordon kept glaring at Todd Garton as he answered Greg Gaul's questions. When the question came up as to what rank Gordon held in the marines, he yelled at Garton, "I was a corporal!" This was an obvious reference to the fact that Todd Garton had lied to him about being a lieutenant in the marines. On the question of Garton's honesty, Gordon said, "Oh, he told all sorts of lies." Then

Dale Gordon responded that he believed him at the time because one marine was not supposed to lie to another.

Gordon talked mainly about the attempt on the life of Dean Noyes rather than the murder of Carole Garton. He testified in detail about the assassination attempt in Oregon and blamed Todd for his present troubles. He clearly said that Todd Garton was the ringleader of the plot and controlled himself, Norm Daniels and Lynn Noyes.

All during the testimony, Dale Gordon's eyes kept shifting back toward Todd Garton sitting at the defense table. Greg Gaul twice told Gordon to look at him and not at the defendant. But angry glares were nothing compared to one of Dale Gordon's responses during cross-examination. Pearce was trying to prove that Gordon had a vendetta against Garton and was lying about him in police documents and in court.

Pearce—You had several meetings with the district attorney in relationship to your testimony?

Gordon—Yes, I have. I have tried to give all the truth and nothing but the truth. I have tried to provide a lot of evidence.

Pearce—You discussed basically how you would testify and what you would testify to?

Gordon—Yes.

Pearce—When you were having visitors at the jail, do you remember having a conversation with Jim Gordon, who is your father, that you testified you had to be a credible witness?

Gordon—Yes.

Pearce—What did you mean "credible witness"?
Gordon—Telling the truth.
Pearce—Did you also indicate to your father that if you came through with your testimony, it could help yourself?
Gordon—Perhaps. I don't remember.
Pearce—Also at one of the visits at the jail, you told your parents that you were going to devastate Mr. Garton in court. Is that correct?
Gordon—Perhaps. I have been very angry.
Pearce—What did you mean by "devastate"?
Gordon—By telling the whole truth and nothing but the truth. But he told a lot of lies. It hurt real bad. I'm telling the whole truth.

And then Dale Gordon turned directly toward Todd Garton and yelled, "I know it hurts, doesn't it, Todd!" As he said this, he gave Garton the finger.

It happened so quickly, everyone was caught by surprise. Nothing was done about it immediately, but it certainly became an issue at the next recess.

Swartz—I just think the record should reflect that during that one portion of the testimony, the witness made a hand sign to Mr. Garton.
Boeckman—I can't articulate exactly what the witness did, Mr. Swartz, because I only saw it out of the corner of my eye. It appeared he raised one hand and made a gesture toward the defense table. That's all I saw.
Swartz—It appeared that he raised one hand with one finger uplifted toward Mr. Garton. What is commonly called "flipping the bird." Giving the finger. A sign of some disrespect.

Gaul—Your Honor, I didn't see it. But Detective Grashoff did. And I would say that Mr.
Swartz has probably characterized it correctly.
Boeckman—I can certainly say that, based on
the tone of voice of the witness at the time he
made the gesture, his manner of speech, it
would not be inconsistent with such a gesture.
So, I think that's the best record that can be
made of it. Again I don't want to admonish
the witness in front of the jury so that it cre-
ates an artificial appearance or attitude on
the part of the witness.

But Judge Boeckman did admonish Dale Gordon
outside the hearing of the jury. He told him to behave himself in court. Judge Boeckman said, "I want
you at all times to keep yourself under control.
You're here to listen to questions and give answers."

Just to make sure that Dale Gordon would keep
himself under control, there were now three deputies and one sergeant from the marshal's office
in the courtroom. It was a wise precaution. Dale
Gordon was so agitated that no one could say what
he might do next, including jumping up from the
witness stand and attacking Todd Garton.

The length and volatile emotions of the trial
were obviously getting to everyone at this point,
and Judge Boeckman had to admonish the counselors also to keep themselves under control. He
said, "Somebody at the defense table, which narrows
it down to one of three, remonstrated in some way
to the court's ruling. I don't need to identify who
it is. I don't appreciate reactions to my rulings. That
includes anyone. Actually, the four of you, because,

Mr. Gaul, you also reacted to one of my rulings regarding something you were trying to get in. You were obviously frustrated, but it's inappropriate. You counsel"—he turned toward Russell Swartz—"and Mr. Garton, need to control yourselves. You don't have to like my rulings, but one way or the other, you're going to have to accept them. I don't want any audible reaction to them. Is that clear?"

Russell Swartz said that he understood, but he also said, "Your Honor, I've never been admonished to maintain a poker face. I will certainly research it."

Judge Boeckman replied, "Let me phrase it another way, Counsel. I don't care what kind of face you make as long as it's not reasonable for a juror to think you're reacting either to the court's ruling or the testimony of a witness. Now, that seems fair to me. If you don't agree and want to do some research, point out errors of this admonition, I'm happy to hear it. In the meantime, I want all of you to adhere to this rule."

Greg Gaul asked, "Does this apply to the defendant? I mean, I hear Todd Garton audibly reacting to things that happen."

Judge Boeckman said, "That's a good question. In this circumstance, if the defendant chooses to react to testimony, I'm going to use a little bit of care before I tell him what to do by way of reaction. I'm not the trier of fact. It could be arguably appropriate for a person who is not guilty to react in some way. And I could hear a prosecutor at the end of the case telling the jury, 'Well, you watched the defendant. He was impassive during all the testimony that he heard at trial. Is that the way an innocent person would react if somebody was on the witness stand lying about him?' So, I feel that if he's not disrupting me or distracting me, I probably should leave it alone."

After this, it was back to the business of listening to Dale Gordon. And he was just as woundup as ever. Pearce tried to have Gordon admit that Norman Daniels was in love with Carole Garton—a love she did not return. And this unrequited love supposedly made Daniels very angry. This line of questioning required a break because of an objection by Greg Gaul. Judge Boeckman asked Pearce, "First of all, the statement that he [Gordon] made to the police is hearsay. And unless it is an exception, then it won't come in."

Pearce replied, "I intend to ask him if he ever thought Norman Daniels had any feelings toward Carole. And if he responds in the affirmative, then I'm going to ask him his impression of those feelings. And intend to go into detail. . . . Could be motive, Your Honor. Norman Daniels is the person that actually killed the victim. It is the district attorney that is alleging the fact there is a conspiracy in this case. Basically, it could be something as simple as Mr. Swartz pointed out, 'If I can't have her, he [Todd] can't, either.'"

Pearce was able to ask some of these questions within limits. And even though Dale Gordon indicated that Norman Daniels liked Carole Garton, he didn't indicate that Daniels loved her romantically.

The testimony of Dale Gordon was a roller-coaster ride for everyone. And even when he got off the witness stand, it didn't mean that this trial would be ordinary by any stretch of the imagination. There were not only debates about witnesses and their testimony among the counsels, there was the debate about the inclusion of movies that jurors would see or not see. These included *Patriot Games, La Femme Nikita, The Professional, The Day of the Jackal* and more. Judge Boeckman had concerns that his courtroom was about to become a version of the neighborhood cineplex.

He asked, "With regards to our venture into the movie *Patriot Games,* where are you going with that, Mr. Gaul?"

Gaul answered, "Well, I think pretty much what I wanted to get from Mr. Daniels in that movie—that the individual worked for the CIA. He's also a retired lieutenant, which is what the defendant's claims were. The main IRA character in there is named Sean. He's a member of Sinn Fein, which is the provisional wing, or the legal wing, of the Irish Republican Army. Later on in the trial, that will become part of the evidence."

Judge Boeckman said, "Let me stop you there before we move on. What is it about the movie that caused you to think that Mr. Garton got the ideas for these names from the movie, as opposed to somewhere else?"

Greg replied, "In that movie, when the main character, Harrison Ford, receives a confidential file on this IRA group—stamped right on the outside of that folder is the name Patriot. It looks strikingly similar to the way the defendant's business card is printed. There is another movie, and that's the movie *Sniper.* Mr. Daniels has seen that movie. He now realizes some of the scenes in that particular movie are strikingly similar to what he claims the defendant made things up about. For example, there is one scene in the movie where there are two snipers. One is a marine sergeant, the other is an individual, I believe, works for the National Security Organization or the CIA. And they are in Panama to kill a reputed drug lord. During the movie these two snipers are standing up in a river area, or pond area, and sleeping while they are standing up. And Mr. Daniels realized that is just what Todd Garton claimed he had done down in South America. Also, they use the term about becoming a 'liability.' That if one of the snipers became a liability, the other one would have to take him out. The movies were in the defendant's house. They tend to connect him to the words and scenes."

Judge Boeckman ruled: "I think that the people are representing Mr. Daniels's realization that Garton's plotlines were very similar to fictional movies that he saw in the defendant's residence is relevant, and I tend to agree."

The movies were in, and the *Record Searchlight* reported: *Harrison Ford made a cameo appearance to jurors in the Todd Garton murder trial.* It also reported that during a court break, Garton quipped, *"Pass the buttered popcorn, please."*

Interestingly enough, both Greg Gaul and James Pearce used the movie *Patriot Games* to bolster their arguments—arguments that were diametrically different in scope. Greg Gaul pointed out to the jury that Garton made numerous references to *Patriot Games* in characters' names and similar scenes. Pearce, on the other hand, said that *Patriot Games* portrayed the Irish Republican Army in a negative light. Outside of the courtroom he told a reporter, "*Patriot Games* is no training film for somebody that's supposed to be an IRA sympathizer." He pointed out that the IRA operatives in the film were the "bad guys."

Another movie shown by Greg Gaul was a home-made video owned by Todd Garton called *Whispering Death*. It was about gun silencers and how to make them. This was pertinent since a homemade silencer found in Gresham, Oregon, was attributed to Todd.

Of the whole movie business in court, Judge Boeckman said, "I looked for every way to avoid them. But I think it's unavoidable." Then he instructed everyone not to make any more jokes about passing the buttered popcorn.

There were other good witnesses for the prosecution, including Collin Colebank, who spoke of Todd's rock days and his ability to "sell a refrigerator to an Eskimo." He also spoke of Lynn Noyes's obsessive behavior with Todd Garton and the way Todd manipulated her. He referred to her as a "bubblehead" whom none of the other band members wanted around. It seemed to him that Garton had strung her along.

Another good witness was Chuck Hawkins, who told of Todd making a fool of himself at the archery shoot and his claims of being a sniper for the U.S. Marines. "Didn't look like a marine sniper to me," he said. "He was about forty pounds overweight."

Hawkins was followed by a videotape of Todd Garton as he talked to investigators on the night of Carole's murder. In it he was caught in one lie after another, lies he had to try and counteract later.

There was everything from the fact that he barely knew Norman Daniels to the fact he never had any kind of relationship with Lynn Noyes.

Finally it was the defense's turn to call witnesses, and their first was none other than Todd Garton. In some ways it was a good choice that he took the stand. He was calm and poised and answered every question put forth to him by Russell Swartz with an easygoing and confident manner. He often looked directly at the jury as he spoke. He even smiled nostalgically while remembering Carole. Todd said, "I felt romantic about her within ten minutes of meeting her. She had short, bobbed hair, expressive green eyes. She was cute. And smart. Articulate. Funny. She had music in her soul. She wrote poetry. She had a lot of talent."

Of course, all of Todd Garton's testimony about what had happened contradicted that of Lynn Noyes, Norman Daniels and Dale Gordon. He said that if there was a conspiracy, it was done behind his back without his knowledge. He had a different answer for everything that the prosecution was accusing him of perpetrating. Of the February trip up to Oregon in 1998 with Dale and Norman, he said he took them along to help him sell camouflage wear. He admitted to meeting with Lynn then, but only to say hello, not to plan any sort of attempt on the life of her husband. And if Dale and Norman did anything in that regard, they did it while he was not with them.

Garton also claimed there was never any package handed to Norman Daniels; he knew nothing about some assassination organization called The Company; the wax impression that Norman Daniels kept could have come from his Navy SEAL pin, but that Norman was inside his house so often, he could have made the wax impression himself. Todd also verified that both Norman and Dale were into violent role-playing games and computer games. They often lived in a fantasy world.

Russell Swartz asked Todd Garton about the evening of May 16, 1998, when he found Carole lying on the floor of their bedroom. "I was so panicked," he answered, "I couldn't tell if she had a weak pulse or it was my own heart beating. When the paramedics told me she was dead, my first question was 'What about the baby?' "

He acted distraught about the death of his child and often choked back tears. When asked about a certain .22 rifle that he had purchased, he grimaced and said, "That was going to be for Jesse."

Todd Garton even managed to dance around the damning phone call that had been placed from the jail by Norman Daniels. The phone call that the investigators taped. Asked why he used the term "big boys" who would help Daniels, Todd said, "That was my father and brother. I called them 'the big boys.' I always have."

Asked to explain about the fact that he offered to give Daniels money, Garton answered, "It referred to the two hundred fifty I owed him for work he did for G and G Fencing."

And asked why he wasn't more angry with Norman Daniels when Daniels said that he had killed Carole out of jealousy, Garton said, "I didn't realize he was admitting to murder at the time. I was still in a state of shock."

A curious thing happened soon thereafter—
just one more incident that seemed to plague the
smooth progress of this trial. Greg Gaul hurt his
back before he was ready to begin the cross-
examination of Todd Garton. Unable to stand, except with a great deal of pain, he was ordered by
his doctor to take off a week.

"I'm not happy about it," Gaul told reporters.
"It's not good timing, but sometimes these things
just happen at the worst of times."

Russell Swartz was sympathetic and said, "We're
all human. Things like this happen and the system
has to accommodate it."

In Gaul's absence, Garton and the jurors got to
watch more movies, including *The Jackal,* with Bruce
Willis, *Pro Sniper* and *Ultimate Sniper.* Todd kept his
mouth shut and didn't ask for buttered popcorn
during these movies.

Finally by February 21, 2001, Greg Gaul was able
to return to court. And it was the moment he'd
been waiting for, a chance to cross-examine Todd
Garton. He pounded away on the fact that Todd
was a habitual liar.

Gaul—During the police interview after your
wife was killed, did you lie to the police investigators?
Garton—I was pretty messed up that day. I
don't think I lied. I think I answered to the
best of my ability.
Gaul—Did you lie on a job application for
the River House Inn in Bend, Oregon?
Garton—I may have exaggerated.

Gaul—When you say "exaggeration," do you mean you lied?

Garton—Yes. It's your word, not mine, but yes.

Bit by bit, Greg Gaul made Todd Garton admit to one lie after another. These included being a U.S. Marine lieutenant, being in the DEA and being a Butte County sheriff's officer. He even got Todd to admit that he'd lied to the state licensing board about G and G Fencing. He had told the board it stood for Greater and Greater Fencing, when it stood for Garton and Garton Fencing. Asked why he did this, he admitted it was because he wanted to keep his father's name off the form so he wouldn't have to pay an extra fee for having a partner. He also admitted he paid employees under the table in cash so that he wouldn't have to pay a workers' compensation fee.

Gaul played the audiotape of the phone call between Norman Daniels and Todd Garton, where the investigators listened in. On the tape it was clear that Garton was upset with Daniels for confessing to the murder of Carole Garton. Yet in a videotape soon thereafter with investigators, he claimed he didn't know that Daniels had confessed to anything. On the audiotape Daniels also asked Garton if his parents hated him for killing Carole. Garton told detectives on the videotape that he'd answered, "I said, 'What do you think! You're sick!' And hung up on him."

But on the audiotape Garton never said these things, and he and Daniels mutually said good-bye at the end of the phone call.

Asked about these discrepancies by Gaul, Garton

answered, "I'm sorry that my emotions don't match the emotions that you think I should have."

After Todd stepped down from the stand, his mother, Pat, was just as important a witness. She was a link to the label maker and the labeling tape—one of the few physical bits of evidence that could tie Todd Garton directly to the murder of Carole Garton. From this label maker there was supposedly a little label that stated, I LOVE YOU, BABE. And Todd had allegedly asked his mother to get rid of this label.

Todd had claimed to authorities that he never owned a label maker and that Lynn Noyes's story of them both throwing it into the Sacramento River was a lie. But a receipt from the OfficeMax in Redding proved that the electronic label maker had been purchased with a check written by Todd Garton on April 27, 1998. This was right before the time Norman Daniels claimed that Todd Garton had given him the package from The Company.

Also purchased that same day at the OfficeMax was a pager, the very same pager that Daniels claimed was in the package. Asked to explain this, Pat Garton said that she and Todd had gone to the OfficeMax that day. But Pat said the label maker was purchased for a friend of hers, a friend who had died in 1999. She said the pager had been intended for her use. She also said she had given the pager to Carole Garton to return to the store, because it wouldn't work with the phone company with which she preferred to do business.

Not buying this story of a friend and the label maker, Greg Gaul said, "Mrs. Garton, you've been sitting in throughout this trial. You know that label maker is a key piece of evidence to the trial, don't you?"

Both Pearce and Swartz objected, and they were sustained.

Gaul then asked, "Why didn't you tell the DA's office or police about the receipt before this?"

Pat Garton answered, "Because I think you're tricky. I think you're sneaky. I think you've lied. My son has an attorney. Anything that I would find, I would contact him first."

Gaul asked if anyone had seen her give the label maker to the friend who had died. Pat Garton said yes, someone had, but she refused to give the name.

Greg Gaul replied, "I think you have to, ma'am."

Pat Garton crossed her arms and mocked him, "Oh really, ma'am?"

Ordered by the court to reveal the name, she eventually did.

Further questioning by Gaul concerned the small bit of labeling that Todd wanted her to destroy. Pat Garton said that she couldn't remember this particular conversation because she had gone to visit her son in jail almost one hundred times since 1998. And then she said she thought that bit of labeling (I LOVE YOU, BABE) actually came from a children's sticker book, not a label maker.

All in all, Pat Garton was a difficult witness for Greg Gaul. But the end of the tunnel was in sight. The trial had gone on for three months now, with movies, outbursts and behind-the-scenes legal matters. It was finally time for closing arguments. Greg Gaul showed the jurors a timeline starting with the events of October 1997 when Todd and Dale had first gone up to Oregon. And he also flashed photographs on a large screen of a dead and bloody Carole Garton lying on the floor of her home. Among these were close-ups of Carole's face, bruised and bloodied from a bullet lodged behind her left eye. Some of the photos were so graphic that a couple of the jurors averted their gaze.

Greg Gaul told them, "We're here because two innocent lives were taken. It was a brutal murder. It was a hit. An assassination. It was very clear that Todd Garton didn't want that baby. He either didn't believe it was his or he just didn't want the little pain around. That's who Todd Garton is. That's all he does—he lies. He wanted his wife dead. He wanted his baby dead. Mr. Garton didn't even want to spend a lot of money on a murder weapon. He bought a forty-four-caliber Rossi. Less expensive than the three fifty-seven he liked or other brands. He wanted to save money when he killed his wife."

Gaul also brought up about the hollow-point bullets Garton purchased at Jones Fort. "If Todd Garton has told you anything, it's that he knows about guns. He knew what kind of damage these bullets would do to his wife."

Then in a shot at Todd's arrogance and insensitivity, Gaul said, "He even placed the picture of a Celtic cross on Carole's memorial-service booklet. This is a slap in the face to Carole. This is a sign to Lynn—look what I did for you."

By contrast, Russell Swartz portrayed Todd Garton as a grieving husband who had been duped by friends and set up as the fall guy. Swartz played a videotape that none of the jurors had seen up to this point. It was a police video of Todd Garton in the interview room in the days after his wife's murder. For about five minutes he was left alone in the room with the videotape still running. Only when the investigators were gone did he break down and start crying. He stopped as soon as they came back.

Swartz told the jurors, "Remember, Todd was taught, 'Hide your emotions. Suck it up. Don't let your feelings show.'" Swartz said this was why Todd sounded so unemotional on other police video and audiotapes.

Russell Swartz depicted Norman Daniels as lovesick and pathetic, a wanna-be assassin under Lynn Noyes's spell. According to Swartz, she had him wrapped around her little finger. Daniels may have been obsessed with her, but she was obsessed with Todd Garton. To prove his love, Daniels would do anything for her, including murder. Lynn Noyes found a target for him—Carole Garton.

Swartz said, "She was obsessed with Todd since she was sixteen years old. She even carved his initials with a razor blade on her thigh. How do you know when Lynn Noyes is lying? When she looks you in the face and says she's telling the truth."

Russell Swartz saved his most scathing remarks for Dale Gordon, saying that Gordon even admitted to being insane in the Shasta County jail: "He dreamed of being a superhero killer. He rewrote his own role-playing game, the World of Chaos. And he played it to a tragedy. We're looking at a person who's been in and out of the rubber room, and should have been there before."

Swartz suggested various alternative theories of what had happened that differed from the one

Greg Gaul presented. One theory was that when Lynn Noyes learned that Carole Garton was pregnant, she was afraid she would lose Todd forever. She assigned Norman Daniels to do the actual killing. Dale Gordon could have helped her send e-mail messages to Daniels from the fictional Colonel Sean and The Company. By his own admission, Gordon was computer savvy and had access to Todd Garton's computer.

Swartz also ran an alternate theory by the jurors. In this one Dale Gordon was the mastermind behind all the plots. He was so obsessed with military games and assassins he decided to carry it over into real life. Swartz also contended that Norman Daniels had never received a package from Todd Garton's hands concerning The Company. He said if the jurors looked carefully on the red wax seal, they would not notice any fibers from an envelope attached to it. Then he said, "I can't prove them [the theories], but it's not my responsibility to do so. If there is any reasonable doubt in this case, you must find Todd Garton not guilty."

Since this was a capital case with special circumstances, each juror was given a handout to take to the deliberation room. It read in part, *If you find Mr. Garton in this case guilty of murder, of the first degree, you must then determine if one or more of the following special circumstances are true. Murder for financial gain and multiple murder convictions. The People have the burden of proving the truth of a special circumstance. If you have a reasonable doubt as to whether a special circumstance is true, you must find it to be not true. If you find that Mr. Garton was not the actual killer of a human being, you cannot find the special circumstance to be true as to Mr. Garton, unless you are satisfied beyond a reasonable doubt that Mr Garton aided, abetted, counseled, commanded, induced, solicited, requested or assisted any actor in the commission of the murder in the first degree.*

When the jury's decision came, it came quickly. After only four hours of deliberation they found Todd Garton guilty in the murders of Carole Anne Garton and Jesse James Garton. Jury foreman Fred Castagna said, "It was pretty obvious from the beginning we were in agreement."

The penalty phase began in March 2001. And things did not look good for Todd Garton. Russell Swartz noted that "Shasta County juries have never exercised their option to grant life in a capital case of this nature." As a matter of fact, neither Russell Swartz nor Todd Garton ever spoke at length at his penalty phase. Instead, Swartz read a paper to the jurors that Todd had written. These words were portrayed on the same movie screen where Harrison Ford had made his appearance in *Patriot Games*. The sentences were a short synopsis of the case as Todd saw it:

1. Norman Daniels had killed his wife, Carole.
2. Norman Daniels had killed his son, Jesse James Garton.
3. Norman Daniels took his family from him.
4. The police took his freedom.
5. The verdict had taken his honor.
6. The only thing Todd had left was his life.

And my life is worth nothing without my family, freedom and honor, Garton wrote.

Then in a very unusual statement, coming from a defense attorney, Russell Swartz told the jurors, "You might as well kill him. He neither asks, nor does he expect more than death from you."

Before this could really sink in, Russell Swartz did add an amendment to his remarks. He said, "Todd Garton will die in jail whether he's sentenced to death or life in prison without the possibility of parole."

Swartz then pointed out that a prison cell was no larger than his bathroom at home. He portrayed some slides on the screen of flowers, sunsets, beaches and mountains while telling jurors that if Todd was sentenced to life in prison, he would never see these things again.

One of the last things Russell Swartz pointed out was that Todd Garton would never be able to go back to Northern Ireland: "The area of green, green islands that were of value to him."

Greg Gaul, on the other hand, argued for the death penalty to be implemented. He said in part, "Death should be imposed in the most extreme types of cases. This is one of those cases. He didn't give any sympathy, compassion or mercy to his wife. He's not deserving of your sympathy, compassion or mercy."

Jim Holman was also there to speak for his daughter, Carole. He choked back tears as he told the jury of Carole when she was a cheerleader, musician and tennis player. He said, "I miss the joy. I miss not having her in my life. I think about her every day. She didn't have enemies. It was such a senseless thing."

Vicki Holman also spoke of Carole. She said, "I loved her dearly and I felt she loved me. She made me feel like a special person in her life, as she was in mine. Now I wish I hadn't been so concerned about minding my own business when Carole announced plans to marry Todd."

Even McGregor Scott, the district attorney of Shasta County, addressed the jury. It was a synopsis of the case and ended with the words "Without question, the murders of Carole Anne Garton and her child were particularly cruel, vicious and callous acts. One can only imagine the extreme shock, pain and suffering she experienced as she was shot five times at close range while resting on her own bed. As she gasped for the last breath of life, she was attempting to seek cover by trying to crawl under her bed. She must have been terrified during her final moments of life and unquestionably died a quick, but very painful, death. For these vicious acts Todd Garton clearly deserves the ultimate punishment—death."

Greg Gaul tried to introduce a photo for the jury to see of the unborn baby's wounds. But the photo was so graphic that Judge Boeckman ruled against its presentation. He called it highly inflammatory and said, "As seasoned as this court is in viewing autopsy photos, this court has a hard time not having that reaction."

Finally when everyone else was through, Judge Boeckman told Todd Garton that he had the right to speak. He answered, "I don't care to, Your Honor."

It was now up to the jury of seven men and five women to decide if Todd Garton would spend the rest of his life in prison or die by lethal injection in California's San Quentin Prison. Surprisingly, they were only in the conference room for seventy minutes. This was an extremely short amount of time for such an important decision.

As Todd Garton sat with his attorneys and stared straight ahead, the verdict was read by the jury foreman, Fred Castagna. The verdict was death. Todd Garton didn't say a word or even flinch when the verdict was read.

Afterward, a nineteen-year-old juror, Paul Toroni, told a reporter, "A thousand other jurors in there would have come to the same conclusion. It was tough, though, to say it."

Jury foreman Castagna agreed: "We spent most of our time trying to construct scenarios that might change the belief that Garton was guilty and deserved to die. But every time we tried, it would just fall apart."

Castagna went on to say that the jurors felt that the fetus was the primary target, because of the window of opportunity that had been given to Norman Daniels in which to kill Carole Garton and thus the unborn baby. Todd's plans had originally been to kill Dean Noyes, but with the advent of a baby, his target switched to Carole and he pushed Norman Daniels by all means possible to carry through on the hit.

After the verdict Russell Swartz told reporters he wasn't surprised about the outcome. He said, "Mr. Garton received what he expected, as stated to the jury. I don't ever like to see a person condemned to death. I don't think anybody should enjoy seeing a person condemned to death."

Fred Castagna had one more thing to say about all the others who had been dragged down with Todd Garton, especially Norman Daniels, Dale Gordon and Lynn Noyes. He said, "We [the jury] felt some sympathy for them. We saw Todd Garton as a puppeteer. Their lives are ruined. I felt without Todd Garton's instigation, they wouldn't have committed the crimes."

Chapter 15

End of the Line

Even though it wasn't much more than a formality and routine procedure, Judge Bradley L. Boeckman presided over the actual sentencing of Todd Garton on April 27, 2001. But nothing concerning Todd was ever routine. Given a chance to speak, he did so with a vengeance.

The proceedings began with Greg Gaul saying, "The victim's family has chosen not to address the court simply because I think that they believe that evidence speaks for itself, and that it was, in fact, overwhelming. They had the opportunity to tell the jury how this has impacted their lives.

"There is no doubt that this defendant clearly planned this out over a lengthy period of time, went through a great deal of effort to conceal his own identity or involvement in this crime at great risk of subjecting three other individuals to punishment. He clearly lied before the court and jury. They saw that he lied and that his mother would lie to protect him.

"This was a very complex case. A complex conspiracy. The lengths that this defendant went through to make sure these murders were carried out before Carole Garton had her baby—it was his own selfish desire not to look bad in the community that caused him to have her murdered, instead of doing what everyone else would do, and get a divorce. He didn't want the baby.

"I think it was pretty clear that, although he was giving outward impressions to people close to the time of the murder that he was very supportive of the baby, he was callously plotting to have Carole murdered before she could have the baby. And some of the indications of the desire not to have the baby were manifested sometime prior to her ever becoming pregnant, in statements he made to other individuals.

"But the thing that strikes me the most is the defendant's own testimony. How callous he is and how he chose to put things on the victim and clearly lied about those things. Carole Garton was by all accounts a fantastic person who did nothing to warrant this type of crime. The defendant had someone else carry out this crime for him because he couldn't face his own wife and do the deed. So he had Norman Daniels do it. And to make sure that Norman Daniels did it, he coerced him, and threatened him with his own death. I truly believe Norman Daniels would not have carried this out if he didn't feel that his own life or his family's life were at stake.

"I think Norman Daniels was under the impression, based on representations of the defendant, that the murders that the defendant claimed that he committed over several years were basically done for the good of everyone to get rid of bad people in society.

"But Carole Garton was not a bad person. She was looking forward to her child's birth. She was very happy about it. People in the community loved her. People that she interacted with on a daily basis loved her. And she apparently loved Todd Garton and had no idea what he was plotting. No clue whatsoever. It's just a very tragic murder.

"I'm glad the jury sent the defendant a clear message. This is the only just verdict and he deserves to die. And I hope it's swift. I hope it does not go on for years and is resolved soon for the sake of Carole Garton, her baby and Carole's family."

Russell Swartz followed with a few comments about Greg Gaul's remarks. He said that Todd Garton agreed with a couple of statements Gaul made, that Carole Garton was a wonderful person and didn't need to die. Then he added, "As to the rest of the matters, Mr. Garton disagrees with the accuracy of the speculation and the comments of the district attorney; in essence, is appalled that the district attorney chooses to defend the man who put five bullets in to the body of Carole Anne Garton and Jesse James Garton, killing them." Swartz went on to say that Todd was grieved by the loss of a wife he loved, and the son he would never see. He added that despite the verdict, Garton still maintained his innocence and was not involved in the horrendous crime.

It was now time for the Honorable Bradley L. Boeckman to pass sentence on Todd Garton. He began by saying, "I have independently considered and reviewed the evidence of aggravating and mitigating circumstances. And I have applied my own independent judgment to determine whether the jury's findings and the jury's verdict are contrary to the law or the evidence presented. I found beyond a reasonable doubt that the defendant is guilty of the multiple murders of Carole Garton and her fetus and the murders were committed for financial gain.

"The defendant intended to kill his wife and his unborn son in order to be free of the marriage and impending parenthood in order to be with one of his co-conspirators, Lynn Noyes. I note that the defendant drew Norman Daniels in this conspiracy, and by a combination of promises of money and excitement, and by threats and intimidations, Mr. Garton caused and encouraged Norman Daniels to kill the two intended victims.

"I note that the defendant assisted Norman Daniels in the choice of, and the purchase of, the murder weapon. I note that on May 16, 1998, as a direct result of the defendant's actions, Carole Garton was lying in her own bed, in her own home, completely vulnerable and defenseless and unsuspecting, when the defendant's co-conspirator Norman Daniels shot her at close range five times with a forty-four-caliber pistol. And that Carole Garton appeared to Norman Daniels to be trying to roll under the bed to avoid being shot further, and that she undoubtedly suffered pain and fear.

"I note that there was compelling victim/witness impact evidence in the testimony of Carole's brothers Michael and Donald, and her father, James Holman, and stepmother, Vicki Holman, regarding the profound and abiding loss each of these persons suffered."

The mitigating factors in the sentencing amounted to Todd Garton's never having been arrested for a felony before, and his service in the U.S. Marine Corps with an honorable discharge. But these mitigating factors were heavily outweighed by the aggravating factors in the case. Judge Boeckman said, "I find that the aggravating circumstances are so substantial in comparison with the mitigating circumstances that it warrants death instead of life without the possibility of parole."

Todd Garton, through his lawyer, announced that he wanted to make a statement, and he was allowed to do so by Judge Boeckman. Garton began, "First off, Your Honor, I'm sickened by the decision this court has come to. Most of all, I'm sickened at Mr. Gaul. Mr. Gaul has presented Norman Daniels, a man who killed my wife and son, as a compassionate, poor victim who was suckered into committing murder. And he's defended Norman Daniels throughout this trial. I think that is sickening and appalling.

"As far as the family goes, I was going to keep my mouth quiet on this, but I can't. The only family that Carole had that's had a loss are the people who loved her the most—people that she called 'mother' and 'father'—Jess Garton and Pat Garton. Her own father molested her to the point to where she ran away from home [a lie]. And his own wife left him because of this [another lie]. And to have him get on the stand and talk about the victim impact, and about how he missed his daughter—when my own mother and father saw Carole more in two weeks then he saw his own daughter in ten years, [it] makes me sick.

"I am innocent of this crime. I will never, ever change that statement. I do not care what the jury found. I do not care what the court found. Especially when I had to sit in court and hear Your Honor say that the Constitution was not enough authority while my lawyers were making motions. That was a statement made by the court.

"I think everything else has been stated by my defense attorney, especially in the closing arguments; that with everything else taken away from me, I don't want to live among people like this. I just can't tell you the deep insult and dishonor I felt throughout this. I think I have said enough."

Judge Boeckman obviously thought Todd Garton had said enough as well. He ordered, "You are remanded to the care, custody and control of the sheriff of Shasta County to be delivered to the warden of the state penitentiary at San Quentin, California, within ten days of this date. To be held by the warden pending the final determination of your appeal in this matter. Once the judgment becomes final, the warden is ordered to carry into effect the judgment of this court within the state prison, at which time you shall be put to death in the manner prescribed by law."

When Vicki Holman left the courthouse, she commented to a reporter about Todd Garton's insults. "It's just like him. He's still trying to inflict pain and he did. That was the meanest, ugliest thing he could say. He knew that it would be a dagger to the heart."

If Todd Garton had no remorse for his actions and continued to proclaim his innocence, the same could not be said for Lynn Noyes. She wrote a long, heartfelt letter to Carole's mother and stepfather. It began, *I know this won't ever be good enough, but I'm writing to try and express to you the sorrow and remorse I feel for my part in what happened to your daughter and grandchild.* She said that she had been caught up in something far larger and more sinister than she knew at the time. She even claimed to have tried to persuade Todd to tell The Company not to go through with the hit on Carole. However, she only pushed him so far because she was afraid for the lives of her own children.

Lynn said that she had let her emotions dictate her actions. She said that her last meeting with Carole had been cordial and they had buried the hatchet. They had even embraced at Carole's parting. *This was all so senseless and sad,* she wrote. *So much loss. Innocent loss. I trusted a very bad person and let my feelings toss all sensibility and rational thinking aside. I could say I'm sorry repeatedly for the rest of my life, and it still wouldn't be enough.*

She promised to educate other young women in prison about certain men who were dangerous liars and the corrosion of their relationships. Lynn Noyes asked that she hoped that one day Carole's parents could forgive her.

To a degree both Virginia Griffiths and Vicki Holman did forgive Lynn Noyes for her actions. And to an even greater degree they forgave Dale Gordon. They looked upon not only Dale, but his parents, as victims of Todd Garton. Virginia said, "Dale's parents sent flowers to us during the trial. They were devastated when they found out Dale was involved in all of this. We actually became friends later. We all had a loss. My husband and I very much liked Dale's girlfriend, Sara Mann. She was a victim, too."

Vicki Holman said, "We also met Dale Gordon's parents at the trial and our hearts went out to them. Dale was a victim. His mother was so sorry that her son was in a way involved with Todd and all that happened. She kept wanting to do something. She finally gave us a gift certificate for a rosebush to put in Carole's garden at our home. I still write her on occasion and pray that Dale will survive his time in prison. He seems so vulnerable."

By January 2002 it was finally time for Norman Daniels to learn his fate. In November 2001 he had reached an agreement with Deputy DA Greg Gaul to forgo a jury trial in exchange for the death penalty being dropped. Instead, he would take his chances with a trial by court, which meant that Judge Boeckman alone would render a decision of guilty or not guilty and pronounce sentence. It was risky in some regards because Judge Boeckman would not be swayed by sympathy. Rather, he would be constricted by points of law and the matter of deciding mitigating and aggravating circumstances.

Richard Maxion, Daniels's attorney, put Norman Daniels on the stand to answer questions about Todd's scheme that included the fictional bureau,

The Company. Daniels admitted, "I was having financial problems at my house and, to be honest, I was thinking about the money. I agreed to do it, but I didn't know who I would have to kill."

As far as The Company and Colonel Sean went, Daniels said, "I took him at his word because it didn't sound too far-fetched." Maxion said of this, "He [Daniels] genuinely feels that he was brainwashed. I think he's genuinely remorseful."

Maxion's defense of Daniels was unusual. He based it on a little-used legal pretext of imperfect duress. For example, regular duress would be someone forced to rob a minimart because a third party held a gun on his family member and threatened to kill that person if the store was not robbed. Since duress is not allowed to be a factor in a murder trial, imperfect duress became its substitute. Maxion argued that during the whole experience Norman Daniels felt that either he or his son would be killed if he didn't follow through on the assassination of Carole Garton.

Daniels's own words from the stand backed up this premise. He said, "I had night sweats. I was afraid of a point-blank execution from customers that I pumped fuel for at the gas station. I thought there might be snipers hidden in the fields. Members of The Company watched my every move. If I said one wrong word, and they overheard it, I would be dead."

Greg Gaul had the very delicate act of striking a balance in how to treat Norman Daniels at this point. On the one hand, Daniels had been the actual killer of Carole Garton and her unborn baby. On the other hand, he had helped Greg immea-

surably in the trial against Todd Garton. Gaul began
by refuting Maxion's argument about duress. And
he did it point by point:

1. There must have been no adequate alternative to the commission of the act—"Norman
   Daniels could have easily reported to the
   police the plan to kill Carole Garton and
   her fetus, and sought the protection of law
   enforcement authorities."
2. The harm caused by the act must not be
   disproportionate to the harm avoided—"The
   harm here is the same, death to one or more
   innocent persons, which is specifically why
   the legislature enacted Penal Code twenty-
   six and stated that duress is not a defense
   when the defendant is charged with a crime
   punishable by death."
3. The accused must entertain a good-faith
   belief that his act was necessary to prevent
   the greater harm—"Norman Daniels could
   have prevented the harm to both Carole
   Garton and her fetus, and to himself and
   his family, by reporting the planned murders
   and threats on his own life to law enforcement authorities. Therefore, he did not have
   a good-faith belief that the act was necessary to prevent the greater harm."
4. That the defendant must not have substan-
   tially contributed to the creation of the emergency—"Here, Daniels clearly contributed
   to the creation of the alleged emergency by
   participating in and planning the murders
   of Carole Anne Garton and her fetus in ex-

> change for personal and financial gain in the future."

All of that being said, Greg Gaul now presented facts about Norman Daniels's cooperation with him in so many key areas. He said, "Beginning with his very first interview with Shasta County sheriff's detectives, Daniels assisted law enforcement officers and the district attorney in unraveling and exposing the conspiracy. Without his willingness to cooperate and do the right thing, the true extent of these conspiracies would never have been known.

"I have personally participated in numerous interviews with Mr. Daniels throughout the investigation and ultimate prosecution of Todd Garton. He testified for several days before a jury and told the truth about both his participation in the crimes, as well as the participation of others. He has been totally forthcoming and has helped me and the detectives to fully understand why these crimes were committed and the true motives behind the murders of Carole Anne Garton and her child. Of great significance was Mr. Daniels's assistance in identifying all the conspirators who participated in the murder of Carole Garton and her fetus, as well as the failed attempt to kill Dean Noyes, the husband of co-conspirator Lynn Noyes. Without Norman Daniels's full cooperation and assistance, the true extent of these crimes would have never been known to law enforcement, and it would have been extremely difficult to obtain a conviction against Todd Garton.

"I am convinced that Mr. Daniels would not have ever contemplated resorting to murder, had it not been for the months of being manipulated by Todd Garton. Mr. Garton took advantage of Mr. Daniels's financial problems and convinced him that he could make easy money in participating in assassinations. In talking to friends and family of Mr. Daniels who knew him well, they were shocked to learn of his involvement in these crimes. However, because of Todd Garton's persuasiveness, manipulation and threats to Mr. Daniels and others, Mr. Daniels apparently felt compelled to carry out his role in the murders and conspiracy to commit murder.

"Mr. Daniels has accepted full responsibility for what he did. He has been honest and forthcoming with me. In fact, I can state without reservation that he has been the most honest and cooperative witness, let alone defendant, that I have ever had the pleasure of interacting with and presenting before a jury. He was extemely credible as a historian and witness. Furthermore, he has on his own initiative provided helpful information without even being asked or prompted. He has also been a model inmate while incarcerated in the county jail for the past three years.

"Based upon all these factors, and assuming he remains a model prisoner while incarcerated in the state prison system, it is my request, and I sincerely urge the Board of Prison Terms and Parole Board, to grant Mr. Daniels release on parole when he first becomes eligible for parole. I do not see Mr. Daniels as ever being a threat to the community and I am confident that this was an anomaly in his life. Mr. Daniels can be a productive citizen, and once he serves his time for his actions, I feel he should be granted parole."

Judge Boeckman took all of this in, as well as the four thousand pages of transcripts and reviewed them during February and March. Then in mid-March he was ready to pronounce judgment upon Norman Daniels.

Judge Boeckman acknowledged that Daniels had feared for his life and that of his son. He had trusted Todd Garton, whom he thought of as a friend. Daniels had also helped law enforcement and the district attorney's office in all aspects of their investigations. But then Judge Boeckman said, "I reflect back, and I remember getting a letter that I considered during the trial itself. I believe it was from your ex-wife, Ms. Praiter, Mr. Daniels. She indicated that this tendency of yours to be gullible, naive, to place greater importance to the statements and assertions of others than you should be placing, your ability to be taken in, on your propensity to be taken in by others, was demonstrated before you ever got involved with Mr. Garton, and it had an impact on the dissolution of that marriage. For some people that's a good thing if it happens in the right circumstances. One can be influenced toward good by somebody who is influential. But our society expects people to withstand influence if it's an influence to do evil. And, nonetheless, you succumbed to that.

"Whether or not you are likely to succeed in probation, I find it otherwise. I find it more likely that, despite your professed willingness to comply with terms of probation, that we're all subject to whether or not you happen to come into contact with another person like Mr. Garton. And, sadly, experience has taught us there are many people like Mr. Garton in our society. I think it's been suggested that you have learned your lesson. I'm not comfortable with that.

"I'm aware that this is going to have a negative impact on you, on your son, and I accept that you are remorseful. I am persuaded that that is a genuine attitude that you hold. Nonetheless, I think the weight of information and factors that I would consider would cause me not to grant you probation.

"Mr. Daniels, you may have been partially motivated, at least at the very end of this conspiracy, by fear and concern for your own personal safety and possibly that of your family. But I also note that you were motivated by greed and by a desire for excitement, and the thrill of being involved in this so-called assassination unit. And that, for most of the time period of this conspiracy, or at least a large part of it, that was your motivation. And, by your own testimony, and by your own statements to the probation officer, you felt that you would be able to go forward with that assassination and that you would not get caught. That your reasons for becoming reluctant once you learned that this quote, target, of the assassination plot was a friend, then you thought it more likely you would get caught.

"In terms of the extent of your involvement, you were the actual killer, not a co-conspirator who was not actually involved in the final decision. I was critical of Mr. Garton at his sentencing because I thought, even for somebody who planned to kill somebody, he took the gutless or easy way out, because he delegated the actual killing to somebody else so that he would never personally have to make that last and final decision about whether he would actually do it. But you had that opportunity. You had the last opportunity of anybody, and an opportunity to exercise some humanity, and you chose not to. You chose to go ahead with it. You indicated that after you fired the first shot, you realized what you were doing. And your response was to fire four more times.

"In the eyes of the law you killed two persons. Carole Garton personally was aware that she was being shot to death and was trying to escape it. So, in my judgment she suffered fear and pain right up until the time she lost consciousness.

"I think when somebody achieves the age of thirty years, that person in our society is expected to conduct themselves within the rules of society. I think you are a gullible person. You were a naive person. You were a person who was given over to, if you found somebody who had greater education, sophistication, experience or simply confidence, that you would put them in high esteem and give greater credence to what they said and did than they deserved. And until you knew that Carole Garton was going to be the victim, you felt cold-blooded about it. You were rebellious. And you were thirty years old at the time."

With all these factors of aggravation and mitigation, Judge Boeckman sentenced Norman Daniels to the maximum of fifty years with the possibility of parole after forty-two years served. If Daniels ever got out of prison, he would be in his seventies.

Showing little emotion at the sentence imposed,

Daniels said politely, as he always did in court, "Thank you. I appreciate you hearing my case and God bless you all."

Even Greg Gaul was moved by Norman Daniels's genuine remorse and his unstinting help during Todd Garton's trial with no deals on the table to help him. Gaul filed a prosecutor's statement to the Board of Prison Terms, recommending that Daniels be paroled at the earliest possible time. He said, "I think he has learned his lesson."

Chapter 16

Epilogue

Greg Gaul continues to serve as senior deputy district attorney in Shasta County, California. He is assigned to the serious offender unit, concentrating on homicide cases.

Russell Swartz continues to take on the most difficult cases. He is considered one of the best defense lawyers in Shasta County.

Jim and Vicki Holman have a portion of their garden set aside as a memorial to Carole and Jesse Garton. They have forgiven Dale Gordon and become friends with Dale's parents. As Vicki said, "His parents are victims, too."

Gary and Virginia Griffiths constantly think of Carole and baby Jesse. Virginia said, "Carole will always be my daughter."

Jesse and Pat Garton still believe in the innocence of Todd. They are supportive of their son's cause in the appeal his conviction.

Dale Gordon is incarcerated in the California

Medical Facility at Vacaville. This penal institution deals with prisoners who have suffered from mental problems. Charles Manson and Sirhan Sirhan have spent time there.

Lynn Noyes serves her time behind bars at the Central California Women's Facility in Chowchilla. She counsels young female prisoners about the dangers of becoming enamored with charming but dangerous con men.

Norman Daniels is serving his sentence at one of California's most notorious prisons—Corcoran State Prison in the Central Valley. Because of many gang members there, Corcoran has a reputation as a dangerous place. During the 1990s, Daniel Mc-Carthy, onetime head of the California correctional facilities, said, "The level of violence was absolutely the highest I have ever seen in any institution, anywhere in the country."

Todd Garton inhabits death row in San Quentin Prison on San Francisco Bay. Opened in 1852, San Quentin sprawls over 432 acres. The general population exceeds 1,500. The numbers of those on death row now exceed 600, in a prison that was built to hold a maximum of 554 death row inmates. As Bob Martinez, a spokesman for the State Department of Corrections, said, "San Quentin's current death row is a hodgepodge of prison facilities, some of which previously were used to house inmates with lesser sentences. Additional cells were switched to death row status as more and more were sentenced to die."

With the average of only one or two executions a year in California, Todd Garton may die of natural causes within its walls before he is ever executed.

In the meantime he lives a life similar to that of a
death row inmate described in the book *A Murder,*
by Gary Fallis. Fallis wrote: *His world had shrunk,
collapsed in on itself. For the most part the boundaries of
his life were the boundaries of his cell. . . . There was absolutely no privacy on death row. Never a moment of
quiet seclusion.*

As with all things concerning Todd Garton, the
final resting place of Carole Garton's ashes has remained somewhat of a mystery. Todd indicated
where they might have been deposited, but then
he was so prone to lying it was anyone's guess if
what he said was true. Vicki Holman, Carole's stepmother, recalled, "We heard different stories about
Carole's and the baby's remains. We tried for a
year to get them. Todd's mother said she still had
them as of the time Todd was arrested. In May of
1999 we got a strange call from Pat Garton. She
said that the Moose Lodge in Anderson was having
a memorial service for all their members who had
died in the previous year, and Carole was one of
them. She said Todd thought we might want to go.
I was dumbfounded. I told her kindly as possible
that we would not be able to attend. I also took the
opportunity to again ask her about the remains.
Her reply was 'Oh, we decided Carole would not
want to return to Oregon, so we scattered her remains up at Burney Falls.' "

In some regards this was an appropriate spot for
Carole Garton's ashes to be deposited. She loved
the outdoors and Burney Falls is a beautiful spot.
Teddy Roosevelt had even declared it to be one of

the "wonders of the natural world" at the turn of the twentieth century. Its double falls thunder 129 feet over a cliff of lava in a natural setting of pines. The shimmering pool beneath the falls is awash with cool spray, and rainbows often arch across the waters when the sun beams down between the pine needles. There is even a very probable spot where the ashes could have been deposited into Burney Creek above the falls. A footbridge spans the waters and is hidden from casual view by the forest and surrounding hills.

Beautiful or not, both Vicki Holman and her husband, Jim, were crushed by this news. They wanted Carole's ashes, and those of the baby, back among people who loved her. But then they heard a story later related by another family member that the Burney Falls story was not true. That it had been invented by Todd Garton—a tale he told his mother to pass on to others.

Just where Carole Garton's and Jesse James Garton's remains were scattered, perhaps only Todd Garton knows for sure. And even if he told someone where they had been deposited, it might be the truth, or it might be a lie—or something in between. Todd was never one to let truth stand in the way when there was an elaborate story to be told. Todd Garton stayed true to only one thing—true to his character right down to the bitter end.

HORRIFYING TRUE CRIME
FROM PINNACLE BOOKS

Body Count
by Burl Barer   0-7860-1405-9   **$6.50US/$8.50**CAN

The Babyface Killer
by Jon Bellini   0-7860-1202-1   **$6.50US/$8.50**CAN

Love Me to Death
by Steve Jackson   0-7860-1458-X   **$6.50US/$8.50**CAN

The Boston Stranglers
by Susan Kelly   0-7860-1466-0   **$6.50US/$8.50**CAN

Body Double
by Don Lasseter   0-7860-1474-1   **$6.50US/$8.50**CAN

The Killers Next Door
by Joel Norris   0-7860-1502-0   **$6.50US/$8.50**CAN

Available Wherever Books Are Sold!

Visit our website at **www.kensingtonbooks.com**.

MORE MUST-READ TRUE CRIME
FROM PINNACLE

Under the Knife   0-7860-1197-1   **$6.50US/$8.50CAN**
By Karen Roebuck

Lobster Boy   0-7860-1569-1   **$6.50US/$8.50CAN**
By Fred Rosen

Body Dump   0-7860-1133-5   **$6.50US/$8.50CAN**
By Fred Rosen

Savage   0-7860-1409-1   **$6.50US/$8.50CAN**
By Robert Scott

Innocent Victims   0-7860-1273-0   **$6.50US/$8.50CAN**
By Brian J. Karem

The Boy Next Door   0-7860-1459-8   **$6.50US/$8.50CAN**
By Gretchen Brinck

Available Wherever Books Are Sold!

Visit our website at **www.kensingtonbooks.com**.